REAL ESTATE FIELD MANUAL

An Official Selling Guide

Barbara C. Nash

CENGAGE
Learning™

Australia • Brazil • Japan • Korea • Mexico • Singapore • Spain • United Kingdom • United States

Real Estate Field Manual, 5e

Author: Barbara C. Nash

Vice President/Editor-in-Chief: Dave Shaut

Director, Products and Services: Scott Person

Acquisitions Editor: Sara Glassmeyer

Developmental Editor: Sara Glassmeyer

Editorial Assistant: Michelle Melfi

Sr. Marketing Manager: Mark Linton

Manufacturing Coordinator: Kevin Kluck

Content Project Manager: Lysa Oeters

Production Service: Integra

Art Director: Bethany Casey

Internal Designer: Brenda Grannan

Cover Designer: Brenda Grannan

Cover Image: GettyImages, Inc/Digital Vision/ Ryan McVay and Jupiter Images Corporation/ CS Productions

For product information and technology assistance, contact us at **Cengage Learning Academic Resource Center, 1-800-423-0563**

For permission to use material from this text or product, submit all requests online at **www.cengage.com/permissions** Further permissions questions can be emailed to **permissionrequest@cengage.com**

Library of Congress Control Number: 2008923300

ISBN-13: 978-0-324-65406-6
ISBN-10: 0-324-65406-5
Book with CD ISBN-13: 978-0-324-65408-0
Book with CD ISBN-10: 0-324-65408-1

Cengage Learning
5191 Natorp Boulevard
Mason, OH 45040
USA

Cengage Learning products are represented in Canada by Nelson Education, Ltd.

For your course and learning solutions, visit **academic.cengage.com** Purchase any of our products at your local college store or at our preferred online store **www.ichapters.com**

Printed in the United States of America
1 2 3 4 5 6 7   12 11 10 09 08

•••••• CONTENTS

It took me years to learn the ins and outs of real estate. In fact, I'm still learning every day. However, from the time I joined the real estate profession 30 years ago until today, I have yet to find a good manual—a self-help book that covers the entire gamut of real estate. *Real Estate Field Manual* is such a book—a book, you can take with you to listings and have the dialogue right there! It shows you what to do daily, how to get that appointment, how to get clients, and how to keep them. It also stresses the importance of disclosure and fair housing, as well as every aspect of professionalism. There are examples from the best in the business of:

- Voice mail scripts
- How to keep your books and run your daily schedule
- Advertising on the Internet
- Designing your own web page
- Generating prospects and keeping them
- Case study dialogues of potential listings
- Ways to simplify and be successful
- Real estate Web address book
- Computer technology

This manual is especially for those who are already in the business who want to make a fresh start!

> Above all, this book will be your complete guide for all of your real estate questions as you start to make lots of contacts and know how to convert them to sales! Have a plan and work your plan!

PREFACE

This book is written for my fellow real estate sales professionals. I hope to help shorten your trial-and-error experiences on your way to becoming successful in the real estate business. This book will act as your FIELD MANUAL on the car seat next to you. It will give you countless sample dialogues, closing techniques, and a step-by-step recipe to list every potential customer! Included are Internet information, web page design, web addresses, and countless other up-to-date developments in this fast-paced industry.

> The real estate business will be as busy as you are!
>
> Your business will be successful if YOU stay disciplined each and every day. HAVE A PLAN AND WORK YOUR PLAN

Just open *Real Estate Field Manual* and learn how easy it is to take charge and follow these leads.

Try to remember the following:

1. Keep your sense of humor.
2. Be disciplined and follow through.
3. Stay enthusiastic. (The dictionary defines enthuos as "inspired by God.")

Only through discipline and enthusiasm each day will you simplify your work schedule and form good business habits. You will save countless hours and waste little time by knowing what to say and when to close.

This is your official *Real Estate Field Manual*—a book filled with positive examples of 30 years of success in the real estate industry.

I hope by sharing all of this information with you, I will help you grow to enjoy the art of selling real estate in the twenty-first century.

> Keep this manual on the car seat next to you and refer to it often!

AT THE START

- What to Buy
- Car Contents
- Sales Strategies
- Weekly Charts

big deal by Lorayne n' Neil

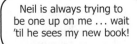

A Twenty-First Century Start

Getting started and staying in business requires one crucial element—DISCIPLINE, followed by organization and enthusiasm!

In today's "super-interconnected Internet highway," anyone can get information on a house in almost any state in a matter of minutes! Times have changed drastically, and a real estate agent today needs to begin with phone numbers, e-mail addresses, and fax numbers. Where, oh where, to keep all these numbers so they are easily accessible?

The practice of real estate generates lots of little odds-and-ends numbers, little pieces of saved paper where this number and that number were hastily scribbled down; all these numbers must be kept in a computer and/or a daily planner. What about a daily schedule? What about specialization? Why would someone choose YOU?

It makes a lot of sense in the twenty-first century to begin to develop an exclusive real estate niche of your own. The way to go in the days ahead is to consider "the senior specialist niche" or another type of "niche marketing." Position yourself as a person who specializes in one part of the real estate market, although you provide full service as well. *Try hard* from the very beginning to develop a unique, compelling marketing message that makes it easy for clients to find you.

When I first started out in real estate 30 years ago, I quickly realized how much business I lost from being disorganized! It took me years of trying various methods before I could determine which tools were definitely needed and which ones could be abandoned.

Some agents believe that getting started means simply completing a "quick-start" program at the company and then diving right in—just go out, list, and sell a house. Little do most agents realize (until it's too late) that they must be prepared to sell themselves first. They must be able to show the strengths and the effectiveness of their current marketing plan—then they can corner any market in real estate. In addition, they must be confident, trustworthy, and enthusiastic! Seldom will they get a second chance with a buyer or a seller.

Real estate is pretty much a sink-or-swim business. It is up to the new agent to be prepared from the start. With computer technology, a business can become far more focused and marketing, more effective. Agents who can market their own unique and exclusive real estate services to their own unique customer base so that those prospects and customers feel that those services were created just for them will reap all the benefits. Remember: Everyone wants to work with a specialist—someone who specializes only in them. Who wouldn't?

What Do You Need to Buy?

The following information is created for a real estate agent. This information should help you to work effectively from one day to the next.

1. Daily planner, size 5" × 8" or 8 1/2" × 11" or any digital planner you feel comfortable using.
2. Calculator, preferably flat to fit into the planner.
3. Good pen and pencil set.
4. Plain pad of white paper to fit into back of planner (5" × 8"), lined.
5. 8 1/2" × 11" or legal-size, ruled daily notebook (perfect for taking notes at seller's house).

6. Large and small paper clips.
7. Highlighter pens.
8. Current map of your city.
9. Stationery with your name, photo, and real estate company printed on it.
10. Stickers for envelopes with your name, photo, and real estate company (order 1,000 minimum).
11. Promotional brochure with your name, photo, and real estate company (1,000 minimum).
12. Business cards and business reply cards with your name, photo, real estate company e-mail and website addresses (order 1,000 minimum).
13. Large construction-grade tape measure.
14. Polaroid® instant camera and/or digital camera.
15. Cell phone/BlackBerry/iphone.
16. Laptop computer/modem/software packages.
17. Fax machine.
18. Tape recorder (for good PMI tapes).
19. Through the company or independently, acquire the following:
    a. lockboxes (12)
    b. signs and name riders (12)
    c. home highlight stands (12)
    d. open house signs (6)
20. Large wall calendar and large desk calendar.
21. Legal-size folders.
22. File folder labels.
23. "Sold" and "initial" stamps, address, and name stamp.
24. Standard-size leather or good vinyl notebook (8 1/2" × 11") with plastic inserts. This will be your promotional book in which all promotional material regarding yourself and your company is kept.
25. Personal assistant.
26. Scanner.

First, get your daily planner

What to Wear

REMEMBER: A REAL ESTATE AGENT SHOULD ALWAYS LOOK SUCCESSFUL.

Whether you have been in the business for one day or one year, dress and look as if you have *always* sold real estate.

How do you do this? Start by acquiring some must-haves:

1. A basic, tailored, dark suit
2. White or cream-colored dress shirt/blouse
3. Well-kept, good-quality dark shoes
4. Women: dark leather purse with a shoulder-strap
5. Good quality (leather) briefcase
6. Leather day planner and/or handheld computer

I could clean up a little bit

Your nails should always be well groomed and manicured. Your hands are used for writing contracts and are always in the spotlight! Your nails and shoes are a direct reflection of how successful you are based on how attentive you are to your appearance.

Spot-check your clothing daily, making sure it is pressed and free of spots and stains. To avoid dry cleaning, use an iron and a wet towel to bring back a fresh look to your clothes, and keep shirts wrinkle-free. Invest in a lint remover, and keep it by the door to use before leaving.

Avoid garish and overpowering colors. Clothing should be conservative enough not to cause the buyer to be ill at ease! Be sure your overcoat is a neutral color. If you must wear jewelry, make sure it is simple and in good taste!

Spot-check your shoes daily to make sure they are shining and scuff-free.

Your total look not only includes how you dress, but also how clean you keep your car!

Your Automobile

Consider purchasing a newer four-door vehicle. Keep the following materials in your trunk:

1. Purchase agreements, net sheets, buyer information sheets. Keep forms in manila folders, with a separate folder for each type of form.
2. Open house signs (3 or 4) with name riders.
3. Children's books for all ages (2 or 3) for clients with children.
4. A calculator, camera, and flashlight.

Keep your personal brochures in the glove compartment. Affix a stick-on notepad and pen to the front of the dashboard, and keep a daily (week-at-a-glance) planner in the car. In addition, keep printouts of current listings from the area in which you work and update the listings weekly. You should have a large tape measure in your car, as well as a car or cell phone (for making appointments). On a weekly basis, spend time cleaning your car and removing all debris.

I stopped at a store and a woman started talking about real estate! She saw my license: HOMES 4U.

Keep healthy snacks—protein bars and bottled water—on hand for times when you are driving in the city, looking for listings or searching for new properties, or exploring new areas.

Consider putting your real estate motto on the side of your vehicle along with your phone number!

How to Work Smart

Organize your daily planner following these guidelines (or carry a BlackBerry containing the same information):

- A yearly agenda calendar that has spaces to write in daily.
- The inside cover flap should hold a flat amortization schedule, up-to-date real estate interest rates, personalized brochures, and a flat calculator.
- The inside back cover, underneath the notepad, should contain a blank listing as well as a blank purchase agreement.
- Use large paper clips to section off calendar dates.
- Have a separate section for your daily mileage records.
- Keep three large legal pads with you at all times, one for each of the following topics:
    1. For sale by owners (FSBOs)
    2. Daily to-do lists
    3. Daily phone messages
- Keep a plastic insert that holds business cards.

> Wow—I don't have any listings. I'd better get organized!

> Take time every day to record everything you do that involves money, your time, and the people with whom you have appointments.

> Keep one or two lock boxes in your car for new listings!

Purchase a good quality pen set for writing up purchase agreements and all new listings, or use a laptop for typing up the agreement!

How to Work Effectively

1. Use your time wisely: start early in the morning!
2. Dissect your day. Prioritize your morning, afternoon, evening. Spend the mornings doing computer research. During the afternoon, show buyers houses. In the evenings, update your daily planner, send faxes, check e-mail, and make appointments.

- Note throughout the day any FSBOs and contact for appointments.
- Contact expired listings for appointments.
- Contact canceled listings for appointments.
- Early in the week, make sure you have two open houses scheduled for the next weekend.
- Contacts: Potential sellers and buyers (call to make appointment).

- Inform FSBOs that there is a Multiple Listing Service filled with contracts already signed by a seller. That is the service you generally work with! Always try to get a FSBO to sign a list contract.
- Keep sending out computer information. Send new listings to buyers and potential clients. E-mail updated information.
- Remind buyers/sellers that you have either Tuesday or Thursday available. Ask them which day would work for them to set up an appointment.
- Are you listening to what your client tells you? Do you consistently take notes?
- Paper clip or rubber band a "cover sheet" on the front of your daily planner to be used as a to-do list.

I'm trying to get up before noon!

Make a transaction list

A transaction list is a list that contains the following information:

- Address
- Date sold
- Date closed
- Agent numbers
- Commissions earned

Getting Started with Contacts

1. Call an architect and request information. You may have a buyer who wants to design a new home (instant referral).
2. Find a good real estate attorney and have lunch. You may need to refer to him/her time and time again. They, in turn, will refer clients to you!
3. Contact good heating and plumbing contractors in your city. Have lunch with them. Give them referrals and vice-versa.

4. Talk to two or three good builders in locations you are comfortable with. Look at their projects. Keep information on hand. Need representation?

5. Go to the local courthouse. Become familiar with records of deed.

6. Call the telephone company and have second line installed for business or get a cell phone if you don't have one.

7. Locate two or three good title companies. Tour the companies and meet the closers.

8. Call two or three moving companies and request information. Give them your name for referrals.

9. Contact the Chamber of Commerce to see if there are openings for community involvement. This is an excellent resource for new clients.

10. Call the Welcome Wagon rep in your area. Offer assistance to incoming buyers they may know of.

11. Call five new companies in town and ask to speak with someone in the relocation department. Take them copies of your personal brochure/resume and promotions of your company.

12. Run a personal advertisement in the weekend edition of the newspaper.

13. Watch the business section of the newspaper. Look for real estate articles worthy of a monthly newsletter.

14. Have a professional photograph taken of yourself. Put it on everything you send out: monthly mailers, pencils, calendars, stationery, postcards, bus bench, and so on.

15. Set up your office, home, and car with duplicates of all necessary forms.

16. Join a health club and meet new people.

17. Join a religious organization. Put your picture ad in the weekly bulletin.

18. Visit estate sales and moving sales.

19. Network with your lawyer, dentist, doctor, and others.

20. Put a real estate logo on your car.

If I were Starting in the Business All Over Again, I Would . . .

1. Select one of the most productive agents at the office. I would ask if I could tag along to a few open houses to watch him or her in action.

2. Find someone who would have my least favorite area of real estate down pat and see if that agent would let me team up for some future business.

I have teamed up with many agents in the past to call on FSBOs, and we usually decide to split all commissions down the middle.

I like associating with a large, reputable real estate firm. This provides credibility not normally found when starting out with a tiny firm.

> **ALWAYS . . . LOOK YOUR BEST! YOU REPRESENT HOW SUCCESSFUL YOU ARE.**

I should have put gas in my car . . . my buyers got angry when I ran out!

Remember enthusiasm is contagious. Become enthusiastic—you will stay that way longer.

The more you worry, the more you lose your self-confidence.

Never leave anything to chance. Make the most of the moment.

I called my new client all week ... finally we have an appointment to see houses!

When you show a home or are ready to list a home, don't wait. By waiting—even until morning—buyers and sellers cool off!

Getting started in the real estate business takes a tremendous amount of perseverance and persistence. Another good word for it is "stick-to-it-iveness." Throughout the day, call:

- a buyer to buy a home
- a seller to sell a home
- a client to see a home
- a seller to list a home

My normal plan of action is to allow six weeks to find a home, and six weeks to sell a home.

Once you are in the business, you will encounter salespeople who do better than you, about the same as you, and much worse than you! Don't waste time wondering why. Don't wallow in self pity if this day Jane J. Jones got one more sale than you did. Don't be envious. Be positive!

It's amazing how jealousy can be conveyed. Be genuine! Compliment a fellow agent on a sale. Don't wonder who is being fed listings and buyers. It doesn't matter in the long run. What does matter is that you are doing all you can do to stay in the real estate business. You will be so busy that when you take a breather, it will be to go to sleep.

One important note in regard to sales commissions: Don't count on them until they are in the bank. Too often an agent becomes overconfident that there will be a closing and that he or she will get a check.

> Real estate is definitely a hands-on business. Real estate is definitely a hand-holding business.

Getting started in the real estate business is similar to getting started in the counseling business. You have to learn to understand people's needs and try to imagine yourself in their place.

Real estate people are looked upon to fix things, such as:

Fix my housing needs when I get divorced.

Let me yell at you because I'm frustrated.

Fix the bind I'm in financially—get me more money.

Fix the pressure because we bought before we sold.

Fix it!

Fix it!

Fix it!

My buyer bought the house with the ugly red carpet!

GETTING STARTED IN REAL ESTATE MEANS:
DISCIPLINE (throughout the day)
DETACHMENT (from disappointment)
DETERMINATION (go after that next lead!)

Getting started in real estate means making large sums of money when you least expect it, having your own hours and literally being your own boss, making wonderful new friends, sometimes for life, and becoming well known and very popular.

Role play the following situations with a "seasoned" real estate agent:

1. Hosting an open house.
2. Asking a buyer to sign a purchase agreement.
3. Asking a seller to sign a listing agreement.
4. Answering an ad in the newspaper.
5. Looking at houses.
6. Overcoming an obstacle regarding listing or buying.
7. Dealing with a client who just walked in.
8. Talking to a friend, relative, or neighbor about real estate.
9. Referring yourself to your local "frequently frequented" establishments.
10. Going over papers at a final closing (settlement and/or close of escrow).

Remember: Real estate generally runs in cycles. Sometimes it is very hot and then there is a cooling-off period. Know when it is important to stay hot and work those buyers and sellers rather than taking off for long periods of time. In the beginning it is much more difficult to take off a lot of time. As years go by, you will develop more and more networking among contacts and lots of referral business!

Perhaps your idea of setting yourself up involves designating duties to another individual. If this is the case, you will want to have a personal assistant. This person can do all of the detail work and usually can be paid by the hour. A personal

It is vital to take time each day just for you—to avoid burnout. Learn to pace yourself and know yourself and have fun with yourself.

Okay, Neil, you can be the buyer ... I will give us a problem listing I Have....

Can we do this a little later?

assistant can leave the networking to you and let you simply sell, sell, sell! (See the Personal Assistant section at end of this chapter.)

. . . and so goes it in the real world of real estate. Overall, it's fun, it's challenging, it's rewarding—and it's never, ever boring!

If a listing doesn't sell, reevaluate the entire program you have instituted with the seller. Begin by trying for a price reduction after 30 days.

If a buyer hasn't bought a home

- other areas should be investigated
- the price should be increased
- the price should be decreased
- the buyer lacks motivation
- the buyer cannot determine what he or she wants

If a seller hasn't sold their home

- the home is overpriced
- the home needs serious attention
- the home is marketed poorly
- the home is difficult to show

In order for you to be successful in today's real estate market,

you need discipline.

Getting started in the real estate business means *you must be informed.* In most states it is essential to complete a certain number of accredited courses every year. Each local real estate board sponsors seminars, conferences, and classes to take for continuing education. Keep abreast of what is happening in the real estate market across the country. Subscribe to real estate journals and periodicals. Become a CRS (Certified Real Estate Specialist). Obtain your real estate agent designation and attend graduate Real Estate Institute classes for your GRI designation.

Keep your eyes open to all that is around you and watch yourself in interactions with clients. Constantly improve your style. Watch for signs of your own weaknesses and work in these areas with self-help tapes and seminars. Discover special strengths that can distinguish you and sell your uniqueness.

CHAPTER 1

Getting started with good habits is extremely important. With the Clean Air Act in force and more and more people aware of air pollution, try not to smoke or offend a client with foul odors of any type. Always keep breath spray or a peppermint in your pocket for close encounters.

They bought from someone else ... they said I talk too much!

Get started with a good attitude (covered in Chapter 2) and a good sense of humor. Many, many transactions have been saved and closed with a good sense of humor and a light touch at the right moment. Learn to become discerning. Learn to listen more effectively and take constructive criticism when it is fair and truthful!

I don't need a plan ... something will come my way if I show up at the office ...

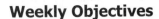

Weekly Objectives

1. Put together your real estate plan.
2. Develop an individual marketing system that you promote through your motto or logo.
3. Close daily on a new buyer or seller.
4. Get a minimum of two new buyers this week.
5. Get a minimum of two listings this week.
6. Call six FSBOs this week, working a 6-2-6 program.
7. Start your own referral sheet with your clients.
8. Prioritize and carefully schedule your time.
9. Weekly, write down 10 ways to improve your time management.
10. Keep a daily comprehensive to-do list.
11. Identify niche market possibilities.
12. Recognize and deal with stress.

It took me a few weeks ... but now I have a plan for my week, month, and year in real estate

"All Star Service"

(Photo of yourself on front of postcard with five stars.)

My weekly Checklist

Yes	No	
☐	☐	I have called and made appointments with buyers.
☐	☐	I have called at least five friends and asked for referrals.
☐	☐	I have added five to ten new names to my prospect list.
☐	☐	I have cut out at least five ads on FSBOs to call on.
☐	☐	I have driven through the area I work and looked for new business.
☐	☐	I have set up at least two open houses for this weekend.
☐	☐	I have set aside time for daily exercise and/or walking.
☐	☐	I call my customers/sellers/buyers and ask for feedback.
☐	☐	I attend any and all weekly real estate meetings and events.
☐	☐	Community involvement is important, and I volunteer weekly.
☐	☐	I call every potential client, and I ask for the next appointment.
☐	☐	I discuss self-evaluation with my sales manager.
☐	☐	I keep a good audio tape for motivation in my car.
☐	☐	I constantly update my daily planner with appointments.
☐	☐	Weekly I "classify" my buyers/sellers as to their motivation.
☐	☐	I try to close on a client, whether it is a buyer or a seller.
☐	☐	I try to meet new loan officers and know their services.
☐	☐	I write thank-you notes to buyers/sellers on weekly basis.

18 yes = excellent attitude	12–14 yes = fair attitude
14–16 yes = very good attitude	below 11 w = poor attitude for selling

Current Buyer List

Name	Address	Phone	Email	Date Met	House Needed	Price $	Area

Daily To Do

Time	Showings	Previews	FSBOs	Phone	Other
7 A.M.					
8 A.M.					
9 A.M.					
10 A.M.					
11 A.M.					
12 P.M.					
1 P.M.					
2 P.M.					
3 P.M.					
4 P.M.					
5 P.M.					
6 P.M.					
7 P.M.					
8 P.M.					

Personal After-Business Hours

Family:

Social:

Exercise:

Shop:

Friends:

Church:

To do:

Current Listings

Address	Name	Phone	Date Listed	Price	Combo Lockbox	Date sold

Transaction Sheet

Address	Seller/Buyer	Commission Paid	Closing Date	Agents Name/ Coop. Company Loan Officer/ Phone No.

Voice Mail Script

Hi, _____ here. I'm away from the phone temporarily. Today is _____ and I check my messages frequently. Please leave your name, phone number, time you called, and how I can help you. Talk to you soon . . .

Hello. Real estate is great today! I look forward to talking with you and helping you with your real estate needs. Please leave your name, phone number, and a brief message. I will return your call soon!

Good day! It's always a good time to take care of real estate! Please be aware that I check my messages often and will get right back to you! Just leave your name, phone number, and a message. I'll call soon.

This is _____ and today is _____. I'm away from this phone only momentarily; if you press 0 the operator will page me and I will get right back to you. Otherwise, leave your name and phone number and I will return your call shortly.

Real estate is moving today and so am I. However, I do check my messages often, so please leave your name, phone number, and a brief message. I will call you back soon.

Everywhere in the country someone is moving now! I am available to talk with you from 8 A.M. to 10 P.M. seven days a week. Please leave your name, phone number, and time you called. You will hear from me very soon.

A tremendous amount of property is now on the market. I am unavailable for a short period of time. If you are calling after 10 P.M. and need to reach me immediately, please feel free to e-mail me at _____. Or, please leave your name and phone number. I will get back to you ASAP.

When there is a home for sale, I find a buyer! Please be kind enough to leave your name, phone number, and brief message, and I will call you back as soon as possible. Have a great day!

It's so much easier to buy and sell today! From e-mail to web page, I take the worry out of real estate. Please leave your name and phone number and I will contact you shortly. Feel free to press 0 to have me paged.

Real estate is moving quickly today. There are so many new listings! Please feel free to leave your name and phone number, and I will call you for an appointment shortly.

This is only temporary! I can get back to you shortly. Just leave your name, phone number, and a brief message. Feel free to visit my website in the meantime at: _____. Or "blog" or e-mail me at: _____. I look forward to talking with you soon.

Sales Strategies

1. Never make the buyer or seller angry. There is nothing to be gained by arguing with the buyer or seller. Try to stick with the truth and stay focused on negotiating to win.
2. Disclose only the truth. Do not volunteer unnecessary information. There is no reason to tell a potential buyer the seller's "bottom line."
3. Trust in yourself. You will develop a good relationship with your clients when they know you possess self-confidence. Know the facts about properties in question.
4. Remember, a house will always sell itself. It is not necessary to try to convince a buyer to purchase a property that does not interest them.
5. It is a waste of time to show a client properties that are priced too high. If you do so, buyers will become disenchanted with what they can afford.
6. The most successful relationship is built on trust. Your client must be able to trust you. Anything you do to limit this trust will hamper negotiations with your client.

7. The majority of people do not want to reveal their true motivations. If someone says something is "non-negotiable," you many need to use a new approach.

8. When people speak in a loud, angry voice, they usually are fearful about something. Investigate this area; find out what the problem is.

9. Although signed contracts are supposed to be binding, in practice frequently the language is flawed or the sellers or buyers have a way out.

10. In order to resolve issues before a client will sign a contract to buy a home, concerns and problems must be addressed one by one.

11. Try to tackle the least important issues first, knowing this will bring comfort to the buyer and will help to develop an outline in the contract.

12. Leave the impossible tasks for last. If you are between a rock and a hard place on the purchase price, ask them to split the difference.

13. Communicate with your clients often; remember that they are waiting for you to present an offer to them ASAP.

14. Always remember that individuals are unique.

15. At any given juncture, try to close on your client to buy or to sell.

Timeless Tips

1. Timing is everything.
2. Once you back down, you can't change your mind.
3. Always set a deadline for negotiating on a purchase agreement.
4. Act quickly if a buyer and a home are a good match.
5. There must be an offer—in writing—before anyone can negotiate.
6. Know your facts and don't assume anything regarding the listing.
7. Be current on all financing and mortgage information.
8. When showing a property, leave the best for last.
9. A house will always sell itself; an agent need only show the buyer where to sign.
10. Asking why gets everything out in the open.
11. You can always make a deal with someone you trust.
12. Never, under any circumstances, offend the buyer or seller.
13. When someone says non-negotiable, negotiations have begun.
14. Just because it is written doesn't mean it is true.
15. Listen, listen, listen to discover what each party wants in a deal.
16. In real estate, knowledge is always power.
17. Pricing a home fairly from the start results in more offers more quickly.
18. Offer bonuses to agents in top brackets to sell a home quickly.
19. Learn all you can about contract for deeds creative financing.
20. Sometimes in order to make a deal, a commission must be negotiated.

Personal Assistant

A personal assistant can perform many duties for a real estate agent. Following is a list of the many jobs I have assigned to my personal assistant:

1. Prepare a FSBO packet.
2. Prepare a listing packet.
3. Prepare a buyer's packet.
4. Prepare seller's weekly report.
5. Call with feedback to all agents after showings.
6. Answer telephone calls and messages.
7. Track all pending files before closing.
8. Input listing, price changes, and so on in computer.
9. Contact title companies.
10. Take photo of property.
11. Help to measure home.
12. Get printout of current new listing, solds, and expireds.
13. Clip and save all FSBOs in newspaper.
14. Update computer daily. Obtain latest interest rates from lender.
15. Send out fax to other company and/or client.
16. Write ad for paper.
17. Write ad for real estate magazine and/or television.
18. Update client list for mailer after closing.
19. Make all appointments for buyer.
20. Send highlight sheet on listing to other agents.
21. Prepare a CMA on the computer.
22. Prepare an area market survey on computer.
23. Purchase cards and gifts for closing.
24. Give all information on property to appraisers.
25. Order self-marketing tools for agents.
26. Send listing renewal to clients ahead of schedule.
27. Note all showings on listing files.
28. Continue to update calendars.
29. Keep files on important real estate articles for newsletters.
30. Use computer for mailings of postcards and mass mailings.
31. Take care of travel arrangements.
32. Set up open houses.
33. Pull comparable listings for FSBOs.
34. Install highlight homes boxes at listing.
35. Call lender for update of buyer's mortgage.
36. Send thank-you notes to clients and/or agents.
37. Send out sheet of new listing to all top agents.
38. Type correspondence; proofread purchase agreements.
39. Keep office neat and orderly.
40. Take notes at office meeting if agent is unable to attend.

I thought I could "Do It All" . . . and now I have no business!

"MAKE THE RIGHT MOVE"

(Photo of you on the front of postcard.)

Following is a list of various functions, compiled by agents in the field. Assigning jobs to an assistant allows you more time to call on NEW CLIENTS!

1. Input the listing, change the price in computer, and send to MLS.
2. Prepare a report to send to the sellers weekly.
3. Label and prepare a listing packet for new business.
4. Label and prepare a buyer's packet for new buyers.
5. Prepare a FSBO packet and pull solds off the computer to carry with you.
6. Track all new files before the closing.
7. Contact title companies. Keep all information current.
8. Photograph subject property.
9. Help to measure the dimensions of the property.
10. Generate a computer printout of current listings, solds, expireds.
11. Send out fax to other companies and buyers/ sellers.
12. Write ads for Sunday open houses.
13. Write ads for other periodicals.
14. Set up showings for new buyers.
15. Clip and get names and additional information on FSBOs.
16. Answer the telephone and take all messages.

My real estate field manual helps me write ads now!

A Daily Planner

The ultimate personal marketing tool that every professional must have!

Chapter Summary

Starting out in the business requires one crucial element: discipline, followed by organization and enthusiasm! As a real estate agent, you need to be prepared from the start. This chapter discussed 26 essentials you should have in your possession in order to work effectively in the real estate business today. A daily planner and a laptop computer are just two of them!

As a real estate agent, you should always look successful—from how you dress to how clean you keep your car! Organize your daily planner with important guidelines, and work effectively with the 20-point plan for getting started with contacts.

Don't forget to take time off periodically; this will help you avoid burnout. Hiring a personal assistant can help with the day-to-day detail work; assistant are usually paid by the hour.

Utilize and put into practice the 12-point weekly objectives discussed in this chapter. Also, use one or a combination of the various voicemail scripts provided in this chapter. These will help to identify who you are and secure a client's return call.

Finally, fifteen important sales strategies are provided to help you identify how to close on your client to buy or sell. Timing is everything. Pricing a home fairly from the start will result in more offers quickly. Listen, listen, listen, and remember—knowledge is always power.

ATTITUDE

- Agency
- Fair Housing

big deal by Lorayne n' Neil

Attitude

Following is a quote from Charles Swindoll:

> The longer I live, the more I realize the impact of attitude on life. Attitude, to me, is more important than facts. It is more important than appearance, gift, or skill. It will make or break a company... a church...a home.

The remarkable thing is we have a choice every day regarding the attitude we will embrace for that day. We cannot change our past. We cannot change the fact that people will act in a certain way. WE CANNOT CHANGE THE INEVITABLE. The only thing we can do is play on the one string we have, and that is our attitude. I am convinced that life is 10 percent what happens to me and 90 percent how I react to it...and so it is with you...we are in charge of our attitudes.

My definition:

> Attitude, either spontaneous or thought out, is the reaction you take to and maintain in any given situation. An attitude is directly attributable to the value you place on happiness and peace of mind. An attitude, more than any other single thing, will make or break you in the real estate business.

Guess what?

Attitude is 93 percent of everything that you do!

Guess what else?

Almost 83 percent of all communication is what you see.

The amount of money you make in real estate depends on how you feel about yourself.

What about Your Attitude

Your attitude might as well sum up your whole career in a nutshell.

Here's an example of attitude that I can think of:

> Don't listen to No!
> Carefully...
> Constantly...
> Consistently...maintain a positive approach.
> Don't listen to No.

If a client mentions that he "really doesn't want to list his home right now," and he's had the best of all real estate agents over to his house and he's "sick and tired of the whole thing," tell him that you understand completely. Then tell him that you really are going to be in his area next Monday, and you really do have either 4:00 or 7:00 P.M. open right now. Tell him you could stop by on Monday; ask him which time would work best for him. If neither time works, then when? If he's not interested in meeting at all, find out why.

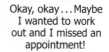

Be kind.

Listen.

If all else fails and he still says no, then that's okay—you won't get all of them.

> Go on to the next one, and the next one.
> And suddenly someone will want you to come over and list his or her home.
> And the wait wasn't so bad after all!
> It works—I know it does because that's how I get all of my business. I SIMPLY DON'T GIVE UP.
> Good luck eventually finds me.

I could write chapter after chapter on attitude, how to stay enthusiastic, how to constantly keep the smile on your face when all around you is horrible. But actually maintaining a good attitude is a bit simpler than that.

Try to remember to stay disciplined! Have a schedule each and every day from which you cannot and will not and do not deviate. Use certain days to call on the FSBOs, certain days to work with your buyers, certain days to call on expireds, and certain days to spend on yourself. In all my years in the business, I still reserve Sundays for "opens." I have two open houses on Sundays: 12:00 to 2:00 P.M. and 2:30 to 4:30 P.M. I call FSBOs on Sunday nights. I still go over all my notes from my opens on Mondays and call buyers to set up showings for the week. I send out mailings and call more FSBOs on Mondays to set up appointments for all week!

You are only as busy, successful, and motivated as your daily calendar shows that you are! Your attitude is your lifeline in the real estate business!

Be your own manager! Set up your own schedule for the *entire week* at the *beginning of the week.* Start with Sunday after your two open houses!

You need to fill in the blanks for the week *by Monday.* Call and work with two buyers a week. Call and work on at least two listings a week. Call and work on at least five future listings (FSBOs) each week. Call and work on at least five expired listings each week. Your attitude should tell you to *just do it*! Don't think about how you feel. Don't think about needing money, not having money, not feeling like it, not wanting to do it, or possible rejection. Don't think beyond the disciplined schedule that you have created for yourself.

Attitude reduces to one equation:

basic hard work = terrific results

A common denominator of life is that most successful people have the habit of doing things that other people don't like to do.

Be all that you can be. Give yourself continual reassurance.

You need to work the business from all of these angles:

1. Out-of-town buyers
2. Local buyers and sellers
3. Corporate relocation clients
4. Expired listings
5. Past customers
6. Retired people

I worked friday night, but I found so many new listings for my clients...

Take on the goal to make a sale, somehow, every day! (Sometimes this means selling a client on making an appointment.)

You will get ahead because most people are unwilling to make even a good effort! To achieve this goal, you must

1. Have a plan, and
2. Prospect all the time.

In real estate, if you come to and leave work without appointments, you are out of business!

All we have to offer people is our product knowledge.

To determine your sales appeal, ask yourself if you would hire yourself to sell your own home.

I've got a hangover today! Wish I didn't have to show houses!

People hire real estate agents for three reasons:

1. To manage their properties.
2. To help with the decorating.
3. To get a property bought or sold.

REMEMBER:

People will always want to work with **enthusiastic** individuals.

People get hung up on ego.

Take control of your own destiny!

Professional Attitude

1. When meeting someone for the first time, try to refrain from calling them by their first name. Personal contact is essential, and understanding how a client wishes to be addressed is crucial. If there is any doubt about how to address someone, use "Mr.," "Mrs." or "Miss," or simply ask, "What do you prefer?"

2. Immediately learn how to pronounce a person's name. Everyone likes to have their name pronounced correctly. Avoid misspelling the name and avoid difficulty with pronunciation. Learn how to say your client's name.

3. If you have a client from a different country, respect the cultural differences. Although it is not necessary to learn everything you have always wanted to know about that country, go to the library first and do your homework. Your client will be much more comfortable after meeting you.

4. Many people wish to keep their relationship with you on a more formal level. Respect this wish. Do not try to familiarize yourself or become too personal. A business relationship comes first. Buying and selling a home is serious business!

5. Buyers and sellers come in all shapes, sizes, and ages! Don't show disrespect to a client who appears to be too old or too young. All clients should be given the same respect regardless of their culture or age.

6. Respect all religious holidays, and schedule appointments around these observances. Many people of the Jewish religion observe the holy day from sundown on Friday to sundown on Saturday. They may not wish to conduct business during this time. With this awareness, many problems can be avoided.

7. Always confirm and reconfirm appointment times. Check with your secretary and be prompt and efficient. Be sure you leave a card with the time, date, and your name on it. This also protects you from any misunderstanding regarding who was the last person to "leave the door open" if there were to be two or three showings on one day.

8. Many countries do not measure by the square foot; some customers may actually prefer the metric system. Charts that convert meters to feet are readily available.

9. Avoid saying "I hardly notice your accent," and using terms such as *handicap*.

10. Practice remembering your client's name!

Training Programs

Real estate training programs are essential to helping an agent become a professional in the business!

Business math, foreign language, English, and office skills are great classes to help you become a professional in real estate.

There are many excellent real estate schools in your area. Many schools will want you to use the *Real Estate Field Manual* as your car companion as you enter into the field of real estate.

Be sure to look for a certified real estate school.

- Most states require a minimum of 60+ hours of prelicensing.
- Each state is free to set its own limits for prelicensing.
- State averages range from 45 to 90 hours.

Prelicense salesperson requirement course

This course normally covers topics ranging from real estate law, property rights, and contracts, to finance, legal language, and contract for deed.

Educational requirement courses

It's too confusing. I should have taken a training program!

These courses include title problems, legal descriptions, closing situations, agency law, evaluations, finance, antitrust, and, of course, fair housing.

Prelicense education requirements include:

- Agency law
- Fair housing
- Disclosure fundamentals
- Contract law
- Principles of real estate
- Total number of required hours in your state: _____

Related real estate courses include:

- Real estate investment
- Real estate trading/auction
- Real estate marketing
- Real estate on the Internet
- Real estate finance
- Listing presentation
- Real estate foreclosure
- Real estate property trends
- Real estate syndication
- Real estate management

Most courses range from three to four credit hours.

Training program questions:

1. What requirements do I need?
2. What are the qualifications?
3. Is the school accredited?
4. How much does the program cost?
5. Will my real estate company reimburse me?
6. Does the school have a child care program available?
7. What classes are offered?

Licensing and Broker Requirements
for Most States

- Must be 18 years of age. Some states require that applicants be 21 years old.
- Must have attended real estate school for a minimum of 90 hours.
- Must have passed a state licensing examination given by a state-approved licensing school on real estate principles and practices.
- Must attend yearly continuing education courses (standards, issues, fair housing, agency law, contract law, and electives).
- Must apply for license with a reputable broker.
- Fingerprinting (some states).
- Must pay all state, broker, required fees.
- Must order name riders, business cards, signs for open houses.
- Must establish membership in national and local board of realtors.
- Must join organizations that are of benefit to real estate agent status.
- Must sign contract with broker and sign various arbitration contracts.
- Must attend weekly, bimonthly, annual real estate broker meetings and conventions, plus additional seminars.
- Must be honest, reputable, and of the highest moral character.
- Must strive to improve the image of real estate agent by exercising the highest of standards in each and every transaction.
- Must treat all clients and potential clients fairly regardless of race, creed, or national origin.
- Must enhance your personal image to reflect the highest degree of personal self-confidence possible.
- Must demand honesty, integrity, and high moral character.
- Must meet a "sales goal quota" for each individual office.
- Must pay for online computer access for MLS.

Fair Housing

In August 1997, The National Association of REALTORS® approved the model Affirmative Fair Housing Marketing Plan for use by all real estate agents in the nation.

Fair Housing is designed to ensure positive outreach and information to people who would be least likely to know about and apply for the housing in question.

> The Fair Housing Act covers all prospective buyers or tenants of all minority and non-minority groups in the housing market area regardless of race, color, religion, sex, handicap, familial status, or national origin. These groups include: Whites (non-Hispanic), Blacks (non-Hispanic), American Indians/Alaskan Natives, Hispanics, and Asian Pacific Islanders.

This program ensures that any group(s) normally not likely to apply for housing without special outreach efforts—because of existing neighborhood racial and ethnic patterns, location of housing in the metropolitan area, price, or other factors—know about the housing and feel welcome to apply and have the opportunity to buy or to rent.

On December 5, 1996, HUD and the NAR entered into a Fair Housing Partnership that replaced the Voluntary Affirmative Marketing Agreement.

A REALTOR® FAIR HOUSING DECLARATION now exists under the terms of which the real estate professional agrees to:

1. Provide equal and professional service without regard to race, color, religion, sex, handicap, familial status, or national origin of any prospective client or resident of any community.
2. Stay informed about fair housing law and practices, improving clients' opportunities and my business.
3. Develop advertising that indicates everyone is welcome and no one is excluded; expand clients' opportunities to see, buy, and/or lease property.
4. Inform my clients about their rights and responsibilities under the Fair Housing laws by providing brochures and information.
5. Document my efforts to provide professional service, which will assist me in becoming more responsible and successful.
6. Refuse to tolerate noncompliance. Take a positive approach to Fair Housing by developing and implementing fair housing practices always.

Fair housing act

The Federal Fair Housing Act became effective March 12, 1989.

This law prohibits any discrimination in the housing market based on any of the following protected categories:

- Race
- Color
- National origin
- Religion
- Sex
- Familial status (presence of child, under 18, or pregnant)
- Disability (physical, mental, sensory, AIDS/HIV, recovered addict)

FHA Resource Center
1 800 225-5342

Following are examples of activities that would be violations of the law, based on a person's protected class. This list is not all-inclusive, but encompasses the most commonly identified discriminatory acts.

- Refused to rent or sell housing, or to negotiate a rental sale.
- False denial that housing is available for inspection, sale, or rental.

- Refusal to make reasonable accommodation for a tenant with a disability.
- Raising inappropriate questions about an applicant's disability.
- Establishment of different terms, conditions, or privileges for sale or rental of dwelling.
- Providing alternative housing services or facilities to tenant.
- Failure to make housing available.
- Steering or directing a renter/buyer to a specific neighborhood, apartment, or house.
- For profit, persuading owner to sell or rent (blockbusting).
- Denial of access to or membership in a facility or service (such as a multiple listing service) related to the sale or rental of housing.
- Advertising or making a statement that indicates a discriminatory preference.

Persons who may not discriminate include, but are not limited to:

> Landlords
> Resident managers or assistant resident managers
> Apartment maintenance crew or other staff
> Property managers
> Property owners
> Newspapers or other sources of advertisement
> Real estate agents
> Lenders or other financial institutions
> Insurance agents or companies
> Appraisers, builders, and architects
> Any other person who designs, constructs, or provides housing

Persons with disabilities receive additional protection under the Fair Housing Act. In order to enable persons with disabilities to realize equal enjoyment of housing, the Act provides the right to request reasonable accommodations, to make reasonable modifications, and to live in accessible housing, depending on the age of the housing.

A person with a disability has the right to request that a housing provider make reasonable accommodations that will enable the person with a disability to have equal enjoyment of housing. Reasonable accommodations are changes in policy that do not change the nature of the program. Examples include, but are not limited to:

- Allowing a person with a working or therapy animal to live in an apartment with a no-pets policy.
- Providing a friendly note on the last day of the month to remind a person with developmental disability the rent is due the following day.
- Providing a sign language interpreter for meetings with a tenant who has a hearing impairment.

> The law does not provide detail regarding what types of accommodations are reasonable, so it becomes a matter of judgment on behalf of both the landlord and the tenant.

A tenant with a disability has the right to request a physical modification to his or her rental unit if such modification is necessary to provide the tenant equal enjoyment of housing. Examples of reasonable modifications include:

- Installation of a ramp
- Installation of grab bars
- Widening of doorways
- Installation of a lift

In most cases, the tenant bears the cost of modifications made to the property and will need to assure the landlord that the work will be done properly and that any permits needed will be acquired. The tenant may be required to make payment to an escrow account to establish funds to remove the alteration, if indeed the change would interfere with the landlord's or future tenant's ability to enjoy the property.

Newer multifamily housing accessibility

Any housing that consists of four or more units that was built for first occupancy after March 13, 1991, must comply with the six technical requirements for new construction. These requirements are:

- Accessible entrances on an accessible route
- Accessible public and common use areas
- Usable doors
- Accessible routes into and within the dwelling
- Switches, outlets, and environmental controls at specific heights
- Usable kitchens and bathrooms: bathroom wall reinforced with grab bar

Agency

What exactly is an *agency*?

The dictionary defines agency as "a means of exerting power or influence." In real estate, agency is the fiduciary relationship that results from a manifestation of consent by one person to another that the other shall act on his behalf and subject to his control and consent by the other to so act. A fiduciary relationship is the highest standard of duty implied by the law. Real estate licensees' fiduciary duties include:

1. Loyalty
2. Obedience
3. Disclosure
4. Confidentiality
5. Reasonable care and diligence
6. Duty to account

I can remember these easily enough....

> **Principal** = the one for whom action is taken
> **Agent** = the one who is to act

In a real estate brokerage firm, an agency relationship is formed between the brokerage firm (including all licensees) and the principal.

Client = a buyer or seller represented by the agent

Customer = a person not represented by licensee but working with licensee. For example, a seller may be represented by an agent; a buyer is not. A buyer may be represented by an agent; a seller may be a FSBO.

> **Seller's Agent:** A real estate agent who is employed by and represents only the seller in the transaction (a.k.a. list agent).
>
> **Subagent:** An agent who is employed to act for another agent who performs duties undertaken for the principal. This person owes the same duties to the principal as the principal's agent. The liabilities created by the subagent for the primary agent and the principal are the same as those that would be created by the primary agent acting for the principal.
>
> **Buyers' agent:** A real estate agent employed by the principal who represents only the buyer in a real estate transaction regardless of who pays the commission. Information must be kept confidential.
>
> **Dual agent:** An agent whose brokerage represents both the buyer and the seller in the same real estate transaction with the informed consent of both parties. One licensee can legally act as a dual agent, although this concept is difficult to put into practice. Dual agents owe fiduciary duties to both buyer and seller. Therefore, there are limits imposed by law regarding the role and disclosure obligations of dual agents (also known as an in-house sale).

Most states require disclosure of agency representation in the purchase agreement.

Disclosure forms issued after 1993 have provided for more complete agency disclosure, including statutory disclosure forms with particular emphasis on extensive dual agency disclosure. The process and forms apply to one-to-four-unit residential property transactions. They also require a written buyer representation contract.

After 1994, some states amended agency disclosure forms by providing that disclosures made in accordance with the statute were sufficient to satisfy common law disclosure requirements, and that agents must disclose specifically if the client is a relative or business associate, or if the agent is the principal in the transaction.

In 1996, some states made modifications intended to streamline and to simplify the process, in part by replacing the four statutory agency disclosure forms with a one-page disclosure form. They also required presentation of new one-page form to all customers and clients at **first substantive contact** (first meeting). First substantive contact does not occur when a client asks how many bedrooms there are in the house. However, when they start talking about the sense of urgency and what is motivating them, then it is wise to provide a disclosure form citing the various agency roles.

The 1996 law also covers listing contracts, buyer representation contracts, and purchase agreements, which must now contain dual agency disclosure and/or consent language from previous forms. These buyer representation contracts must be signed before the real estate agent performs any act to represent the buyer and before a purchase agreement is signed. If no representation contract is signed, the party is treated as a customer and is not represented by the broker. The broker is then a **subagent** of the seller or a **nonagent**.

> **Agency law** applies to all transactions, whether residential or commercial. Statutory form and process applies to *residential real property*, which is property occupied.

Agency Options

Seller representation

In *seller representation* one acts for and in the best interests of the seller's principal, agent, and subagent relationships. This relationship is created by written contract. Multiple Listing Service creates relationships implied from statements or conduct. There are loyalties and responsibilities toward the seller. There also exists a vicarious liability for statements made and conduct of agents and subagents that can bind the sellers.

The duties toward the buyer are to disclose material facts about a property to buyers and to disclose that a party intends not to perform in accordance with the terms of a purchase agreement.

Buyer representation

In *buyer representation*, the agent acts for and in the best interest of the buyer's principal-agent-subagent relationships. This is a relationship created by written contracts. Multiple Listing Service creates an agency relationship implied from statements or conduct. There are loyalties and responsibilities toward the buyer that contrast with seller representation.

Dual agency

In *dual agency*, the broker acts for and in the interests of *both* the buyer and the seller. An *in-house transaction* is created when one or more agents licensed to a brokerage represent *both* the buyer and the seller. Disclosures and consents are now *required*: explanation and initial consent in listing contract and buyer representation contracts and confirmation and consent in purchase agreements. A responsibility still exists to the buyers and to the sellers. A fiduciary duty is owed to both buyer and seller. Dual agency contrasts with exclusive buyer representation and exclusive seller representation. In dual agency, one cannot "advocate exclusively for either party" and cannot "represent the interests of either party to the detriment of the other."

Nonagency transaction broker

A nonagency transaction broker facilitates the transaction but does not represent either party. This arrangement requires a *written* contract. The relationship with the buyer or the seller provides services *specified in the written contract* to facilitate this transaction. The role of a nonagency transaction broker is limited in that there is no advocacy or negotiation on behalf of a party.

With the new year upon us, new laws state that agents must disclose their "relationship with buyers and sellers." They must be able to answer questions on accompanying forms regarding behavior and separate requirements thereof. If their role changes, they need to redisclose their relationship.

Statutory one-page agency relationship disclosure forms are used, for the most part, in all residential transactions and they replace the four statutory agency disclosure addenda. The new forms include the following provisions:

- Addition of dual agency provisions
- New nonagency services agreement
- No agency relationship established
- Confidential information about price, terms, and motivation to be kept confidential
- Compensation agreement
- Term of contract, with services to be provided
- Caution in looking at other states for guidance. Different roles can be taken without dual agency occurring (the absence of representation on one side of the table or the other).

In-house sale: A property is sold by an agent licensed to the listing company. Dual agency exists in an in-house transaction only when agents of the brokerage are representing both the buyer and the seller. No dual agency exists when the selling agent represents the seller as a subagent.

Nonagent: A licensed real estate broker who represents neither seller nor buyer in the transaction, owes no fiduciary duties to either party, and whose duties to the party and method of compensation are spelled out in a nonagency service contract. The nonagent facilitates the transaction, but does not act in a representative role (for example, does not advocate or negotiate for the party).

What exactly are *fiduciary duties*?

1. Loyalty: An agent must act at all times solely in the best interests of the principal to the exclusion of all other interests, including the agent's own self-interest.
2. Obedience: An agent is obligated to obey promptly and efficiently all lawful instructions of the principal.
3. Disclosure: An agent is obligated to disclose to the principal all relevant and material information, unless obtained through a previous fiduciary relationship, that the agent knows and that pertains to the scope of the agency. In a dual agency, the law imposes limits on the kind of information the dual agent can disclose.
4. Confidentiality: An agent is obligated to safeguard the principal's confidences and secrets.

5. Reasonable care and diligence: An agent is obligated to use reasonable care and diligence in pursuing the principal's affairs.

6. Accounting: An agent is obligated to account for all money or property belonging to the principal that is entrusted to him or to her.

The importance of creating an agency relationship:

1. There must be express written or oral agreement.
2. Listing contracts, buyer representation contracts.

Commitment

The real estate business is you! To be in the business unconditionally in rain, sleet, snow, hard times, good times, high interest rates, low interest rates, happy customers, and so on, you must have an unconditional desire to succeed.

Some time-saving devices include:

1. Cell phone/BlackBerry
2. Computer (laptop)
3. Fax machine
4. Phone mail/voice mail/e-mail
5. Personal assistant
6. Blogging
7. ichat

I try to start over every day...let go of the ones I lost...

Increase productivity without increasing your activity.

Life is a gift and a game you've already won. *To maintain a lead, be true to yourself!*

Is there a best attitude to approaching real estate? Is there such a thing as being able to turn a positive attitude on and off? Can a person actually achieve success in the real estate business, even when his or her life is in a quandary and depression is weighing heavily on one's mind?

Let's just say the answer for myself, to all of the above, is Yes! I have developed a formula for success for myself over the years by applying a technique that works well using a time management solution for buyers, home, office, open houses, and sellers.

Attitude toward Buyers

When I meet with a buyer through a phone call, an open house, or from a referral, I try to use the following formula to keep them as clients:

> I sit down with my clients and have at least one meeting during which I can listen to their needs. I listen to what is important to them and put a time limit on how long they want to look for a house. I frame a time limit from the very beginning.

I let buyers know that my attitude toward selling them a house is based on when they want to be in a property. I do not allow myself to listen if they tell me that "if and when" they find the right house they will buy. This is not appropriate dialogue for either my clients or for me. I find it imperative that I get across to them how important it is to be working within a timeframe for all parties concerned.

> I stress the fact that, once a home is found, usually a mortgage commitment is affixed at or around 60 days, and that the interest rate is usually set for that period of time.

> I also stress the fact that good properties are usually uncovered immediately and sell fairly quickly. Buyers need to have, especially for themselves, some sort of timeframe.

I explain to my clients that I assign them to one of *three categories: A, B,* or C. The A buyers are the buyers who get the *majority* of my attention—and rightly so. Once you establish boundaries on your own *way of working*, the respect that comes from your buyers is *automatic.* Buyers instinctively don't want to miss out on a good deal. If they feel that they can get the best from you just by rerouting their own thought patterns on how and when to buy, it will be in everyone's best interest to have a timeframe to work within. (The B and C buyers are not in a hurry.)

Important Rule Of Thumb: Find Out Your Potential Buyer's Schedule.

Make sure that you allow yourself time in the beginning to discover client flexibility and to set up future appointment times. Also cover the ground rules from the start.

Have an attitude that is *enthusiastic, fun,* and *exciting* in order to entice potential buyers to want to be with you more than any other real estate agent. How can you achieve this? *Tell them that you are the best agent for them.* Keep your personal life separate. Don't allow the buyer to peek into your private life! Talk about *them.* Ask lots of questions. Be cheerful, talkative, and upbeat about real estate.

Attitude at Home

Is your business life tied with your family life? How important is it to mix? Should and can you take real estate calls at home at any time and allow them to overlap with family time? The answer to all of the above questions is Yes.

You simply need to know how to do this. Your attitude regarding real estate must be very broad-minded. You must be able to cope, bend, and be flexible in ways that you were not required before. This is all okay if you can allow yourself the opportunity to say No at the appropriate times and work within a fixed schedule for yourself and your family.

Your family should know that the home phone is essential to success in real estate. The phone at home must, should, and can be answered in a professional manner at all times. Let your family know how important it is for everyone who calls to hear an appropriate response at your end. Let them know that good manners come across with a good attitude on the telephone. Many missed calls and wrong numbers and much loss of time can be eliminated simply by making the following statement when answering the telephone:

"Hello, this is the Johnson residence, Jim speaking." Or "Anderson residence. May I help you?"

Keep a pencil and pad of paper by each phone in the house. Instruct all people living at home how important a telephone message is and that not only the name and phone number, but the time of the call is very important! Tell your family how important phone calls are to you and that you *do not* intend to let business interfere with family time during certain times of the day. Try to work around this timeframe. If the dinner hour is from 6:00 to 7:00 every night, make this the time that the answering service automatically receives the calls at home. With an appropriate message on your recorder, this should not be a problem.

When people come through one of your open houses, they immediately *size you up*. It isn't fair, but *life isn't fair*. That's the way it is. Buyers will decide—sometimes on the spot— whether or not they want to work with you.

Your Attitude Cannot Be Compromised.

You must decide when preparing for an open house that your attitude will be upbeat, cheerful, and **enthusiastic!**

When meeting buyers at an open house, act and talk the way you would want to be treated if you were them. Attend other open houses to gauge how impressed you are with the attitudes of other agents. What turns you on or off?

Never take anything for granted.

You most likely will not have another opportunity to impress them!

I told them
I went fishing...
I did't get a chance
to wash the car!

Attitude Toward Sellers

Should you treat all sellers the same? Should you answer a seller's question just to satisfy him or her, even before you have checked into it? Should you assume that you probably will not get the listing from a seller because he or she mentioned another company?

THE ANSWER TO ALL OF THE ABOVE QUESTIONS IS NO.

The correct attitude to have regarding sellers is to treat every potential sale as a unique situation. Rely on your good judgment to tell you when to back off and when to ask more questions. But have the attitude that you can help them regardless of their difficulty with selling their home. Do your homework first. Your attitude should consist of genuine concern and undivided attention to their entire situation. You should demonstrate an understanding nature about what has brought them to this point, and let them know that you are the professional and you will make every conceivable effort to help them in the best way you can. Be sure to convey an attitude of trust and assuredness. Your demeanor should be impeccable, and your appearance should be professional at all times. You should reflect an attitude of irreproachable honesty and unique style. Sellers should be left feeling that you are the best professional that they could hope to find—a confident person whom they can trust.

Your attitude toward sellers will be a deciding factor in your success in the real estate business.

Never, under any circumstances, take anything for granted. Follow up on all information.

> **You Should Be the Best Groomed. Your Attitude Should Be the Best in the Room.**

Seven important statements for real estate salespersons

1. Stop focusing on what is not, and start creating what can be!
2. Take an honest look at all the negative practices in your life and business, and eliminate them.
3. Revoke your membership in the "Knock Yourself Down" Club.
4. Start all over again with the basics.
5. Look ahead instead of backwards. Spend time in your past only if you really must.
6. Change your mental diet by watching what you feed yourself (TV, radio, paper, magazines, etc.). Spend 30 minutes daily outdoors.
7. Do something that you normally wouldn't do or couldn't afford to do. In other words, *take a risk!*

The Key To Growing Is Expanding Your Knowledge.

If You Want Success in Real Estate, You Can Have It !

How to Work Best with Your Body's Timeclock

> It is important to know how to make use of the best hours in each and every day. Did you know that your body has a natural timeclock and that you subconsciously follow what your body says, regardless of what you want to do?

Following is a general guide for taking full advantage of your body's daily rhythm.

7:00–9:00 A.M.	Short-term memory is at its peak. Problem-solving skills are at their peak. Overall alertness is generally very high.
8:00–10:00 A.M.	Pain tolerance is highest.
9:00 A.M.–12:00 P.M.	Analytical and reasoning skills are high. Good time to solve problems. Good time to map strategy. Good time to balance books. *Good time for thinking things through.*
10:00 A.M.–12:00 P.M.	You are wide awake. You are most alert and most aware. Your speaking skills are at their peak. Excellent time for business meetings. Excellent time for presentations. Good time for closing arguments and important lunches and brunches.
1:00–3:00 P.M.	You naturally feel dull and sleepy; exercise at this time revitalizes you. Good time for walking, jogging, or swimming.
3:00–4:00 P.M.	Alertness rises again. Long-term memorization skills peak. Time to deliver a speech or sell job. Recall of material is 8 percent higher. Hand-to-eye coordination is at its peak. This is a good time for a game of tennis.
3:00–5:00 P.M.	You might expect to experience a mood swing. Disposition improves throughout the day. Cheerful afternoon high.
4:00–5:00 P.M.	Your ability to handle confrontation is at its highest.
4:00–6:00 P.M.	Your manual dexterity is the sharpest. This is a good time to type contracts.
6:00–9:00 P.M.	Your thinking skills and reflexes are winding down. Not a good time to exercise. You need to regroup. Good time for mental affirmations. Low key.
7:00–9:00 P.M.	Your five senses are most acute now. Great time to appreciate music. Excellent time for rescheduling activities for the next day. Excellent time to meet with people because you are so responsive to their needs and wants.
11:00 P.M.–1:00 A.M.	Late night genius creativity burst is possible. Good time to write snappy, catchy ads. Compose copy for self-promotion.

Scientists have found that the afternoon dip persists regardless of whether people skip lunch, eat at odd times, or eat at identical times every day. We are at our sleepiest every twelve hours, typically in mid-afternoon and a few hours before dawn. Include some distraction in your afternoon—a walk, a short time out—whatever works for you!

Real estate agents must work long, hard hours into the evening. Shorter, time-managed periods make the most out of the entire day.

Find a Way to Relax Your Mind and Body.

ABCs of a Successful Attitude

A Arguing with a seller or buyer is unacceptable.

B Begin a sales effort with full knowledge of the customer's needs.

C Careful in the way the agent dresses *at all times.*

D Deliver answers to buyers and sellers without dodging them.

E Emphasize the right statement at the right time.

F Follow through after a sale to keep in touch with the buyer and seller.

G Guarantee top performance at all times.

H Have heart in the business at all times.

I Interested in the customer and asks lots of questions.

J Join the buyer and seller together successfully. Jot down notes from meetings with clients.

K Know what to do *every* day.

L Look at all possible alternatives in a transaction.

M Manage business in a professional manner.

N Number "to do" items daily.

O Organize time daily in making appointments and sales.

P Praise oneself for good effort.

Q Quit only when the job is done.

R Realize that success in real estate depends on personal hard work.

S Service clients with 100 percent dedication to the business.

T Time management in all things.

U Understand the situation of the buyers and the sellers.

V Vacation at least one full weekend a month with family and/or friends to avoid burnout.

W Walk, jog, or exercise during the week to eliminate stress.

X Xerox all necessary information as clients' needs arise.

Y Yearly review of all goals and ambitions and reorganization of files.

Z Zestful whole-hearted interest, gusto, and spirited enjoyment of life.

Affirmations: Alternative Ideas for Negative Attitudes

I am doing the best job I can to succeed in real estate.

Every day I will try to better myself in some way.

Nothing can disturb my thinking or upset me if I do not allow it to.

In all ways, at all times, for all purposes, I will guard against negative thoughts and negative behavior.

I will survive through all kinds of adversity and discouragement.

Today and every day, I commit to loving myself and forgiving my mistakes.

Decisions I make are based entirely upon the truth that is.

All people and all things depend upon good. I will seek to do good.

I am completely filled with good feelings, good thoughts, and good intentions, at all times.

These positive affirmations can be used on a daily basis. Try one at a time for a week at a time.

Anything Good Is Worth Trying Once.

Ways to Improve Sales

1. Replace a negative thought with a positive one.
2. Read a positive motivational book.
3. Buy a *"real" piece of jewelry.*
4. Discover what makes you *look your best.*
5. *Change your diet* by eliminating sugars, meats, alcohol, tobacco, caffeine, and salt and go for low fat.
6. *Eat more foods high in fiber* like fruits and vegetables.
7. *Exercise* 15 to 20 minutes every other day.
8. *Say something positive to yourself* every day, such as, "I am important."
9. *Update your finances* and budget twice a month.
10. *Try to laugh* more than frown each day.
11. Tell yourself *something good* about yourself.
12. When showering each morning, *say positive affirmations to yourself.*
13. Do *something nice* for somebody each and every day.
14. *Listen to good motivational tapes* (keep them in your car) and limit TV viewing time.
15. When frustrated, take deep breaths and relax by replacing negative thoughts with positive ones.
16. Find a *hobby* other than your job. Work on it weekly. (Consider volunteer work, something you've always wanted to do, or lessons of some kind.)
17. Become aware that you can control your own destiny.
18. Every *third* weekend, *plan a special event* or trip.
19. *Try smiling* more each day.
20. When you schedule your work, *schedule your fun.*
21. Keep lists of your goals.
22. *Keep lists of things* that you want to do daily, weekly, and monthly.
23. Before you leave the office, make sure that you *feel good about yourself.*
24. Take time for your family with a *planned event.*
25. *Surprise someone* with a gift.
26. Make or attend a good sit-down dinner with friends or family at least *twice a week.*
27. *Let go of grudges.*
28. *Learn something* new each day.
29. *Replace a bad habit* with something you have always wanted *to do for yourself.*
30. Introduce yourself to your neighbors.
31. *Join an organization* that makes you feel satisfied.
32. Give someone a compliment *each day.*
33. Talk to people who are *positive.*
34. Avoid gossip.
35. Subscribe to a magazine that reflects inner growth.
36. Keep a journal to record your thoughts and to see how you change.
37. Keep your daily planner current.
38. Maintain *good posture.*
39. Buy yourself something to improve your looks once every month. (If money is tight, sometimes getting a haircut, a new tie, a new hair clip, or even a new color of lipstick or nail polish will suffice.)
40. *Read this book again!*

Twenty-One Questions

1. What is your logo?
2. When will your personal brochure be ready for distribution?
3. How can you set yourself apart from other agents?
4. What is your personal motto?
5. What area of real estate will you specialize in?
6. Where will you farm?
7. What is your self-marketing plan?
8. What will you offer sellers?
9. What will you offer buyers?
10. How will you promote yourself and your company through community involvement?
11. What is your personalized marketing plan?
12. What is your sellers' marketing plan?
13. Have you purchased lockboxes? Do you take your lockbox with you on every second appointment with potential sellers?
14. How many listings will you get this week?
15. How many buyers will you sell this week?
16. How many listings will you sell this month?
17. How many buyers sold this month?
18. How many listings will you get this year?
19. To how many buyers will you sell this year?
20. Do you want to work with a partner? FSBOs?
21. Do you have a four-week schedule in your daily planner?

I constantly add new things to my marketing plan...

Have you practiced **closing on a buyer** this week?
Have you practiced **closing on a seller** this week?
How many **appointments** do you have for this week?
Where have you **promoted yourself** this week?

What's your attitude regarding money?

Would you rather have $1,000,000

Or

a penny that doubles itself in value each day of the month?

Day					
1	$.01	11	$10.24	21	$10,485.76
2	$.02	12	$20.48	22	$20,971.52
3	$.04	13	$40.96	23	$41,943.04
4	$.08	14	$81.92	24	$83,886.08
5	$.16	15	$163.84	25	$167,772.16
6	$.32	16	$327.68	26	$335,544.32
7	$.64	17	$655.36	27	$671,088.64
8	$1.28	18	$1,310.72	28	$1,342,177.28
9	$2.56	19	$2,621.44	29	$2,684,354.56
10	$5.12	20	$5,242.88	30	$5,368,709.12

31 (Last day)…$10,737,418.24

How Do You Spend Each Day?

CHAPTER 2

A "best attitude" regarding life...

Risk...

To laugh is to risk appearing the fool
To weep is to risk appearing sentimental
To reach out for another is to risk involvement
To expose feelings is to risk exposing your true self
To play your ideas and dreams before the crowd is to risk their loss
To love is to risk not being loved in return
To live is to risk dying
To hope is to risk despair
To try is to risk failure...
...but risk must be taken,
Because the greatest hazard in life is to risk nothing
The person who risks nothing does nothing, has nothing, and is nothing
One may avoid some suffering and sorrow
But one simply cannot learn, feel, change, grow, live, and love
Chained by one's certitudes,
One is a slave, one has forfeited freedom
Only one who risks...
...is truly free

—author unknown

Attitude Sums It Up

> The most important thing you can do each day is have a plan. Start the morning off with ORGANIZATION. Whether you have two or four things to do first thing in the morning—DO THEM!

- Make a client call-back list and have a reason to call.
- Know how to answer any objections your clients may have.
- Make sure you ask for an appointment before you hang up.
- Keep written time logs on potential clients. Know when to call.
- If you send direct mail, make sure you follow up with a call.
- If you get a new listing, have a great attitude. Spread the word!
- Let FSBOs know you have a client for their house.
- Ask a FSBO if they know of anyone who is selling.
- Have an attitude of success in everything you do daily.
- Create excitement for real estate in the clients you contact.
- Be happy to look at new homes on tour. Keep clients in mind.
- Ask your neighbors—with a smile, "Can I help you find a home?"
- Energetically apply yourself to learning more about real estate.
- Be enthusiastic about taking advanced real estate courses.
- Offer to hold your fellow agent's listings open if you have none.
- Maintain an attitude of balance in everything you do each day.
- Let go of a bad day and make the next one a great day.
- Choose an attitude of forgiveness for clients who make you sad.
- Have a professional attitude and handle daily dilemmas.

Chapter Summary

Your attitude is 93 percent of everything that you do! So the amount of money that you make in real estate depends on how you feel about yourself. Don't listen to "NO" and carefully maintain a positive approach. Try to remember to stay disciplined. Have a schedule each and every day from which you do not deviate. Try to work with two buyers a week. People will always want to work with enthusiastic individuals. Always confirm and reconfirm appointments.

Prelicense education requirements include Agency Law, Fair Housing, Disclosure Fundamentals, Contract Law, Principles of Real Estate and a certain number of required hours each year. Remember to establish membership in a local and national board of REALTORS®. Be honest, reputable and of the highest moral character. Pay for online computer access.

Fair Housing consists of providing equal and professional service without regard to race, color, religion, sex, handicap, familial status or national origin of any prospective client or resident of any community. The Fair Housing Act prohibits any discrimination in the housing market based on race, color, national origin, religion, sex, familial status (presence of child under 18, or pregnant), or disability (physical, mental, sensory, AIDS/HIV, recovered addict).

Agency is the fiduciary relationship that results from a manifestation of consent by one person to another that the other shall act on his behalf and subject to his control and consent by the other to so act. Fiduciary duties are loyalty, obedience, disclosure, confidentiality, reasonable care and diligence, and accounting. Make a commitment to be in the business unconditionally—in good times and in bad.

Keep a pencil and a pad of paper by every phone in the house. Learn how to work with your body's timeclock. Find a way to relax your mind and body. Learn the ABCs of a successful attitude. Affirm alternative ideas for a negative attitude. Know that there are 40 ways to improve your sales daily. Practice closing on a buyer and seller weekly and have a professional attitude in handling daily dilemmas.

CHAPTER 3

ADVERTISING

- Ads to Write
- Banner Ads
- Internet Fliers
- Virtual Tours

big deal by Lorayne n' Neil

Advertising

When writing an ad for the seller of a particular piece of property, I try to include the following important items:

1. Number of bedrooms and baths
2. Style of the home (especially if it has a walkout lower level)
3. Main floor family room and/or den and fireplaces
4. Major new improvements
5. Interior square footage
6. Special amenities of the lot or interior
7. Price or price range
8. Location

Ads are to Expensive!!! I'll wait and see if it sells itself.

These items reflect the overall type of home that you are selling.

An ad that reflects the above items will target potential buyers for this particular home. Inclusion of the price range and description of the particular style and area narrow the market to a more specific buyer who can qualify for the home. Therefore, you will be more likely to keep a potential buyer who calls.

Placing Ads in Newspapers

When designing a newspaper ad, I try to use a short headline with no more than seventeen letters. The second line should also be short with no more than seventeen letters. This line might reflect the times the home is open, such as Sunday from 2:00 to 4:00 P.M. If the home is not being held open, you might describe the style and area of the home, such as:

Newspaper heading suggestions

Just Listed!	Country Charmer!
Great Listing!	Classic Colonial!
Gorgeous Home!	Brick Beauty!
None Like It!	Designer's Treasure!
It's the Best!	Hidden Wooded Retreat!
Colonial in Woods	Hillside Haven
Lakeside Retreat	Two-story Sun-filled
Country Rambler	Breathtaking View
Sensational Split	Unique Area
Beautiful Bungalow	Close to School

Writing ads

- *Remember* your two-line headline.
- *Get across* to the reader that this home is a real bargain.

  Examples: "no home with this square footage for the money…"

  "lowest priced home in the neighborhood…"

- *Stress* a particular feature.

  Examples: "park across the street…"

  "located in desirable area of…"

  "lowest maintenance around…"

- *Be specific* on the address and provide clear directions.

  Example: 425 Maplewood Drive (2 blocks So. of North St. and 1 block W. of Alameda, left to 4th house)

- *Be specific* in the body of the ad.

  Example: "3 BR, 2 bath, family room off kitchen, formal DR, huge finished lower…"

- Make the ad *interesting* as well as specific.

  Example: "3 huge BRS! Fantastic family room off country kitchen…"

- Find something *unique* to the home.

  Example: "no other lot like this one"

  "very unusual floor plan"

  "a gourmet cook's dream kitchen"

- *Ask yourself* if you would call on your own ad.
- *Remember* to include your name and phone number and the price of the home.
- Short and sophisticated ads = satisfied clients who call!

1. Give the facts.
2. Don't exaggerate.
3. Be descriptive.
4. Avoid hard-to-understand abbreviations.
5. Include the price.
6. Be available.

Advertising Real Estate on the Internet

Lots of agents believe that if you give too much information about a home, the buyer will not need you. Many agents think they need to control what the buyer looks at. Those days are gone! A wealth of information available on real estate property is available all over the world, via Internet advertising!

> Advertising on the Internet is *crucial* for real estate agents. Technology today provides an agent the opportunity to market him/herself to literally millions of people.

People are demanding one-stop shopping!

Even though FSBO sellers already have chosen to list their homes on their own over the Internet—www.owners.com—the number of Internet listings run far behind the majority of more sophisticated sites that are developed by big real estate producers in the country today.

How an agent advertises over the internet

1. Individual website
2. Banner advertising
3. Links to other sites
4. E-mail literature
5. Internet newsletters
6. Blogs

Individual website

A big advantage in having your own website is giving out your web address! People can be at home, in their car, in their office, or on vacation and if they hear about you, they can look you up right away. Plus literally hundreds of additional people could be browsing the Web at any given time, and if your site were linked to another real estate site of interest, you would get more notoriety! On your website, you can give sample listings and information deemed critical to a home buyer or seller.

Your **Credibility** Is Established Immediately!

Perhaps a relocation client or a mom with time on her hands during the afternoon is coming to town…or an office worker taking some time to browse the Web late in the day wants some real estate information. Your website could make you a commission!

> THE WORLD WIDE WEB is a phenomenal tool for selling real estate today. The International Real Estate Digest (www.ired.com) rates most of the real estate websites today and gives agents much-needed online help.

Internet advertising tips

I just e-mailed my relocation buyers info on houses…They saw one they love!

- Make sure your business cards have your website and e-mail address, as well as all phone numbers.
- Check your e-mail at least twice daily.
- Send prospective clients real estate updates via e-mail.
- Create a worthy newsletter for your website—and update it often.
- Use your own voice mail message at your home and at your office to promote your website.
- Create a stamp containing your web address and e-mail address. Stamp envelopes, stationery, newsletters, and business cards that do not show these addresses.
- Add e-mail addresses of your clients to your computer address book. Keep updating lists.
- Encourage your customers to visit your website often. Update often to provide new information.
- List your e-mail/website in advertisements in the newspapers and in other print media.
- Spread the word about your website and e-mail address to family, friends, businesses, neighbors, and everyone you meet on a day-to-day basis.
- At open houses, encourage potential customers to e-mail you and visit your website for real estate news.
- Remember: Your website should promote and promise customer benefits that only you can give!
- Keep in mind: People visiting your website are seeking less information about you and more information about real estate.
- Show your company logo at the top of your home page on your website.
- Create an inviting "Welcome to my home page." Text should be exciting, informational, and above all, easy to follow.

- A good guideline is: Two full screens of information = one printed page of text.
- Go to other real estate websites. Make a list of the things you like and dislike about the sites. Be sure your site does not include anything offensive.
- In order to have an interesting website, it is important that you have original art. Be sure your website includes pictures and graphics as well as printed material.
- You may want to include an online chat group about real estate in your site.
- To be able to advertise online and receive e-mail, you must have a modem and access to the World Wide Web (WWW). You will need to sign up with an Internet service provider (ISP).
- Many agents include programs that allow for translations at their websites.
- Remember to register your domain name (the name of your website).
- There are many ways to promote your website besides word of mouth. You can rent a booth at conventions, offer premiums and real estate gifts, advertise via direct mail, and continue to advertise in the media.
- Real estate advertising networking means taking the time to network over the Internet. Try to link your site with banks, businesses, and professionals that complement you as an agent.
- Strive to take more Internet classes and learn about new and more powerful opportunities that are being created every day over the Internet.

My buyers want my website address. What's that?

Banner Advertising

This type of advertising is most often seen at the top of commercial websites. Many residential real estate agents also use banner advertising.

- Aim your message at a specialty audience.
- Make your ad appear exciting.
- Give your audience a strong desire to click to your site.
- Average banner ad is 60 × 468 pixels.
- GIF = very simple banner ad.
- Animated GIF shows animated images (obviously, an animated ad stands out).
- Keep size under 15 Kbytes. An ad larger than 15 Kbytes takes too long to download.
- Contact advertising departments of large portal sites (Google, Yahoo, etc.).
- Find out the CPM: Cost per thousand impressions. An impression occurs each time your ad is brought up by someone visiting a site with your ad. Currently, CPM is under $100 for 1,000 impressions.

OK...I figured out how to advertise online.

- Make sure you limit banner ad spending! Check out the service that limits banner ads to a ZIP code: Flycast.
- Before placing a banner ad, learn about the following:
  1. CPM—cost per thousand impressions
  2. CTR—Percentage of impressions that are actually clicked on
  3. CUS—Cost of unit sale (money that generates a sale)
  4. CR—Percentage of clicks that result in a sale

Ask someone who has a banner ad for suggestions. A great banner ad will bring more and more visitors to your site.

> There is even a service that asks the visitor to call you now: InstantCall. Just place a button on your website and when a visitor pushes it, they are asked their e-mail address, name, and, of course, their phone number...another click...and they reach *you*.

Most of the advertising companies on the Internet today will promote real estate agents...for a wide range of pricing. However, it is wise to check out the company in depth and find out whether or not they can tell you that real estate agents have been successful in moving property over their particular site. There is so much competition in the industry today to get clients that the fees are all over the board. Many companies claim to get as many as "a million views per month." One particular company claims to sell ads at a rate ranging from $10 to $25 plus about 50 cents per click-through. **Remember, the clicks can really run up your total cost!**

Key Point, for Advertising on the Net

- Join as many real estate mailing lists as you can.
- Offer real estate marketing tips and e-mail/website addresses.

> In your e-mail address, include a **"signature slogan,"** for example: Nash Real Estate
> FREE Real Estate TIPS by e-mail!
> e-mail at: lifeaware@aol.com

- For all your direct mailings, include your e-mail and your website address.
- Always answer your e-mail promptly. Your voice mail can include a statement such as this: "Please visit my website at www.awarebear.com or e-mail me at lifeaware@aol.com. I check my e-mail twice daily."

Where to allocate advertising dollars

- 25 percent aimed at getting new business
- 65 percent aimed at your current customers
- 10 percent aimed at old business/inactive leads

> Whether advertising on the Internet or utilizing the print media, radio, or television, it is important to remember that **image is everything.**

- What kind of real estate agent are "you" promoting?
- What kind of a logo have you designed for yourself?
- How can you advertise yourself uniquely?
- How many sources are out there to link to and piggyback with?
- What "complete package" are you ready to advertise?
- Have you made a direct marketing business plan for print media, radio/TV, and the Internet?
- Are your ads informative and exciting…and are you ready to field calls?

A recent survey of 1,000 websites across the United States yielded these statistics:

> 39 percent of consumers said they visited sites after seeing ads in magazines
> 29 percent said they visited sites after seeing ads in newspapers
> 27 percent said they visited sites after seeing ads on the Web

"Sponsoring" someone else is more effective than banner advertising.

Your website address and your e-mail should be on every piece of promotional literature you send out—everything that leaves your office. It should be on your listings and on all your highlight sheets.

More and more people are using the Internet for classified ads. Make sure your website address and your e-mail address are on all of the classified advertising you do.

Some agents include **virtual tours** of homes on their websites. Other agents feature online home searches and evaluations, local service directory, and dozens of links to local and international sites with extensive buyer and seller information on site.

Any person searching for a new home can click on a website and view listings in that city or town and automatically be directed to other websites! Agents already are posting announcements, updating their sites, editing and removing messages, sending out real estate articles, and giving virtual tours of homes in living color!

> Advertising to the public that you have a **destination web page** is essential. This is a web page that provides information and services to fill the prospect's needs. The more links to your website that they encounter, the easier it is to find you. They must be able to see a link to your website in the first couple pages of search engine results or a prospective client will rarely find you.

Check out these advertising sources

- House and Home Real Estate pages http://www.results-net.com REAL ESTATE WEB PAGE PROVIDER
- Agents Online Real Estate Idea Center http://www.agentsonline.net ONE MORE AGENT ADVERTISING TOOL

> When advertising and promoting your website, be sure to add a counter at the bottom of the page to see how many people visit your web page.

Prudent advertising ideas for the internet

A myriad of search engines are available to search for real estate over the Internet today. A search for "Minneapolis real estate" would likely turn up a few thousand web pages. With the Internet expanding every day, the major search engines and directories are forced to update their programs constantly. It should be possible to list your site and get a good position in a couple of days. Striving to have good placement in all the major search engines at the same time is ideal but not realistic. To be placed in two or three top search engines at the same time is a much more realistic goal. However, to be able to do this, a website must be designed so that it ranks very well in all of the major search engines. The competition is so fierce that **daily updates are** essential. Failure to update constantly can cost you a sale.

It is perhaps most important to develop a strategy that leads others' paths and other sites to your website. Advertising with the companies that complement who you are adds tremendous credibility to your web page. These companies may include: moving companies, insurance companies, mortgage companies, dentists, doctors, and schools. Over the Net you can start a domino effect that is constantly coming back to you with more and more positive results.

One of the best ways to bring clients to your site is to advertise as an EXCLUSIVE REAL ESTATE AGENT SPECIALIZING IN...and then consider all of the elements that connect to what you are specializing in. For instance, let's say you want to specialize in new homes. Contact builders, moving companies, appliance companies, garage door companies, designers, and furniture stores. The big ones all have web pages. Link to their sites!

Remember:

Anybody searching for an agent or property for sale in your city will automatically click on the city you live in and then through various LINKS to you; they will be directed to your website.

Another way to advertise as an EXCLUSIVE AGENT SPECIALIST for your area is to join as many Internet directories as possible. Usually there is a very nominal annual fee. The minimal up-front costs are extremely well-paying in the long run. Think of it as being listed in the Yellow Pages of your phone book...there is only one Yellow Pages. Advertise wherever you can over the Net.

Most buyers today are not interested in picking up the telephone and talking with an agent—they want to visit a website and then, if they are interested, they will e-mail you.

Thesaurus for Real Estate Advertising

ACREAGE

private land

rolling greens

luscious estate

acres of wooded privacy

hobby farm enthusiasts

prestigious private parkland

AIR CONDITIONING

zoned heating and cooling

climate controlled

window-unit air conditioning

temperature control

two-zone heating and cooling

ALCOVE

secluded area

music alcove

hidden corners

secret spots

AMENITIES

assets of the home

pleasantries the home includes

updated throughout

sensational upgrades

APPLIANCES

like new

built-ins

subzero refrigerator

top-of-the-line appliances

deluxe appliances

Julia Child's appliances

APARTMENT

mother-in-law apartment

lower level apartment

teenage apartment

in-law quarters

nanny apartment

live-in apartment

separate entrance apartment

AVAILABLE

take advantage now

accessible immediately

move in tomorrow

close immediately

AVENUE

wide thoroughfare

ivy-covered lane

tree-lined path

approach to home lined with trees

BASEMENT

lower level

downstairs den

crawl space under house

lower family room

lower level walkout

walkout entertainment level

BATHROOM

master bath

jacuzzi in master bath

therapeutic whirlpool spa

private spa

his and her vanity

sumptuous Roman bath

health club with spa in your own home

BEDROOM

master bedroom suite	teenage hideaway
skylite master suite	beautiful, big bedrooms
paneled bedroom or den	dormitory-size bedroom
extra bedroom ideal for rental	second master suite
private, palatial suite	bunk beds go great in this room
master suite with fireplace	secluded master

COLONIAL

two-story center hall	Currier and Ives colonial
charming southern colonial	picture-book colonial
four-bedroom Dutch colonial	Williamsburg white colonial

CONDOMINIUM

corner unit	private end unit
upgraded designer unit	strategically located end unit

CONTEMPORARY

classic contemporary	art deco contemporary
provocative contemporary	exciting and open contemporary

COUNTRY

over the meadow	short drive to country seclusion
country estate	rustic and rural countryside locale
country cottage	country charm galore

CLEAN

model condition throughout	impeccable interior
superbly maintained	flawless condition
refreshingly mint condition	white-glove condition
sparkling, move-in condition	designer's interior

CARPETING

all-wool carpet throughout	genuine berber carpet
plush, luxurious carpeting	neutral carpet throughout entire home
white wool carpeting	wonderful wool carpeting

CEILINGS

vaulted and soaring	beautiful and beamed
softly lighted ceilings	cathedral and open-beamed ceilings
soaring ceiling	crown molding
spectacular ceiling	soaring and spacious
skylights	

CIRCLE

cul-de-sac location	dead-end street!
private courtyard	only 6 homes in circle!
cozy circle location	

CITY

in the heart of town	the center of it all
community involvement	central location

COLORS

neutral colors throughout
wonderful white tones
bathed in soft pastels
softly decorated throughout
decorator decor

earth tones prevail
warm, soft colors prevail
muted tones
fresh, cool colors
cocoas and creams

DECK

private, sunny deck
sunrise deck
BBQ on your dynamite deck
fully landscaped deck
multiple-leveled deck
spacious terrace

oversize cedar planked
relax and watch sunsets from your . . .
wonderful, wraparound deck
extensive deck
dynamite deck overlooks woods

DEN

home office
music room
separate entry for home office
sneak-away spot

separate study
cozy library
convenient office, bedroom, den
convertible office/bedroom

DINING ROOM

elegant formal dining
New England formal dining
entertainer dining
French doors off formal dining
light, airy, formal dining
unique formal dining room
informal dining room
combination living and dining room

gourmet dining room
oversized, grand dining room
cozy formal dining
intimate formal dining
massive, open, formal dining
full-windowed dining room
sensational formal dining
bay windowed dining room

ENTRY

palatial entrance
stone archway
impressive entry
graceful foyer

gleaming marble entry
dramatic entry
massive double-doored entrance
decorator's doorway

EXPOSURE

southern exposure
sun-drenched

sun-filled
sun-splashed

EXTERIOR

maintenance-free
wonderful wood
stunning stone
vinyl siding
genuine cedar slabs

brick beauty
sensational cedar
stone and stucco
low-maintenance masonite siding
stone and brick beauty

FAMILY ROOM

informal family room
leisure room
private studio
enchanting family room
shuttered family room windows
drawing room

handsome hearth accents family room
classic kitchen off family room with
    fireplace
combination kitchen and family room
two-story family room/great room

FENCING

split rail fencing

protective privacy fence

chain-linked fencing

fabulous fenced grounds

white picket fencing

cross-fencing surrounds property

ranch rail fencing

wrought iron fencing accentuates

FINANCING

below-market owner financing

owner financing

no qualifying mortgage to assume

assumable loan below market

assume huge mortgage

terrific terms!

FIREPLACES

beautiful brick hearth

fieldstone fireplace

corn-poppin' fireplacemaster

cozy hearth

woodburning fireplace

old-fashioned featherstone fireplace

toe-warming fireplace

suite with fireplace

Franklin stove

firelit breakfast

FIXER-UPPERS

make this livable

realize huge profit

only cosmetic surgery

fix-up and flowers needed

how would you paint it?

needs lots of love

paint a little, make a lot

prepare to paint

repair and plaster

loads of potential here!

barrels of paint—barrels of return!

fabulous fix-up charmer!

small investment—huge return!

a treasure underneath!

FLOORS

handsome hardwood floors

wonderful wood floors

authentic oak-pegged floors

Italian tile floors

Mexican quarry tile floors

marvelous maple floors

original oak floors

prestigious parquet floors

country-planked flooring

sensational ceramic tile floors

tremendous terrazzo tile floors

FURNISHED HOMES

turnkey lifestyle

total furnishings stay

interior furnishings stay

decorator furnished to stay

furnished by designer to stay

just your suitcase needed

decor all-inclusive

gorgeous inclusions to stay

lavish appointments included

exciting accessories included

GARAGES

oversize double garage

holds three cars

adequate single garage

complimentary carport

garage with workshop

gigantic garage

terrific triple garage

attached, heated garage

fully finished tuck-under garage

surprise tandem garage

garage with separate storage room

heated workshop garage

GARDEN

perfect perennial gardens

inviting English ivy garden

gorgeous landscaped gardens

healthful organic gardens

GARDEN (continued)

perennial flowerbeds
areas for annual garden
lavish, lush gardens

farm-size, gigantic garden
masses of tulips
gorgeous grounds!

GOLF

across from golf course
one shot from the fairway
golf-oriented area
just bring your golf clubs

golf balls in your yard
golf in your backyard
world class golf course
on the green!

HEATING/AIR CONDITIONING

high-efficiency furnace
two-zone heat
economical hot water heat
super solar heat
economical natural gas

zone heating and cooling
state of the art heat pump
environmental climate control
wood furnace—heat home free
oil heat

HOME

luxury lake address
world class residence
magnificent estate setting
unparalleled beauty
one of the rarest pearls
classic country security
from a bygone era
reflects colonial times
right out of history
ready to retire
intimate hideaway
a simpler lifestyle

most envied address
no better lifestyle
understated and elegant
gracious and grand
embassy-size residence
romantic and charming
brings back memories
timeless and elegant
beautiful bed and breakfast
comfortable and cozy
sophisticated and small
perfect getaway home

INTERIOR

meticulously maintained
Old World charm
exciting accessories
lavishly appointed
aura of elegance
ingeniously arranged
prestigious interior
cosmopolitan allure
enduring loveliness
exquisitely renovated
richly detailed

classical loveliness
sublime tranquillity
extravagant appointments
dazzling innovation
impressive details
dramatically designed
decorator delight
magnificent interior
light-away
elaborate interior

KITCHEN

firelit breakfast
genuine gourmet kitchen
sun-drenched kitchen
solid oak cabinet kitchen
English country kitchen
kitchen with a French flair
exquisite decorator kitchen
beyond-belief kitchen
elegantly upgraded kitchen

Julia Child's kitchen
European kitchen
cherry cabinet kitchen
skylit-windowed kitchen
Old World, charming kitchen
kitchen accents breakfast room
style prevails in perfect kitchen
five-star-rating kitchen
conversation area kitchen

KITCHEN (continued)

sensational center-island kitchen
breakfast bay-windowed kitchen
charming, cozy kitchen
handsome rich-tone kitchen
unbelievable condo kitchen
your best foods kitchen
southern charm kitchen
sensational ceramic kitchen

wall of windows kitchen
massive country kitchen
contemporary open kitchen
best-applianced kitchen
perfect Pullman kitchen
traditionally timeless kitchen
meticulously white kitchen
dramatic deck off kitchen

LAKES

sunset over the water
luxurious lakeshore
landscaped lake views
luscious lake dwelling
beachfront property
wonderful waterfront
magnificent lakeshore
docking and beach
deeded lakeshore
beautiful boat slip

waterfront residence
looks out on lake
scenic pond views
fish from your yard
sunrise and sandy shores
float from your dock
sun-kissed shoreline
lake access
deeded docking

LAWNS

artfully landscaped
sensational setting
magnificently manicured lawn
priceless, manicured grounds
terraced, landscaped beauty

formal gardens
grandiose gardens
premier landscaped lot
wonderful wooded grounds
lush landscaping

LOCATION

distinguished address
nestled on the fifth fairway
set back in the woods
this location is a must
expansive views
captures the essence
marvelous, majestic locale
executive retreat
remarkable residence
backdrop of woods
expensive views
in the heart of town
view majestic mountains
gracefully situated
very important address
unsurpassed locale
secluded approach
revered address
breathtaking views
velvet lawn embraces home

waterfront residence
high on a hill
best country club locale
unparalleled views
storybook setting
distinctive address
exclusive area
private seclusion
sequestered behind trees
golf course community
award-winning locale
superb views abound
fabulous foothills
oak-covered hill
priceless views
perfectly poised
year-round view
picture-book setting
elegant edge of acre
ideal locale

LOFT

sun-filled studio loft
a real art studio
likable library loft
designer art studio

superb Swiss loft
hidden, high loft
balcony design studio
sleeping/studio loft

MASTER BEDROOM

sensational master suite
fireplace accents master
master bedroom overlooks
master bedroom hideaway
exciting master spa
firelit master suite
magical master boudoir
master suite indulges
banks of windows — bask in sunshine
    throughout master

master bedroom with jacuzzi
beamed ceilings in master
master bedroom with walk-in
superb master suite
master suite glows
spacious master suite
embodied in sunshine
master suite displays genius
sumptuous master
majestic master suite

NEIGHBORHOOD

tree-lined street
rewarding and rural
winding boulevard
exclusive enclave
private preserve
country charmer

prestigious locale
intimate cul-de-sac
coveted community
successful address
estate setting
hidden pocket

OFFICE

at-home office
open, airy office
optimum office
Old English office
old-time office
obscure office

oak-floored office
bay-windowed office
office opportunity
old-fashioned office
octagon office
number one office

PORCH

prestigious porch
private and peaceful
great garden room
classic conservatory
terrazzo tile porch
summer days porch

a perfect porch
sun-filled solarium
superb Arizona room
patio off porch
New England porch
pretty private porch

PRICE

unbelievable value
rare offering
priced to sell
incredibly priced
uncommon find
carefully priced at

unduplicated in price
obvious value
don't hesitate
solid value-priced
investment-priced
properly priced at

PRIVACY

hidden corner
forest haven
God's little acre
sounds of silence
whispering woods
rare private setting
hidden hill
pampered in privacy

golden pocket
secret sector
wooded dream
acre of privacy
ultimate seclusion
private end unit
end of the road
no one around

REMODELED

old with new	modern and antique
yesterday and now	dramatic updates
handsome renovation	imaginative updates
restored to capture	yesterday's charm, today's decor
artistically restored	up-to-date elegance
partially restored	restored to original elegance

ROOFS

cedar tile shakes	split shake roof
Spanish tile roof	French mansard roof
authentic slate roof	mission tile roof
hand-split cedar roof	brand new roof!

SCHOOL

by schools	don't play chauffeur
don't ride the bus	elementary school areas
super school district	walk to school
perfect playground	walking distance

SECURITY

Westinghouse security	secret security system
hidden security system	protection guaranteed
feel safe and warm	ultrasonic security
central security	video security
24-hour security	monitored security
controlled access	gate guarded
peace of mind	worry-free living

SHUTTERS

plantation shutters	oriental shutters
Bermuda shutters	full-windowed shutters
colonial shutters	privacy shutters
decorator shutters	white wood shutters

SPAS

inviting jacuzzi	wonderful whirlpool
heated hydrotherapy	tantalizing hottub
sensuous hot spa	a private spa
health club bath	Hollywood hot tub
elite super spa	

STAIRS

carved banisters	circular stairway
dramatic staircase	cherry balustrades
spiral staircase	sweeping stairway
grand staircase	floating staircase
center stairway	eighteenth-century stairs

STYLE

English Tudor elegance
European style
elegant Georgian colonial
traditional two-story
rewarding rambler
simplified split entry
exaggerated split level
beautiful brick bungalow
restored Renaissance
from bygone era
Dutch colonial
monumental colonial
Williamsburg colonial
Nantucket colonial
English country estate
English country Tudor
dramatic architecture
country cottage
ivy-clad classic
storybook Victorian
lavish lifestyle
French influence

Knob Hill distinction
exquisite contemporary
Cape Cod charmer
sensational saltbox
wonderful walkout
distinctive style
storybook one-story
expansive two-story
sophisticated traditional
Currier and Ives
gone with the wind
federal colonial
timeless colonial
provocative contemporary
flawless tudor
Mediterranean villa
sumptuous French
Spanish adobe
crannies and collectibles
award-winning architecture
landmark residence
intimate retreat

SWIMMING POOL

inviting pool
backyard vacation
year-round workout
steps to swim
want the water?
like to swim?
diving pool/spa

luxurious pool
private pool
vacation at home
sunshine and swim
miss the lake?
free-form pool

TENNIS

steps to the court
your tennis court
treat yourself to tennis

home to tennis
definitely tennis
trees and tennis

TREES

your own orchard
firewood forever
you'll love fall
hidden forest
exclusive retreat

ask for apples
private woods
trees and trees
enchanted forest
private and romantic

UNFINISHED ROOM

space to create
hobby room area
walk-up attic

full storage attic
easily converted
artist's creation

VACATION HOME

holiday living

family reunion?

weekend getaway

summer hideaway

happy retreat

enjoy fishing

summer relaxing

a simpler life

enjoy the water

live at the lake

VIEW

see forever

whitewater view

tantalizing treetops

sensational night lights

get your binoculars

treetop treasure

majestic mountains

sunset views

million-dollar view

overlooks the city

capture the landscape

commanding views

hilltop haven

panoramic view

WALL COVERINGS

imported paper

textured treatments

richly covered

picture frame paneling

designer walls

wonderful walls

lavish wall coverings

padded in silk fabric

WINDOWS

beautiful bay windows

wall of glass

bring in the outdoors

leaded glass windows

solar-bronze windows

French Provincial

stained-glass windows

skylighted ceilings

soaring windows

intricate etched glass

palladian windows

greenhouse windows

country style windows

clerestory windows

WORKSHOP

wonderful workshop

handyman workshop

hammer and nails hideaway

perfect for projects

carpenter work area

crafts and arts room

time for tool box here!

build anything here!

My ads are better. People are calling now!

While it would be ideal if all your business could be generated just from an ad, you still would like to retain the call-in as a client.

Rules for answering an ad call

1. Give the *facts*.
2. Say something *unique* about the home.
3. *Describe* the home in a positive tone.
4. *Articulate* carefully.
5. State the *price*.
6. *Be available* to show the home as soon as possible.

Dialogue for Answering the Phone

Hi! This is Barbara from _____ Realty. This particular home that you are calling on is one of my favorite properties because...

Examples: "of its big country kitchen."

"it has a gorgeous family room off the foyer."

"the lot is simply gorgeous and loaded with trees."

"it reminds me of going to my grandma's house."

"it has more character than any home I've seen in a long time."

Pick something *special* just for that home, and be sure to accentuate it. If the property is extremely plain and you are having difficulty finding an outstanding quality, imagine what you would *do* to the home if it were given to you. Spend a few minutes focusing on its potential and hidden amenities.

ENTHUSIASM IS CONTAGIOUS!

If *you* are **EXCITED** about the property, then you can **EXCITE** a buyer.

Whenever you answer an ad call, try the following techniques.

Ask the buyer

1. Have you been *prequalified* for this price range of property? OR: Is this a price range that you feel comfortable with?
2. Have. you been *looking* for a home for very long?
3. Do you have a home to *sell* first?
4. Is this the *area* you are looking in?
5. Do you have a *timeframe* for when you want to move?
6. Have you seen *any homes* that have come close to what you want?
7. Have you made any *offers* on homes yet?
8. Can you *meet me* at the *property* later in the day or would after 2:00 P.M. tomorrow work better with your schedule?

If the buyer is authentic, set up an appointment to meet the buyer at the property, keeping the schedule suited to your own needs.

An ad call can be converted easily with just four questions

1. Have you been looking for a home for a long time?
2. When do you want to move?
3. May I show you homes in your price range?
4. Have you visited our website?

AN AD CALL CAN BE CONVERTED EASILY WITH JUST THREE STATEMENTS:

1. I have some excellent properties in your *area* which I will bring for you to look at.
2. I specialize in your area and can take a look at your property sometime this week between the hours of _____ and _____.
3. I enjoy uncovering new properties for clients I meet and helping them find the best home possible.

Be sure that you include in your home answering machine message the fact that *you will be checking in frequently for calls.* Example: "Hi, this is Barbara Nash from XYZ Realty, and I check in frequency for my calls. If you will leave your name and phone number, I will call you back shortly with the information you need. You can also e-mail me at lifeaware@aol.com."

Additional Advertising Pointers

Remember, you are always advertising. You are in the public eye and can meet a new buyer simply by *wearing a lapel pin* that reads:

> **XYZ REALTY**
>
> **BARBARA NASH**

Accentuate your own name; put it in large print!

I cut out *my* Sunday ads from the newspaper and paste them in my *daily planner* on the date that they ran.

I *keep track of when* I ran the ad for each seller's listing in a column on the outside of a legal-size folder, with their name on it.

I *call the sellers* weekly to tell them what activity I had on the ad and if and when there were calls. This is also an opportune time for a price adjustment.

I keep track of *how many clients* were generated from each ad I ran.

Ads should describe the kind of home, number of bedrooms and baths, interior square footage, and something about a special feature that *you* like about the home!

> I always remember to *keep making appointments* from ad calls.
> Keep calling buyers and sellers from ad calls.
> *Get right back to them*... e-mail them...
> fax them... phone them...

> **STAY CURRENT WITH CLIENTS**
> Talk to them weekly

Sample ads

ADVERTISING

7-29
BEST BUY!
OPEN 2-4
Owner transferred–will look at all offers! Great location! In the foothills of Indian Hills. Custom bit 3BR, 2BA split, 1st flr fam rm, 2 fplc, neutral decor.

8-12
"BELOW INDIAN HILLS"
PRICE SLASHED!!!
Owner transferred–leaving beautiful 3BR, 3BA home w/1st flr family rm, 2 fplcs, att dbl garage, gorgeous lot, huge deck.

8-19
SUPER BEST BUY
OWNER TRANSFERRED
Chance of a lifetime; 3BR, 3BA, beautiful home–2 fplc, first floor family room, formal dining room, lovely lot, below Indian Hills.

9-2
OPEN
INCREDIBLE
OFFERING!!!
INDIAN HILLS AREA…
Below Indian Hills nestled on beautiful landscaped lot sets this 3 BR, 3 bath home! FIRST FLOOR FAM ROOM, 2 fplcs.

9-9
INCREDIBLE FIND
INDIAN HILLS
surrounds this 3BR 3BA one-of-a-kind find!! FIRST FLOOR beautiful family room loaded w/wonderful windows! 2 fplc. Att dbl gar. Hurry–offered only for reasons of transfer!

9-23
IT'S OPEN 12-2
JUST PERFECT
INDIAN HILLS…
…AREA boasts 3BR, 3BA with all WINDOWED & WALKOUT family room off kitchen!! Over 2300 Sq ft fin. Att dbl gar. Hurry–Transferred.

3-11
NEW LISTING
OPEN 1-3
"Picture-Book Colonial" Fabulous spacious New England colonial in-demand Morningside area, but bordering the country club district. Main floor formal living room w/marble fireplace, first floor formal library w/built-ins and richly paneled, first floor family room, spacious dining room, adorable kitchen w/laundry facilities adjacent, lower level amusement rm w/fireplace and lovely master suite w/ abundant closet space. Beautifully appointed and meticulously maintained. Hurry–won't last long!!!

3-25
JUST LISTED!
IT'S OPEN 12–2
NEW ENGLAND…
…charm prevails in this gorgeous TWO STORY 1940 home!! UNBELIEVABLE floor plan with formal living room & marble fplc–formal DR 3 season porch w/ French doors–handsome library off Lv. room–1st floor fam. room–breakfast room w/floor to ceiling window!! Bay window 1st floor laundry!! Two beautiful BRs, 2 bathrooms–dbl garage.

4-1
1ST OPEN 2-4
Charming 1-1/2 story home in one of Edina's most desirable & convenient areas. You'll love the warm & gracious feel of this one! Coved ceilings, fplc, bay window, updated mechanicals. All levels finished. Kit. appl. included.

4-8
OPEN 2:00-4:30
COUNTRY CLUB AREA
PRESTIGIOUS New England colonial PERFECT for the professional couple looking for lots of 1st floor living space w/two HUGE 2nd flr bedrooms–EACH with its own private deck. You will be absolutely delighted with the 1st flr library or study, Fam Rm, grand size entertaining Din Rm, CHARMING country kitchen plus breakfast Rm w/china cabinet & convenient new laundry Rm. Lovely FRENCH DOORS lead to a 3 season porch from the formal Liv. Rm. w/marble fplc. The fine millwork & many AMENITIES make this home truly SPECIAL!

4-15
JUST LISTED!
COUNTRY CLUB AREA
Such a fabulous flr plan boasts formal LR–DR– library/study–1st flr Fam Rm–SCREEN PORCH–2 HUGE BRs up–Amuse Rm w/extra BR down–dbl gar.

Conclusions for Writing Ads

- Start with exciting headline.
- Make the body of the ad easy to read.
- Use descriptive words in the body.
- Create interest with a "clincher." For example: "Come to the open," "Stop by office."
- Put your photo in the ad.
- Put your e-mail address in the ad and/or blog.
- Put your website address in the ad.
- State proximity to shopping, schools, etc.
- Use persuasive words: discover, healthy, loving, results, proven, you, easy, light, new...
- Be truthful and include price.
- Place ad early in the week.
- Abbreviate only when necessary.
- Use exclamation marks wisely.
- Utilize "white space." It attracts attention.
- Start with the basics: style, location, number of bedrooms and baths, fireplace, square footage, price, amenities.
- Be available to answer your ad calls! Ad calls should generate appointments.

My clients call on "open" ads!

Remember:

82 percent of readers look for area first

72 percent want the price and terms

64 percent want bedrooms and condition

44 percent want location, kitchen, rec room

- Read other eye-catching ads in the paper.
- Keep most ads short, descriptive and to the point.
- Stay away from overused phrases.
- Address one "strong feature" about the property.
- Be sure to highlight any/all best amenities.
- Return any/all ad calls as soon as possible.

PLACE YOUR AD EARLY IN THE WEEK

Virtual Tours

What is the definition of a virtual tour?

A 360° picture, horizontal and vertical with panoramic images that stitch photos together, creating a complete view of the inside and/or outside of a home.

So WHY IS IT SO IMPORTANT TO HAVE VIRTUAL TOURS IN REAL ESTATE?

Not only do virtual tours differentiate a property for an agent, but they completely reinforce a new image or quality and professionalism. A virtual tour is specific in its attention to detail. It reflects a proven competitive advantage, especially in residential real estate. They have proven to help sell listings more than ever, as well as helping the real estate agent acquire new listings. Virtual tours have a way of increasing the perceived value of a property, as well as the value of using a particular real estate agent. Buyers are using the Internet with more and more frequency and the listings that have virtual tours are having great success once they are viewed online. Telling a potential seller that you will have their home on "virtual tour" is a powerful selling tool. Virtual tours help agents find new customers.

Virtual tours are changing the traditional open house. In an article on Realtimes.com it was stated that:

- 72 percent of 3,000 buyers surveyed in a recent study drove by or viewed a house for sale as a result of searching the Internet.
- 46 percent walked through a house after first visiting the home online.
- 78 percent found photos of the houses they saw listed on the Internet very useful.
- 46 percent said that virtual tours are very useful.

Every year homebuyers are using the Internet more and more to search for properties for sale. People who are relocating rely on online research before traveling to see a home in a particular area.

> **VIRTUAL TOURS SELL MORE HOMES!**

Chapter Summary

Did you know that 5 percent of all homes are sold from an ad? Always include your name, phone number, and the price of the home in the ad. Make the ad interesting as well as specific. Give the facts. Advertise on the Internet. Make sure that your business cards have your website and e-mail address on them, as well as all your phone numbers. Check your e-mail at least twice daily. Keep in mind that people visiting your website are seeking less information about you and more information about real estate.

To be able to advertise online and receive email, you must have a modem and access to the Web. You will need to sign up with an Internet service provider (ISP). Join as many real estate mailing lists as you can. Offer real estate marketing tips and e-mail/website addresses. Your website and your e-mail should be on every piece of promotional literature you send out—everything that leaves your office.

Some agents include virtual tours of homes on their websites. Advertising to the public that you have a "destination web page" is essential. One of the best ways to bring clients to your site is to advertise as an EXCLUSIVE REAL ESTATE AGENT SPECIALIZING IN . . . If you are excited about a property, then you can EXCITE a buyer. Always remember to keep making appointments from ad calls. Make the body of the ad easy to read and use descriptive words, be truthful, and include the price. Be available to answer your ad calls! Ad calls generate appointments.

CHAPTER 4

BUYERS

- Closing Guidelines
- Relocation

big deal by Lorayne n' Neil

Cold Calling for Buyers

"Mr. or Mrs. _____ , please. Hello, my name is _____ and I'm from _____ company. I am doing a special survey in our city, and I would like to ask you a few questions."

1. "Are you *thinking of moving* sometime within the next year?"
2. "May I ask you about *when?*"
3. "Will you be *staying here* in the city or moving out of town?"

"Thank you so much for *your time,* and have a nice day."

Additional cold call questions

1. "Would you like me to put you in touch with an excellent relocation firm in a different state? Have you visited our website?"

2. "I (or our company) just listed a home in your area. Do you know of any friends, business associates, or relatives who might be interested in my (our) services?"

3. "I'm having an open house in your neighborhood this Sunday. Would you be interested in dropping by?"

4. "Would you be interested in a free written analysis of your home? I could drop by for about 15 minutes sometime this week."

5. "I (or our company) have a great newsletter, brochure, schoolhouse magazine, map, etc. of your area. Would you like me to drop one off?"

Calling Apartment Renters for Buyers

1. Call until you find a buyer.
2. Make an appointment. Ask for a referral.
3. Make your conversation light and professional, but to the point.

> "Hi, my name is _____ and I'm with _____ real estate company. This call will be very short but very helpful to me. We are looking for people who might be interested in buying or selling a home. Interest rates are extremely low right now, and there are some good properties available. Could this interest you?"

If yes...

Get their name. Set up an appointment with them. Talk a little about their needs. Talk a little about their *finances.* Buyers need a good yearly gross to buy a reasonably priced home, and their house payment should be a little more than one-fourth of their gross monthly income.

Example: If the payment is $1,000, they should gross $4,000/month (4:1 ratio).

If no...

> "Thanks so much for your time. If you should be interested in the near future, I am located at an office near you."

Important questions for buyers

How important is the **number of bathrooms?**

How important is the **number of bedrooms?**

How important is the **closing date?**

How important is the **condition?**

How important is the **lot? (flat, hilly, fenced, corner, cul-de-sac, etc.)**

How important is the **style?**

How important is an **eat-in kitchen?**

How important is a **finished lower level?**

How important is **closet space?**

How important are **older bathrooms?**

How important is a **formal dining room?**

How important is a **fireplace?**

How important is a **two-story (vs. one-story)?**

How important is a **busy street?**

How important is a **backyard?**

How important are **garages (attached/detached)?**

How important is an **office?**

I don't need to write this down, do I?

How important is a **first floor laundry?**

How important is a **bath off the master bedroom?**

How important are **new mechanics (roof, furnace, electrical, etc.)?**

How important is **structural condition?**

How important are **hardwood floors?**

How important is a **main floor half bath?**

How important is the **neighborhood?**

How important are **taxes?**

How important is **assumable financing?**

How important is **interior decorating?**

How important are **room sizes?**

I keep two sets of homes we look at: one for buyers and one for me. Each home they see, I ask them to rate it 1–10 . . .

Learn to Read Your Buyers

When working with two buyers, try to listen between the lines. It is imperative to find out who is controlling the situation. One or the other will take over. If a man tells you he prefers a ranch style and his wife says she prefers a colonial, listen to the conversation. *Don't volunteer any comments.* Show them both styles of homes. They may surprise you and settle on an English Tudor instead!

Where are good buyers?

Whether or not you are new to the business or have been in it for a long time, you will be out of business if you do not have buyers and listings. How do you *get* buyers? The first step is to *have at least two open houses next weekend.* If you do not have any listings, ask two fellow agents in the office if you might hold their listings open. Once at the open house, absolutely resolve to find one or two couples from each open house who sincerely want to buy a house in the near future. How do you identify these people? *Ask a lot of questions.* Write down everything they tell you. Don't let these people leave your open house *without* making an appointment sometime in the coming week.

If they have a house to sell . . .

you are available either Monday or Tuesday night. Which would be better for them?

you can come over and look at their house, walk through, take notes, and come back with a market appraisal for them.

you also will bring your listing book, and they can look through it with you to help decide what price range and area would be most appealing to them.

If they don't have a house to sell...

you have either Monday or Tuesday evening open, and you would be happy to meet with them at your office to help prequalify them for the price range that would be best suited to them and the area they want to consider.

Buyers Are Not Always Knowledgeable about What They Want.

Buyers are *often confused* about areas and price ranges best suited for them. Buyers are generally more interested in *aesthetic* appeal than potential.

Buyers are incredibly *unpredictable.*

Buyers are apt to go through open houses *without* you.

Buyers are often *difficult to read* at the first meeting.

Buyers, more often than not, have a house to *sell first.*

Buyers don't always feel *loyalty* to their agent.

Most buyers stand firm on one point: They want to move *eventually.*

Because buyers are often *contradictory*, they often need help in determining the type of home best suited for them, through:

> My buyer bought a two-story home! They said they didn't want one at first...

1. Process of elimination (viewing at least six homes).

RATE EACH HOME 1-10.

2. Paint a scenario beforehand of a hypothetical transaction using a certain dollar breakdown (such as: $100,000 mortgage with $2,000 annual taxes and $600 annual insurance would result in a specific PITI (principal-interest-tax and insurance). This breakdown provides buyers the opportunity to see exactly what their specific payment would be based on a specific price of a home.

THE MONTHLY PAYMENT

MOST BUYERS have a home to sell
Ask for the listing first

1. It is *imperative* that you prequalify buyers.
2. Set *limitations* and boundaries for geographic areas.
3. Identify a *schedule* and time frame to work within.
4. Secure the buyer's *trust* and *loyalty*.
5. *Outline* the fact that because your salary is commission-based, you depend upon the resources from the time spent on each and every client. Some agents have buyers sign *buyer agreements*.
6. Set up a *minimum* of one *in-office* appointment to go over all of the above.
7. Provide potential buyers with a buyer's book which includes:
   a. map of your city
   b. highlights about yourself
   c. personal brochure and card
   d. highlights of your company
   e. sample properties that are for sale and/or sold
   f. some information about your city and/or suburbs
   g. sample purchase agreement contract
   h. sample financing addendum (explaining terms of their purchase)
   i. buyer timeline, from start to finish, for purchasing a home
   j. buyer inspection cards
8. Use *inspection cards* with a rating system of one to ten as a systematic process of elimination for homes. Keep track of good and bad points on inspection cards.
9. At the end of each appointment day, ask the buyers, "If you had to move into or make an offer on one of the homes we saw today, which one would it be? Why?"

My clients read my buyers book while we drive around...

Important questions for buyers

How important is the **number of bathrooms**?
How important is the **number of bedrooms?**
How important is the **closing date?**
How important is the **condition?**
How important is the **lot? (flat, hilly, fenced, corner, cul-de-sac, etc.)**
How important is the **style?**

Watch and listen carefully

If one of the parties asks a question of the other, don't volunteer information for either of them. Listen to them to figure out what they both really want. Soon you will see that, even though they may not know *exactly* what style they want, they are participating as a couple in the process of elimination.

> *Try not to volunteer your own opinion on a home. Once I showed a property to some people to whom I had already shown 10 or 12 homes. Before we opened the first door, I could tell the home had red carpeting. I was about to say how dreadful the color was, when I heard my buyer say, "Don, honey, look! The red carpet will go perfectly with our Mediterranean furniture."* **They bought it on the spot!**

NEVER try to sell a buyer on a style of a home. The home should, and will, *SELL ITSELF.* You are there to sell the *mechanics* of the entire situation. Learn to *listen* to the buyers' needs. Learn to stay focused on what they need. See them wanting *your expertise.*

Types of buyers

QUICK TO MOVE	*Know just what they want.* Be ready with a purchase agreement so they won't surprise you. They are the best at knowing what they want.
SLOW AND EASY	Want to look at lots of properties. They are very detail-oriented and concise, so bear with them. They will buy, but be prepared to show them 15 to 20 properties.
KNOW EVERYTHING	Have seen *lots* of properties; have bought *lots* of properties. There isn't much they *haven't* done. They'll run out of hot air eventually. Bear with them. They just want to prove their knowledge to you and themselves. They may need to search for a *full eight weeks* and to see lots of homes. Set boundaries.
PIG-HEADED	Very set and determined. Try not to force them into a corner. They will be convinced eventually, but stand firm on your beliefs. A sale becomes a matter of earning respect.
QUEEN OF SHEBA	The wife (or one of the parties) runs the show. Make sure that you find the opportunity to ask the other party's opinion.
LOVE THEM ALL	These clients like all the homes you show them. It's hard to get *any opinion* from them at all! Try to pin them down and eliminate by asking them to close their eyes and imagine if they had to move into one of the homes they saw today, could they make an offer and be happy with it?
HARD TO TELL	These clients are devoid of expression. Regardless of what you show them, it's difficult to get a reaction from them. They do not know how to give you a direct answer. They cannot be specific. It is best to try to get to know them on a *different* level. Learn about them and what interests them. Talk a lot and ask them a lot of questions.

How to Get Buyers Now

1. Hold at least two open houses a weekend in an area that is in a price range you are comfortable with, and preview the homes first if they are not your listings. *Drive the area.*

2. Consider wearing a name tag with your name and company on it; a nametag is an automatic conversation opener.

3. Call a FSBO (for safe by owner), an expired, or a canceled. Make sure you get an appointment now and visualize the listing as yours. *Three appointments maximum* should get you the listing, hopefully before the end of the week!

4. Make a list of all the people in your *warm farm* (people you know or have known). Call as many as you can, starting the conversation off with:

> "Hi, Bob. I haven't talked with you for a while and thought I would let you know that I have some extra time for a new client. If you know of anyone thinking of buying or selling a house, I would be happy to work with him or her now."

5. Do a mailout in an area that you have chosen to farm. This means mailing real estate data to a select number of homes throughout the year, sometimes 400 to 600 or more. If you decide to mail out 1,000 or more, your chances of hearing back from one to five people in the next couple of weeks are *excellent!*

6. Drive to work a *different* way and look for FSBOs.

7. When you get gas or groceries or are involved in any purchase situation throughout the day, bring up *real estate.*

8. Make a deliberate attempt to *go to the source!* It will bring you more than just one client. Contact presidents of companies, lawyers, doctors, community leaders, teachers, coaches, ministers, hairdressers, barbers, PTA members, employment agents, builders, and apartment landlords.

9. Read the *business section* of the newspaper and collect names of people who have been promoted. Chances are excellent that they are considering moving.

10. Call your *past customers;* they already have a rapport with you. Ask them who they know that you may be able to help move.

11. Contact sellers who are FSBOs to offer *relocation* services.

12. Ask *fellow salespeople* if there is a buyer whom they are not able to work with and whom you would be able to help. Work out an agreeable arrangement with the salesperson regarding commission before you work with the buyer.

13. *Meet your neighbors.* A great way to do so is through volunteer work. All of your neighbors should know you are in real estate and should be on one of your farm lists to receive mailouts.

14. Ask relatives if they know anyone who may want to move through their work or other organizations or activities.

Working with buyers in the field

1. Meet them at the office *first.*
2. Give them the *buyers book* for their own records.
3. Give them photocopies of the homes you plan to show them the first day.
4. Never set up more than *six houses* to see at one time. The only exceptions are out-of-town buyers, who may have little time.
5. When showing a home that is open by another agent, make sure you have that agent's permission and have *called him or her first.*
6. Start working with your buyer by setting limits and time frames.

   Examples: "Should we find the home that you like today, would you feel prepared to *make an offer on it*?"

   "Have you *reviewed the sample purchase agreement* that I included in your buyer's folder, and do you carry your checkbook with you?"
   (This is important in eliminating reasons for not making an offer.)
7. *Never leave a buyer at the end of your first appointment without* setting up the next appointment.

   Example: "Should we not be successful after we look at these homes today, would Thursday or Friday be better to *get together again*?"
8. *Never leave the buyer after the first appointment without asking, "Which one of the properties did you prefer*?"
9. Remember to *watch for emotional reactions* to homes.

   Example: "Oh, honey, our furniture would fit perfectly in the master bedroom!"
10. *Remember that* timing is crucial *if they like it! "Once they sleep on it, they won't sleep in it."*

Relocation buyers—guidelines

A wonderful way to generate new business is to work with relocation clients from across the state or across the nation. Start out by getting a "relocation book" from your broker of the various agents and real estate brokers nationwide. There are also international brokers that are more than happy to provide you with their resource books. Relocation companies that are moving people across the country are usually large corporations. They can also be a small company or an individual person seeking to relocate. Following are some guidelines to keep in mind when working with relocation clients.

1. Identify the agent that is sending you the lead.
2. Make sure to get the company's name/address/phone.
3. Find out how much the "referral fee" is to your company.
4. When is the client coming to your city?
5. What are the basic needs and requirements in a home?
6. How is the real estate market in your city, different from the city the client is coming from?
7. Is there a specific part of the city that your client is relocating to?
8. Put together a folder with: your brochure, maps, school information, shopping, cultural activities, sample houses from various areas—for your client.
9. Study the corporate relocation process—with special attention to international clients/languages/needs.
10. Telephone/e-mail/blog your client with your website.

Who is the Best Buyer to Work With?

Buyers are the same today as when I started out in the business almost 30 years ago. They fall into *three* categories:

1. *Buyers who want a home now!* These are *A buyers.* They either don't have a home to sell or, if they do, they want a new home now.
2. *Buyers who want a home soon!* They have a definite time frame in mind and will tell you so. These are usually *A/B buyers.*
3. *Buyers who want a home maybe!* These are usually *C buyers.* These buyers will buy if
   - *they can get top dollar for their present home*
   - *they retire*
   - *a certain home in a certain area with a certain floor plan comes along*
   - *they both decide to agree on what both of them want*

A Plan for Working with a Buyer

Buyers you meet at an open house

1. Introduce yourself with your card and ask for his or her:
   a. name
   b. address
   c. phone number
   d. write it down!
2. Tell the buyer you will immediately put him or her on your computer to receive a mailout of all active properties available in the areas in which he or she is looking.
3. Tell the buyer you will call when you mail the list to see when he or she wishes to set up an appointment during the next day or week to see homes.

If a buyer says, "we are just starting to look..."

Tell him or her:

I will send you information on homes I think you'll be interested in. I will wait for you to call me on the homes you are interested in. If you do not call me, I will wait to send you additional information until we touch base.

This is so important because it will *help you immediately decide* on whether your buyers are *legitimate*.

If a buyer calls on an ad...

After you tell the buyer about the home, ask these important questions:

1. Does this home sound interesting to you? (If the buyer says no, ask the next important question.)
2. Would you like for me to send you some of my favorite properties currently listed in the areas you have in mind? I could have them in tonight's mail. (Most people, if they are serious, will say yes.)

It is critical to categorize buyers. It is crucial to *eliminate* wasted time.

> I do not spend more than *two months* with a buyer unless I have their *undivided loyalty* and they sign an agreement!

To get undivided loyalty, *ask for it*—but not until you have earned it and proved by *at least one meeting* that you deserve total loyalty.

Pledge of Performance to Buyers

Whether this is their first or fifth home-buying experience, *any* home purchase is, for most people, *their largest single expenditure.*

Following are some pledges I'll make, should you choose to utilize my services as your sole buying agent:

Twelve-step plan

1. I'll help you identify the level of *affordability* you would have on a new home.
2. I'll give you the most *vital information* on available homes.
3. I'll *recommend the price range* most suited to your finances.
4. I'll *keep you aware of changes* in the real estate market.
5. I'll *arrange a tour* of areas, schools, and key points of interest.
6. I'll *help you preselect* homes that are most suitable to your price range.
7. I'll give you *all the information* available on any home for sale.
8. I'll help you *arrange an inspection* of that "right" property and assist you in getting financing and homeowner's insurance.
9. I'll see that you get a *complete estimate of all costs* involved in the purchase of a home.
10. I'll help you *write a purchase agreement*, I'll present it to the sellers, and I'll coordinate all negotiation and communication between you and the sellers.
11. I'll *stay in touch* from the day you start the search for your new home until the day you move in.
12. I'll be reimbursed with a commission *only* if you choose to purchase a home through me.

Date: _____

Real estate agent: _____

(PHONE)   (HOME) _____

                (CAR) _____

                (OFFICE) _____   (E-MAIL) _____

What to Give to a Potential New Buyer

1. City map*
2. City and state information
3. Information about specific areas of interest
4. School information
5. Directory of religious organizations
6. Credit information sheet
7. Information about you and or your brochure
8. Information about your company
9. Brief guide to help them to determine amount of mortgage they qualify for
10. Listings of some sample properties that are available for sale in areas that may be of interest to them
11. Names and numbers of some good mortgage loan officers and lenders
12. Internet/website information, e-mail address

Present this material in a *glossy folder* with the potential buyer's name typed on a sticker on the outside. Staple your card to the outside also.

> Most buyers really want to know two things right from the start:

1. ***How much*** **and what (condo, townhome, single-family home) can I buy?**
2. **What can you *show me* in my price range?**

*Most buyers really do want to see a map of where the specific properties are, along with descriptions of the neighborhoods. So keep *copies* of a mapbook with inserts of subject properties.

Buyer Evaluation Form

Name _____

Address _____

Phone _____

Comments/condition:

RATING SYSTEM:

5 = superior
4 = above average
3 = average
2 = below average
1 = poor

Price _____

_____

Price _____

Offer price

_____

Rating

These forms can be incredibly helpful in many ways:

1. When showing homes to a new buyer, give the buyer as many forms as the number of homes you are showing. At each house, ask the buyer to complete each card. After showing properties, ask the buyers to give you the cards to help you evaluate which homes the buyers are leaning toward and which ones are absolutely not of interest.

2. The *evaluation card* is also helpful at your open houses. If you feel there is a problem with the asking price, ask visitors to leave their opinions on the card. They needn't give their name, so they will not feel pressured. This can also tell a seller how a buyer feels about a home without compromising your own relationship with the seller.

I got so many evaluation cards about the price being too high...My sellers lowered it on their own!

I usually watch football during my open houses.

Sample Closing Dialogue with a Buyer

Did you like that home well enough to cook dinner in the kitchen?

Do you think your furniture could fit well in the living room?

Can't you just see yourself trimming a Christmas tree in the family room with a fire in the fireplace?

Why don't we go back to the office and see if the numbers can work for both of you?

Why don't we sit down and see what the monthly payment would be on this particular property?

Let's go back to my office. I'll show you some information that could work for you to get you into this property easily.

Let's call a favorite loan officer of mine to see how she thinks you would qualify for this new listing.

Why don't we go back to your house, and I'll give you a quick idea of what your home might bring in order to get into this property?

Why don't we drive over to my office and go through the additional information I have on this home to see how the numbers add up
for you?

Why don't we go back to your apartment and see when your lease expires in order to get a good closing date and a low interest rate on this home?

Let's follow each other back to the office and put the numbers together to see if we can get this for you tonight?

Why don't we sit down so I can show you how easy it would be to move into this home within the next couple of months?

Why don't you take a minute and go over a purchase agreement with me to see when would be a good possession date for the two of you?

Let's take a few minutes to see whether or not your offer might work. You just might be able to get into this home!

Buyer Information Needed for a Mortgage Application

1. Seven-year address history that includes names, addresses, and phone numbers of landlords.
2. Two-year employment history that includes names and addresses of all employers, a copy of the most recent pay stub, and W-2 forms for the past two years. If commission-employed, federal returns from last two years; if self-employed, federal tax returns, profit and loss statements for last two years.
3. Banks names and addresses, account numbers, current balances, and last two or three months' account statements for checking, savings, and investment accounts.
4. Monthly payments and balances for debts and liabilities, mortgages, personal and auto loans, credit cards, and student loans. Creditors' names, addresses, phone numbers, and account numbers.
5. Child care information, including names, addresses, monthly expenditure, verification of amount, and terms of child support and/or alimony payments and/or income.

At the application appointment, the buyer should be prepared to provide a personal check for

1. *property appraisal* and
2. *credit report on buyer*

Buyer Closing Cost Guide

1. Origination fee—1 percent of the loan amount.
2. Credit report—approximately $100.
3. Appraisal fee—$250 to $350 (FHA/VA usually less than conventional).
4. Title insurance—approximately $500 (mortgagee should talk to loan officer since owner policy is optional).
5. Plat drawing—approximately $55 to $65.
6. Recording fees—under $100.
7. Name and judgment search—approximately $25 to $35.
8. ARM title insurance endorsement fee—approximately $50 (applies only to conventional ARM mortgages).
9. Mortgage registration tax—(MN) $2.30 per $1,000.
10. Settlement closing fee—The VA will not allow the buyer to pay the closing fee for a VA mortgage; it must be charged to the seller.
11. Discount points—each discount point equals 1 percent of the loan amount (example: 1 point on a $40,000 loan = $400).
12. Commitment tax service fee—approximately $200 (not charged on VA mortgages).
13. VA funding fee—1.25 percent of the loan amount with less than 5 percent down, .75 percent with at least 5 percent down but less than 10 percent down, and .50 percent with 10 perent or more down.
14. Buyer Inspection Report $200 to $400 (could be more/less).

Additional fees

1. The *daily interest* on new mortgages from the day of closing through the end of the month will be collected at closing.

2. *One full year of homeowner's insurance* must be paid for prior to closing and a receipt must be brought to the closing.

3. *Private mortgage insurance* is usually required on all conventional loans if the buyer makes less than a 20 percent down payment.

4. *Two months* of homeowner's insurance is collected at closing to start an escrow account. This account is maintained in addition to payment in advance for a one-year policy.

5. If private mortgage insurance is used with a conventional loan, two months of the renewal premium is collected to open the escrow account.

6. Flood insurance is required if the property is located in a specific flood zone. *A full year's* premium is required, usually with two additional months for the escrow account.

Types of Mortgages for a Buyer

1. CONVENTIONAL MORTGAGE
   - *usually amortized over 15 to 30 years*
   - *loan usually available for home purchase or refinance*
   - *fixed rate, adjustable rate, or balloon loan*
   - *minimum down payment as low as 5 percent but usually 10 percent; less than 20 percent down payment requires PMI mortgage insurance*

2. FHA MORTGAGE
   - *loans insured against default by the United States government*
   - *down payment usually less than 10 percent*
   - *FHA adjustable rate mortgage has a 1 percent rate increase with 5 percent lifetime rate increase*
   - *all FHA mortgages require mortgage insurance*

3. VA MORTGAGE
   - *buyer can finance up to 100 percent of sales price*
   - *buyer must have VA eligibility certificate*
   - *veteran can use VA program more than once*
   - *funding fee to guarantee the loan can be financed into the loan or paid in cash by buyer or seller*

4. CONTRACT FOR DEED
   - *seller may hold the mortgage for the buyer*
   - *usually a balloon payment to the seller in five to seven years*
   - *seller determines amount of down payment*

Purchasing Process: From Start to Finish

1. Purchase agreement is accepted and copies are delivered to buyer and seller.
2. Meet with a loan officer at a good mortgage loan company to apply for a mortgage loan.
3. Give check to loan officer for an appraisal and credit report. (Appraisal is ordered, credit report on buyer is ordered, title work is ordered, and employment verifications are made.)
4. Credit report is received.
5. Employment verification is reviewed.
6. Appraisal is reviewed by underwriter and value on the property is issued. Work orders, if any, are issued.
7. Title work process in place to give clear title.
8. When all verifications are received, value is confirmed by the appraiser, and title work is completed and deemed acceptable, file is sent for loan approval. Borrower must sign final application.
9. Loan file is submitted for underwriting review and returned as:
   a. *approved*
   b. *rejected, or*
   c. *additional information required.*
10. If loan is approved, sales associates, sellers, and buyers are notified.
11. Listing agent schedules closing with the title company.
12. Attend the closing, sign all documents, and receive the keys.
13. Move into new home (later that day if per contract).

> Normal time to complete all of the above:
> 30 to 45 days

Interest rate lock-in: normally 60 to 90 days.

It is essential for the agent to *communicate with the lender weekly* on the progress of the loan.

How to Get Referral Business

1. Many good leads come from estate and garage sales. Don't hesitate to stop and visit.
2. Talk to your relatives and your friends. Are people marrying, retiring, divorcing?
3. Refer to your mailing list daily, not only during the holiday season.
4. Neighborhood people are sometimes the best referral sources.
5. Perhaps a favorite sales clerk at a favorite store knows someone who is moving.
6. Your best friend, spouse, or significant other always has a separate pool of referrals that could help.
7. Hair stylists sometimes give great referrals.
8. Pyramid businesses near you (Fuller Brush, Amway, Mary Kay, etc.) always have lists of people.
9. Calling the Human Resource Department of companies near where you live might provide you with future clients.
10. Wearing a name tag with your company logo when you go to your gas station or your grocery store can be great for business!

Referral business in real estate is tricky. Referrals can pass you by unnoticed. Yet every day there are more leads from referrals than you can imagine. So you must *always look the part of a professional* and you must always ask for business.

> *Think of real estate in every facet of your day.* **Aim to get at least two good new leads a week, and keep calling them for appointments.**

Involve yourself in your neighborhood, even if you live in an apartment. You can become involved with a monthly newsletter and provide tasty real estate treats: a monthly recipe favorite or latest real estate trends—the latest scoop in what's happening in housing.

Where Do Buyers Come from?

40 percent come from meeting a salesperson on site
20 percent come from a for sale sign
18 percent come in response to an ad
8 percent come from meeting at an open house
7 percent come from relocation services
3 percent buy an advertised property
1 percent buy the open house they see
3 percent buy for a combination of reasons

Everyone in the office said it was a bad day for an open. I had one anyway and sold it!

Sample Master Buyer's List to Keep in Daily Planner

Name:	Ann Smith	Name:	
Address:	4200 10th Street	Address:	
Phone:	721-2444	Phone:	
Area:	West suburbs only	Area:	
Price	150+ tops	Price	
Contacted:	4/10—5/6—6/3	Contacted:	
Originated:	Open house 4/6	Originated:	
Name:	Jim Jones	Name:	
Address:	1200 W. 3rd Street	Address:	
Phone:	227-1044	Phone:	
Area:	Inner city only (t-house)	Area:	
Price	100+	Price	
Contacted:	4/6—5/3	Contacted:	
Originated:	Call on ad 4/4	Originated:	
Name:	Jeff James	Name:	
Address:	314 N.E. Maple	Address:	
Phone:	342-7717	Phone:	
Area:	Suburbs (east)	Area:	
Price	125 tops	Price	
Contacted:	5/10—5/15	Contacted:	
Originated:	Sign call (Girard prop.)	Originated:	

Keep entries on this list active for *six weeks to two months*, and then move them to an alternative file, depending on when they will buy.

Within the next *three to six months* (depending on how you decide to keep this list), *replace* names.

Use sticky 2" × 3" Post-it Notes to add or replace a new quick addition to temporarily transfer it onto your master sheet.

> Keep active *A buyers* on a list in front of a daily planner. Check it *daily*.

> Keep Daily Planner current!

Sample Buyer Legal File Folder

Property address: _____

Sale price: _____   Selling date: _____

Closing date: _____

Buyer: _____

Address: _____

Phone: (H) _____   (W) _____

Information: _____

Seller: _____

Address: _____

Phone: (H) _____   (W) _____

Information: _____

Agent's name: _____   Company: _____

Address: _____

Phone: _____   Fax: _____

Additional information: _____

Make Copies of all Purchase Agreements and Addenda for:

1. **BUYER**
2. **SELLING AGENT AND SELLER**
3. **MORTGAGE COMPANY AND LOAN OFFICER**
4. **YOUR OWN FILES**

Chapter Summary

When "cold calling" for buyers, try to get their name. Make an appointment and ask for a referral. The first step to getting new buyers is to have at least two open houses next weekend. At the open house, resolve to find one or two clients from each open house who sincerely want to buy a house. Ask a lot of questions. It is imperative that you prequalify buyers. Identify a schedule and timeframe to work within. Meet the buyers at your office first. Give them copies of the homes you plan to show them. Never leave a buyer at the end of your first appointment without setting up the next appointment. Buyers who want a home now are the "A" buyers. Introduce yourself to a buyer and give them your card. Ask them for their name, address and telephone number. WRITE IT DOWN. Categorize your buyers and eliminate wasted time. Make a pledge of performance to your buyers and give them a "Twelve-Step Plan," pledging to utilize your services as their sole real estate agent. Make up a folder for your buyers that includes: city map, city and state information, school information, your brochure, and some sample properties of various areas. Show them what is in their price range. There are important "closing cost" guidelines to give to the buyer which include an estimate of the closing costs. There are various mortgages a buyer can obtain which include conventional, FHA, VA, and Contract for Deed. The purchasing process from start to finish can take as little as 30 to 45 days. Interest rate lock-ins are normally 60 to 90 days. It is essential for the real estate agent to communicate weekly on the progress of the loan. Aim for two referrals a week.

CHAPTER 5

COMPETITIVE MARKET ANALYSIS

- CMAs

big deal by Lorayne n' Neil

What's the Best CMA?

I *get* just about every listing call that I go on!

I attribute 80 percent of my business to *the way* I do business!

I start with a professional-looking *market analysis* brochure.

I pull three properties that I feel are most similar in the following areas:

1. *location*
2. *floor plan type* or style
3. *square footage*
4. *age*
5. *number of bedrooms* and baths
6. *unusual amenities* (such as pool, security system, etc.)
7. *garage* size
8. property improvements (such as *additions; larger garage; new roof; furnace; electrical system; central air; new appliances; and cosmetics*)
9. unusual financing opportunities
10. potential negatives (such as busy street or steep hill)

In the subject property part of the CMA, be sure you fill in the highlight section (the top left portion of the form) in descriptive, enthusiastic terms. Then immediately write an ad on the home!

When you do a CMA, write the information about the subject property in a *different color ink.* Often much of the information is provided to you by the seller, who has already completed a fact sheet on the home, copies of which are available at the property.

Completing a CMA is relatively simple. As you look at the following CMA, you will notice some very specific information. I make it a point to accentuate the *most important information* about a home by writing it *in the margin.*

Example:

L.P.	list price
S.P.	sale price
Days	days on the market
BR	bedrooms
Bath	number of baths
Yr. blt.	year the home was built
Lot	lot size
Taxes	amount of yearly taxes
Fplc	number of fireplaces
Garage	number of garages
Exterior	exterior of the home
W.O.	walkout basement
**	space for extras, such as pool
Sq. ft.	main floor square footage
Ttl. sq. ft.	total square footage

> NOTE: I also do CMAs on my laptop computer at the seller's home. I show them website information, current listings, and relocation on the Internet...

Comparable price: original listing price

Difference: sale price

Indicated value of subject: difference between the home's asking price and the sale price. The difference can be used as a good marketing tool because the sellers can see that the comparable listings sold only after they adjusted the price or took a lower offer on the property.

Write notes about your properties all over the CMA!

The More Notes You Take, the Better!

For example:

new roof
totally remodeled interior
attached triple garage
in-ground heated pool

If one particular home is the best comparable, note it by writing the words "best comparable" above it.
Write notes and highlight information in red pen.

When you have finished filling in the information on all three comparables, go to the bottom of the page where all the comparables on the subject property are listed.

Use a different color pen to fill in the information about the subject property. Under "Miscellaneous," write the year the home was built, its style, its best feature, additional amenities, and any outstanding points of interest.

Do the same for the following comparables with the same color pen.

SUBJECT PROPERTY

Prepared for:

Price _____ Terms SUBMIT # Bedrooms 3 # Baths 3

1 Add
2 Mun EDINA Zip _____ Cty HENN | HS Tax $ 5445 | Map 33 4C
3 Dist 585 Lt Sz 63 × 137 | Tax W/Spec $ SAME | Lake —
4 Brk # | HS Filed Y 19 98
5 Of Ph 920-1960 Apt Ph | Unpaid Spec $ — | Poss ARRANGE
6 Agt NASH-PRICE Hm Ph | Pend Spec $ — | Yr Blt 38
Key CLB C 3.15 T I #

7 SIMPLY ELEGANT NEW ENGLAND TUDOR LOADED WITH CHARM AND FLEXIBLE FLOOR PLAN ON MAIN
8 FLOOR. BEAUTIFUL BEDROOMS LOADED WITH CHARACTER. ENTICING BREAKFAST ROOM OFF FAMILY ROOM
9 OR FORMAL DINING ROOM. LOWER LEVEL WITH ADDITIONAL BR AND BATH AND FAM. ROOM.
10 THE BEST!

	L	C	D	Ap Rm Sz	Dir				
11									
12 LR	M			27 × 14	WSO	Heat FAG	Mtg $ PRIVATE		Type
13 DR	M			INCLUDED	Ext STUCCO	AE$	#		ASM
14 ID	M			AREA	Bsmt YES (FULL)	AC CENT	W	OD	DV
15 Kit	M			11 × 12	Bsmt Bth YES	Fpl YES	PI $	R/S NEW FINANCING	%
16 Fm	M			14 × 15	Mster Bth YES	Refrig YES	2M/CD$		%D
17 MB	2			20 × 14	G DBL Gdo Y	R&O YES	New Finance Possibilities		
18 BR	2			12 × 13	CW YES	DW YES			
19 BR	2			12 × 14	CS YES	SD			
20	L			12 × 14	PID		★ NEW ROOF (1998 - TIMBERLINE)		
21 DEN				8 × 10	SFML/TFF		1997- NEW CENTRAL AIR / FURNACE /		
							COMB. WINDOWS		

While efforts have been made to project an accurate market evaluation, it cannot be guaranteed that the information contained herein is free from errors and omissions.

PICTURE

Suggested List: 309 - 319,000

Suggested Sell: 290 ⁵
(DEPENDING ON
HOW LONG + THE MARKET)

COMPARABLE "A"   ITEM

photo

ITEM	
LP:	309,000
SP:	299,500
DAYS:	17
BR:	4
BA:	3
TAXES:	4927 ⁹⁸
BLT:	1937
LOT:	59 × 158
FPLC:	2
EXT:	SHAKE

REMODELED KITCHEN (NEW APPLCS)

NEW FURNACE - CENTRAL AIR - HUMIDIFER

NEW ROOF ++

SUNROOM + SQ FT: 1263 TTL
TOTAL OF ITEMS

"A" COMPARABLE PRICE (+) or (-) Difference **Indicated value of SUBJECT**
$ 309,000 $ 299,500

	SQ. FEET	GARAGE
SUBJECT PROPERTY	2078 TTL	DBL
COMPARABLE "A"	2661	DBL
COMPARABLE "B"	2550	DBL
COMPARABLE "C"	2500	DBL

I had help putting this form into my database... But now I can print it off my computer!

I might take a night class and learn computers next year...

		COMPARABLE "B"		ITEM			COMPARABLE "C"		ITEM		
				LP: 282,500					LP: 275,000		
				SP: 275,000					SP: 275,000		
				DAYS: 85					DAYS: 1++		
				BR: 4					BR: 4		
		photo		BATH: 3			photo		BATH: 2		
				TAXES: 4303 ºº					TAXES: 4979 ºº		
				BUILT: 1929					BLT: 1938		
				LOT: 80 x141					LOT: 50 x158		
				FPLC: 2					FPLC: 2		
				EXT: STUCCO					EXT: BRICK/STUCCO		

NEWER KITCHEN - FENCED YARD   MAIN FLOOR SUNROOM

JACUZZI TUB/SAUNA - ATT. DBL. GAR.   FINISHED LOWER LEVEL

(MAIN FAM. ROOM) + DINING ROOM   APPLC'S INCLUDED - DBL ATT. GAR

2661   NEW BATHROOM UP+   SQ FT: 1170   TTL 2550   SQ FT 2500 (TTL)

TOTAL OF ITEMS   TOTAL OF ITEMS

$	"B" COMPARABLE PRICE	(+) or (–) Difference	Indicated value of SUBJECT	$	"C" COMPARABLE PRICE	(+) or (–) Difference	Indicated value of SUBJECT	$
-9500 ºº	$ 282,500		$ 275,000	-7500 ºº	$ 275,000		$ 275,000	5-1-98 Ø

LOT SIZE	NO. BRs	BATHS	CENT AIR	FAMILY ROOM	MISCELLANEOUS	BASE TAX	YR. BLT.	LIST TERMS	DAYS MKT.	ASKING PRICE	SALE TERMS	SALE PRICE
63 x 137	3	3	YES	MAIN 14 x 15	LOVELY MAJESTIC TUDOR - 3 BR - 3 BATH - NEW C.A/FURN/ FPLC -DEN-	5445	1938	SUB	NA	NA	NA	NA
59 x 158	4	3	YES	9 x 13	2 STORY NEW ENGLAND 4BR - 3 BATH COLONIAL - MASTER SUITE W/NEW BATH	4927	1937	SUB	17	309,900	CONV	299,500
80 x 141	4	3	YES	17 x 12	2 STORY - 4 BR - 3 BATH WITH MAIN FLOOR FAM. ROOM & FORMAL DR.	4303	1929	SUB	85	282,500	CONV	275,000
50 x 138	4	2	NO	SUNROOM	STUCCO 2 STORY ENGLISH TUDOR W/ 4 BR 2 BATH - 1ST FLOOR SUN ROOM	4979	1938	SUB	1	275,000	CONV	275,000

A good CMA works every time...I get the listing!

Blank CMA

SUBJECT PROPERTY

Prepared for:

Price				Terms			# Bedrooms
							# Baths

1 Add					HS Tax $		Map
2 Mun		Zip		Cty	Tax W/Spec $		Lake
3 Dist	Lt Sz				HS Filed 19		
4 Brk			#		Unpaid Spec $		Poss
5 Of Ph		Apt Ph			Pend Spec $		Yr Blt
6 Agt		Hm Ph			Key	C	T	#
7							
8							
9							
10							

11	L	C	D	Ap Rm Sz	Dir					
12 LR					WSO		Heat		Mtg $	Type
13 DR					Ext		AE$		#	ASM
14 ID					Bsmt		AC		W	OD	DV
15 Kit					Bsmt Bth		Fpl		PI $	R $	%
16 Fm					Mster Bth		Refrig		2M/CD$	%D
17 MB					G	Gdo	R&O		New Finance Possibilities
18 BR					CW		DW		
19 BR					CS		SD		
20					PID				
21					SFML/TFF				

While efforts have been made to project an accurate market evaluation, it cannot be guaranteed that the information contained herein is free from errors and omissions.

PICTURE

Suggested List: _____

Suggested Sell: _____

COMPARABLE "A"   ITEM

photo

TOTAL OF ITEMS

"A" COMPARABLE PRICE	(+) or (-) Difference	Indicated value of SUBJECT
$ _____	$ _____	

	SQ. FEET	GARAGE
SUBJECT PROPERTY		
COMPARABLE "A"		
COMPARABLE "B"		
COMPARABLE "C"		

Grid key:

WSO	= water softener	AE$	= average elec.	W	= where loan is located
EXT	= exterior	AC	= air conditioning		
G	= garage	R&O	= range/oven	ASM	= assumable
Gdo	= garage door opener	DW	= dishwasher	PITI	= monthly payment
		SD	= school district	2M/	= second mortgage
CW	= city water	Mtg.	= mortgage	%	= interest rate
CS	= city sewer	#	= loan number	TSF	= total square feet

		COMPARABLE "B"		ITEM			COMPARABLE "C"		ITEM	
		photo					photo			
			TOTAL OF ITEMS					TOTAL OF ITEMS		

$	"B" COMPARABLE PRICE	(+) or (−) Difference	Indicated value of SUBJECT	$	"C" COMPARABLE PRICE	(+) or (−) Difference	Indicated value of SUBJECT	$
	$_____	$_____			$_____	$_____		

				**								*	
LOT SIZE	NO. BRs	BATHS	CENT AIR	FAMILY ROOM	MISCELLANEOUS	BASE TAX	YR. BLT.	LIST TERMS	DAYS MKT.	ASKING PRICE	SALE TERMS	SALE PRICE	

*Note: Sale Terms = FHA/VA/Conv./Cash
How did the property sell?

**Miscellaneous = Summary of the house's important features.
Example: "3BR/3BATH * 2FPLC * 3GAR * 3400 Walkout Square Feet"

Comments on CMA

The following comments were made by an owner who listed two properties totaling half a million dollars with an agent who called him off of an owner ad in the newspaper:

"First of all, you did your homework."

"It was very well presented."

"You sold us on you that evening and you were so enthusiastic."

"You were so professional and thorough and had such a history on the house and did it in a concise, consolidated manner."

"You have a sense of humor."

I told them I'm their neighbor...they gotta list with me!

Chapter Summary

For the best CMA, pull three properties that are most similar in the following areas: location, floor plan (type or style) square footage, age, number of bedrooms and baths, unusual amenities (such as pool, security system, etc.) garage size, property improvements, financing opportunities, and potential negatives. Note the difference between the homes' asking prices and the sales prices.

For best results

Pull three properties similar in:

A. Location

B. Style

C. Price

D. Amenities

CHAPTER 6

COMPUTER TECHNOLOGY

- Blogging
- Email
- Internet
- Laptops

big deal by Lorayne n' Neil

In order to stay up-to-date and informed on the latest technology, a real estate agent must be willing to TAKE TIME OUT EACH DAY to develop computer skills and SPEND A MINIMUM OF ONE HOUR A DAY learning new computer programs.

More and more transactions are being completed over the Internet. The real estate professional today must be familiar with REAL ESTATE CYBERSPACE.

Create your internet marketing plan

1. Customize your own web page
2. Utilize your online server
3. Search the Internet for information
4. Customize e-mail mailing lists of clients
5. Find buyers for properties
6. Generate new leads for real estate business

Selling Real Estate on the Internet

Search engines

- Allows you to find information on the Web.
- Similar to the Yellow Pages in the phone book.
- Google and Yahoo are popular search engines.

You can type in a real estate request such as "apartment buildings for sale" and you will get immediate results!

BUT STILL THE MOST POWERFUL TOOL TODAY ON THE INTERNET IS:

YOUR E-MAIL!

YOUR BLOG!

YOUR WEBPAGE!

The Internet allows you to create **instant** communication with anyone in seconds!

Computer Uses

Benefits:

- You can use your computer at your open houses to show buyers homes that are currently listed.
- You can look up sold properties near and around your open house.
- You can access the MLS system from your personal computer and hook up to the qualifying program to qualify clients quickly.
- You can use your laptop computer to set up a geographic farming system and type in the names (alphabetized) and addresses of people listed in the cross-reference directory to make a list for your own reference.
- You can install a database program with names and addresses of clients and mail letters to those you have visited.
- You can use software that will enable you to check with people who will be moving in three, six, or twelve months.
- You can create a perfect newsletter on your computer in little time without worrying about typewritten errors because you can modify and spell-check automatically.
- Your computer calendar can remind you to send clients postcards for anniversaries, birthdays, thank-yous, or whatever.

My laptop and website have brought me tons of business!

- New PIM (Personal Information Management) programs allow you to contact up to hundreds of people a day. You can log when you will call them back and automatically look up their telephone numbers. You can even dial the phone number automatically. Some PIMs even have time planners that allow you to schedule your entire day and note (with bookmarks) when to call your prospects back.
- You can create a reference chart of all your past clients, showing when their houses sold and closed.
- A computer helps you become extremely effective and professional when you call on potential clients.
- A program connected with a desktop publisher allows you to create a message to a client and use specific graphics to create any image you like.
- Graphics programs specifically allow you to include charts, graphs, and special artwork to promote specific listed properties.
- Individualized programs enable you to personalize your presentations.
- A database program enables you to keep track of exactly what is required for 25 to 100 listings at a time. You may want to write an ad, send a letter, or change a lockbox code. This is important for time management.
- Specific software enables you to inform your seller how the listing is doing and to send him or her a detailed report regarding your advertising marketing plan.
- A spreadsheet program gives you an overview of your listings and closings on one sheet. This enables you to see what you have spent for advertising, marketing, and all areas of service to any and all of your listings. You can use your computer to show a potential buyer the pros and cons of refinancing. The computer will compare the current rate of interest and payment to a lower interest rate and payment.
- A computer will quickly show a client the advantages of owning versus renting and analyze the differences.
- You can show your buyer the advantages of a 15-year mortgage versus a 30-year mortgage and the amount saved in payments over the years.
- A spreadsheet program can analyze the best loans at the current rate of interest, including points and origination fees.

What about the Computer and Follow-Up?

Having a computerized program set up is essential when going into a buyer or listing presentation.

The benefit of a computer is not just to keep up with the Joneses, but rather to realize the time savings and the many tasks that can be done once you are comfortable with a computer.

Although real estate is a *person-to-person business,* many functions that must be performed by the agent can be accomplished by a computer to save time and energy. Computer use can also make the agent appear more professional to the seller and the buyer.

Following are important abilities and features that are available on the computer:

Computer features

1. Tapping into an MLS (Multiple Listing Service) system.
2. Preparing a CMA (*Competitive Market Analysis*).
3. Searching the *solds* in the areas of interest.
4. Searching the *expireds* in the areas of interest.
5. Searching the *current actives* in the areas of interest.
6. *Internal phone* for calling other companies.
7. Internal *calculator.*
8. Geographic *farming* tool.
9. Various *mailing* systems.
10. Sending out a *newsletter* to clients.
11. Listing *presentation.*
12. Creating charts using graphic programs.
13. *Filing* system.
14. Day/time *reminder.*
15. Monthly *calendar* and world clock.
16. Listing files and escrow/*closing files.*
17. Tracking *expenses.*
18. Printing *informative* reports.
19. Various *financial* help, such as qualifying buyers.
20. Word processing programs such as *fact sheets* and letters.

I e-mail and visit websites all over the country...daily!

You may ask yourself how these individual programs can actually help you when you already know how to do all this. The answer is that the computer saves time and performs a multitude of functions for you.

A computer is a time saver!

A good computer financial program can:

- create a CMA (Competitive Market Analysis)
- create a rent versus buy program
- qualify a buyer quickly
- create a loan rate comparison report
- show buyers monthly cost breakdown quickly

A good word processor program can:

- produce a *letter or postcard* quickly
- produce a fact/highlight sheet quickly
- produce a newsletter for your farm area quickly
- produce a buyer guidebook quickly
- produce a listing presentation book quickly

A good data base program can:

- schedule all listing needs and tasks
- add a listing to your file system quickly
- add a closing to your file/database system quickly

MLS program:

- searches all printed comparable properties for solds, expireds, and actives. It also does an area market survey that lets the seller know how long it has taken for similar properties that have been on the market to sell.

When you start the process of purchasing a computer, you may or may not be knowledgeable as to what you should buy. When I first walked through the door of the computer retailer, I thought I had suddenly been transported to another country! I had virtually no idea of what I wanted to buy!

Computer items to purchase

- an IBM-compatible computer with a color monitor
- a Hewlett-Packard laser printer
- a modem (internal) in my hard drive
- WordPerfect software and Windows
- Lotus 1–2–3 software
- various books to learn about computers (*Windows for Dummies*)
- boxes of computer paper
- a mouse
- an extra phone line installed in my house for the modem on my computer and my fax

Now...I've bought the computer. what's, next?

Now I was set—or so I thought.

It took me quite a while, and a fair amount of money paid to a computer assistant for me to learn *basic features* and most *basic commands. At the least* I needed to know how to *boot* my computer and use some of the functions! I eventually did learn to prepare a complete program, type out a report to my clients, and prepare to print it when...

I accidentally pressed the wrong button!

Everything disappeared! This completely frustrated me, and I decided to regroup. I bought a Windows operating system, which save me hours of aggravation. Even though I love to sell real estate, I realized I had to have a computer. Since I am not very mechanical and I don't often take the time to *learn details,* I need to have things simplified for me.

My computer class helps me a lot ..!

A computer program setup that works for me in a very simplified fashion is the Windows operating system.

Here is everything you need to know to set yourself up with a computer, the software, the printer, and the modem. Once all the components are installed, all you have to do is:

1. Follow directions
2. Give your computer business each day
3. Let your computer be your guidebook and your secretary
4. Check your e-mail regularly

If you invest in nothing else in the next decade, try to own the following five items:

1. Laptop computer and printer
2. Cell phone
3. Fax machine
4. Digital camera
5. Scanner

These five items will enable you to keep abreast of a changing market by giving you access to changing terms and conditions on properties and on purchase agreements.

A laptop computer and a good, small printer (I prefer IBM-compatible) should cost you approximately $500-$800.

You should be able to purchase a cell phone for approximately $200 or less. Oftentimes, a cell phone is free with a contract.

Good second-hand FAX machines are available for $200.

Watch for ads in the classified section of the newspaper for second-hand components. Very often people purchase these items and discard them shortly thereafter with hardly any wear and at a great savings to you!

Your total dollar outlay should not exceed $2,000, and you can usually find a few good software programs for a few hundred dollars.

A good program for under $100 is the Windows operation system.

Multiple Functions of a Computer

1. Desktop organizer: tracks appointments; outlines address book; outlines strategy points before you begin.
2. Word processor: fully edits and formats all documents.
3. Spell checker: 100,000-word dictionary captures 99 percent of spelling errors.
4. Spreadsheet: with 30 functions for financial analysis.
5. Database: searches any field and creates reports on the information on file.
6. Graphics: creates different types of illustrations, such as bar charts and line graphs.
7. Communications: uses a modem (telephone) for autodialing and full- or split-screen options.

I installed Windows on my laptop. I also installed a modem to enable me to call into the MLS system. Some real estate agents prefer to have a computer *at home* also.

I have a laptop *and* an IBM-compatible computer in my home.

Someday I hope to have a better understanding of computers. However, since the majority of my time is devoted to the real estate business, I also have a tendency to do things mechanically—the easy way. I found it helpful to take a lot of computer classes at night.

I use my laptop a lot because it is simple and easy to figure out.

- It *adds to my image* as a high-tech professional.
- It saves me huge amounts of time and guesswork.
- I can show clients new listings in color in their home.
- I can take my clients on virtual tours of new properties.
- I can do CMAs (market evaluations) in sellers' homes.
- I can check my e-mail throughout the day.
- I can visit other websites.
- I can e-mail contracts from my car with a wireless connection.
- I can check for new listings.
- I can use mapping software to get directions to any location.

Purchasing a Laptop Computer

After a lot of trial and error, I realized that I can meet all my real estate needs using a laptop computer.

A laptop computer can, at the touch of a button, provide you with all the information that you need!

Most laptop computers are fully compatible with desktop computers and use the same software and disk drives. They average in cost from $500 (used) to over $5,000 (new and fully equipped).

There are two types of screens for a laptop computer:

1. Liquid crystal display (LCD) screen—gray display
2. Gas plasma screen—amber display

The gas plasma screen offers fine resolution, but your investment will be about $1,000 more.

The keyboard of a laptop is a lot smaller than that of a desktop and isn't quite as easy to use. Also, the layout of the keyboard will take getting used to. When you are looking at keyboards, try to find a layout that is close to what you are accustomed to using.

The memory storage of a laptop operates the same way as that of a desktop. More memory will cost a more money (possibly thousands more). You might want to purchase a Pentium with an 80GB hard drive. Many laptops come with a CD-ROM drive. This allows compatibility with a desktop also.

> One of the best features of a laptop computer is that it can operate on either AC (electricity) or DC (battery-operated) power.

A portable printer (around $200) can be used anywhere. You want to consider a desktop printer as well as a portable printer because the portable printer usually is much slower, printing only one page per operation.

Types of printers include:

1. Dot matrix printer—approximately $150–$200
2. Laser printer—approximately $1,000

Note: I have a Hewlett-Packard laser printer and love it!

A Pentium processor will enable you to do mass mailings.

A laptop computer will pay for itself time and time again. It is also a business expense and is entirely deductible!

Benefits of a laptop

1. Keep track of your *appointments*. Sound an alarm!
2. Print your entire *schedule*, and replace it.
3. Provide instant *financial analysis programs* for buyers.
4. *Prequalify* buyers.
5. Produce professional letters.
6. Create *mass mailings* to homeowners and purchasers.
7. Keep track of all your *farm information*.
8. Keep current clients, listings, etc. available for *instant recall*.
9. Send homeowners *letters*.
10. Figure *net sheets* instantly.

Computer Points of Interest

1. When buying a computer, always find out what the purchase price *does not* include.

2. Buy an *upgraded version* of a computer now rather than later only if the upgrade will save you at least $400.00.

3. A *complete computer system* includes: CPU, RAM, keyboard, disk drives, printer, software, modem, and fax.

4. The *advertised price* of a computer does not usually include much of the software for the computer.

5. Purchase *various kinds of software*, an operating system (which teaches the computer how to handle the keyboard, monitor, printer, and disks), and a basic application program that includes word processing.

6. When you buy software, *make backup copies* of the disks in case the original disks are damaged or lost.

7. Duplicating software disks and sharing/selling them is against the law. *It is called* pirating.

8. A few of the *biggest reputable software companies* are Microsoft, Lotus, WordPerfect, and Novell.

9. Sometimes you can download demos of the software, which allows you to sample the software before you purchase.

10. There are amazing (software) programs that save hours of work, many of which are made for real estate agents.

11. Ask a reputable dealer to help you put together a computer package.

12. All information stored in a computer is called *software*.

13. You can buy many informative real estate programs on *disk*.

14. The business section of the daily newspaper will tell you anything you need to know about the computer industry today.

15. *ComputerWorld* is a weekly newspaper that covers the entire computer industry: $2.00/issue, (toll-free) 800-669-1002.

16. Computer magazines feature ads for *discount dealers* that can save you as much as 50 percent on hardware and software.

17. Every Tuesday *The New York Times* Science section has ads from all of New York's most aggressive discount dealers.

18. Several giant mail-order discount computer companies sell software and some hardware. Two of these dealers are:

    Telemart   800-426-6659

    PC Connection   800-AID-8088

Index of Some Computer Companies

Company	Web/Phone	Comments
Computer Plus	www.computersplusnyc.com online orders only	discounts on merchandise
Gateway 2000	www.gateway.com (800)-LAD-2000	IBM clones
Egghead Discount	www.eggheadsystems.com (632) 727-8577	chain of software stores
New York PC	http://www.nypc.org/ (212) 643-7005	New York's computer club
PC Connection	www.pcconnection.com (888) 800-0323	most software
USA Flex	www.usaflex.com (800)-872-3539	monitors, printers
Apple	www.apple.com (800) MY-APPLE	(Love ichat, iphone, iphoto)

More on Computers

IBM PC programs come on CD-ROM or floppy disks. A *software program* comes with a CD or floppy disk and a manual explaining how to use it.

The disk operating system (DOS) teaches your computer how to handle disk drives.

IBM worked with Microsoft to invent MS-DOS. It is the most popular operating system for the IBM PC and clones.

Be sure you get a Pentium processor. Programs can be purchased from a discount dealer: PC Zone 800-ALT-8088.

You will want to have CD capabilities.

Actually, using a computer is not as difficult as you think.

Real Estate and the Internet

Since 1993 computer use has changed drastically with the introduction of the Internet. Masses can now access an interactive medium that explores the universe. One of the most appealing facets is the ability to purchase goods and services over the Internet. The Internet is projected to bring in over a trillion dollars over the next few years. A huge amount of this money can be attributed to real estate.

Instead of paging through lengthy books with various Multiple Listing sheets attached, you can now go to the Internet and instantly access a particular real estate company's website and pull up a variety of properties you may be interested in viewing. Brokers, agents, sales managers, and clients now have a brand new way of approaching real estate.

Consumers of residential housing now have instant access to multimedia information that shows them available properties and gives all the information regarding the property. This puts the real estate agent in a far more vulnerable position...agents today MUST BE completely up-to-date on the latest material regarding the inventory available for the areas in which they are working. Over the next few years, everyone connected with real estate will be expected to navigate over the Web, seeking out properties for sale in any given market.

Although real estate agents are the core of the real estate business and there are over one and a half million licensed agents in the country today, only a few of these agents are doing the majority of the business in real estate transactions. Agents who have made the decision to learn computer skills are completing computer training quickly and realizing large profits because of it.

Even though real estate is a people business, the computer allows the agent to devote more hours in the field to researching desirable properties. A quick tap of the finger and multiple properties are brought up on screen for the potential home buyer to view.

Across the country agents are using laptop ingenuity to design new and more creative programs for the sellers/buyers to take advantage of. Buyers are quickly prequalified with any number of online mortgage loan officers and are shown a variety of properties (through online MLS access and screens that accommodate up to 32 pictures per frame)—all in an affordable price range.

Being in real estate today is far more complicated than it was years ago. More and more smaller companies have merged with large corporations to form alliances that enable higher and higher technology to be brought about within the organization.

The new reality in real estate is the Internet.

Most all real estate markets in the United States are able to have continuous access to the Internet. Because of this technological breakthrough, the volumes of paper that are used in real estate transactions have been reduced dramatically. Eventually there will be a universal form for use by all real estate agents throughout the country, thereby removing barriers that exist currently in working with agents across the United States. An agent will be able to fax a universal purchase agreement to another agent across the country.

Real estate forms are sent via e-mail or viewed via a web browser as customers shop over the Internet and browse different properties.

Here's a scenario that is commonplace in the market today: Barbara Nash of Minneapolis, Minnesota has decided to move to Chicago, Illinois. Her job offer is immediate and she must find a home quickly. She does not even have time to travel to Chicago to search for a new home. She decides to start her search over the Internet.

The first thing she does is buy a good map program for her computer. (Using a newly updated map program, she is able to search, in depth, any city in the country.) She becomes fairly familiar with the area in which she decides to live. All she needs to do is enter her work address and tell the map program that she wants no more than a 15-minute drive to and from the office. She can choose her home and neighborhood by eliminating or adding areas that are more or less attractive, depending on demographics, shopping, crime, and proximity to churches and other amenities.

Next she goes to a program that allows her to punch in the kind of home that she wants. She can choose the style, the number of bedrooms, the number of bathrooms, fireplaces, and extra amenities. She can then quickly scan the properties that come up in the location she desires, and almost immediately her agent will be able to send her back pictures of a few properties that almost meet her specifications. Once her agent sends her more data on any of the three homes on which she has narrowed her decision, she can then zoom in on the neighborhoods and get more specific information as needed. All this is done from the privacy of her own home, on her own computer.

If she so chooses, she can take a virtual tour of any one of the properties to see the inside of the home. Her agent is now giving her a virtual vocal tour of the entire home.

Now that she has narrowed her search to one of the three properties, she is able to zoom in on more elaborate details such as the window treatments in each room, the bathroom fixtures, the kitchen cupboards, the hardwood floors, and the new appliances. Finally she needs to see a little bit of the neighborhood and the houses around the subject property. There are larger views of the park close by and the school across the street. All of these factors have influenced her decision, and she now feels comfortable enough to make an offer.

The termite report and the home inspection are instantly sent to her via fax or e-mail, and she peruses them quickly before deciding to make her offer via e-mail.

She can also search the Internet for a bank with which she wishes to do business. Once she has secured a good lender, this lender can prequalify her for the above-mentioned property.

When Barbara decides to write up her offer, she can be walked through the offer over the Internet at a website that has specific contracts and forms for her to fill out while the agent speaks with her on the phone. They are able to complete the entire contract and decide to put a 48-hour contingency inspection into the contract once it has been accepted. At this point, Barbara will be able to go to Chicago, meet with her new employer, and view the home that she has contingently purchased—all in one visit. Her time has been utilized to the fullest.

From the time that Barbara contacted her agent over the Internet via e-mail, searched for a home, got approval from a mortgage lender, and made her offer, it has been less than two hours. She also finds the best flight possible and is ready to leave the next day.

* * *

Once you become familiar with the Internet and are comfortable using your e-mail, you may want to design a web page for yourself. Having your own web page is extremely beneficial to you and can bring in more referral fees and commission checks than you may have believed possible.

Many agents specialize in relocation clients. These are clients moving back and forth across the country because of job transfer or current job position. These agents find a niche with the human resource department of various corporations and are constantly given leads as employees/clients move about. Many agents no longer feel the need for a regular business office. They are working more and more from their cars and are creating a new type of office: a virtual team with a virtual office. They connect only by e-mail or over a video conference to talk about agendas.

Real Estate Internet and Your E-mail

What is the most valuable feature of e-mail to a real estate agent today?

…E-MAIL ALLOWS YOU TO GET YOUR MESSAGE OUT *INSTANTLY*…

With one push of a button, your message is sent. Real estate communication depends on being up to date.

Checking your e-mail messages daily allows you to respond to clients from work, from home—even while on vacation!

The majority of top agents in the field today contact their clients via e-mail and relay offers, contingencies, counters, and other valuable information that **must be documented.**

NEW LISTING Leads are generated almost immediately! Prepare a brief description of the property and get to thousands of buyers at once!

NEGOTIATING Allows the computer to be the middleman. The negotiation runs more smoothly with only seconds between counters and instantaneous communication.

CONTRACTS Swiftly e-mail contracts and drafts of contracts back and forth for client approval and acceptance.

PURCHASE AGREEMENTS Now you can type up a purchase agreement, store it on computer, and attach the file to an e-mail to a client for immediate signatures if they are out of town or at work and don't need the extra hassle.

HOME PICTURES Let's say you have an out-of-town client who wants to see a picture you just took of a new listing. You can scan the picture and e-mail it to your client **instantly.** Or photograph it with your digital camera.

REAL ESTATE FILES Perhaps you started a file on a listed property over six months ago and have tried and tried to get a price reduction. Now the seller wants documentation of showings, comments, and the date of the last price reduction. You can instantly e-mail parts of your file to the seller for his or her perusal.

Let's say a new buyer is coming to your town and wants to buy a new house. What are the things they are going to be most interested in upon arrival? What would you be most interested in?

Buyer interests

1. Where are the schools located in a certain area?
2. Where is the best shopping in a certain area?
3. What hotels are nearby?
4. Where is good dining? Ethnic dining? Vegetarian dining?
5. Where are the churches located?
6. What is the cultural climate?
7. What fun things are there to do in the city?
8. Where can they work out and play tennis?
9. Where are the best golf courses?
10. What clubs are available to join?

Search the topics and click on the websites that come up.

- Look at the home page for the e-mail address.
- Send them your message about reciprocal linking.
- Try to send at least 35 to 50 real estate messages EACH DAY.
- Spend time **daily** on improving your own real estate website.
- After connecting with local websites, establish metro and then statewide connections.
- Establish more contacts **daily.**
- Connect with other agents who have websites and ask for reciprocity. By linking with other agents, your business will multiply.
- Always remember to add your e-mail address to all your links.
- Some lucrative ideas for website addresses are as follows:
  www.soldbybarbara.com
  www.homesthatsell.com
  www.Barbarasellshomes.com
  www.nashsellsfast.com

There are many sites to visit, once you become familiar with the Internet. Real estate can become more fun than ever before!

Success in Real Estate through the Internet

Real estate companies need powerful software tools in order to create productive solutions for their agents and the company. Business over the Internet allows for:

My buyer wants my e-mail address. I said it's just a fad....

- Virtual real estate tours of homes all over the world
- Videoconferencing regarding transfers, including speech recognition
- 3D renditions of model homes with instant send-offs (links to other sites)
- Browser plug-ins that extend multimedia applications
- Ability to link up with other websites and surf the Net
- Opportunity to show video presentations of new properties to prospective clients, enhancing buyers' interaction with a property!
- Virtual teams allow agents to
  —work from home and/or a corporate office
  —automatically give information to a specific website
  —e-mail throughout the day
  —have live online training sessions
  —complete online forms

A very important rule of thumb on and off the Internet is to **become a specialist in real estate.**

Try to find a niche that suits you best. Perhaps you like specializing in **senior citizens,** or new home buyers, or relocation clients, or "My Neighborhood," or first-time home buyers, or the Lakes areas, or the west side, or townhomes, or downtown.

Whatever the field you choose…MAKE A BIG DEAL ABOUT IT!

Design your web page with your specialized field in mind and stick to it…promote it…believe in it…contact as many websites as possible and start watching your business grow!

Today and from now on, real estate professionals will be using the Internet for more and more of their daily business. They now have the opportunity to tap into a worldwide market from their car or from their desk. It is now possible to reach thousands of buyers and sellers at virtually no cost.

My business is booming…I have my own web page!

New programs become available via the Internet every day. E-mail techniques now allow a real estate agent to leave home and forward all faxes onto their laptop, with just a click of a switch!

Real estate internet resources

- Worldwide residential/commercial real estate directory
- Map locations and directions to any location with aerial photo
- Up-to-date listing of mortgage lenders and mortgage qualifiers
- Access to business names, addresses, and phone numbers
- Access to any client's (buyer/seller) e-mail address online
- International real estate directory and resource guide
- Latest commercial properties for sale worldwide
- Latest residential properties for sale worldwide
- Up-to-date real estate articles, conferences, event planner
- International real estate conference calling with clients
- Amazon.com book search for any real estate book
- Immediate access to competitive market analysis
- Latest software and computer packages
- Background information on lawyers (Lawyer Locator)
- Translate any relocation client, buyer or seller

*See chapter on "Niche Marketing."

Creating a Website

1. If you are not versed in this technology, find a reputable person to help you design your site. First, ask yourself the following questions:
   a. How much can I spend for my website?
   b. How large should it be?
   c. Who is my audience going to be?
   d. What essentials do I want to include?
2. Read the comments of International Real Estate Digest (www.ired.com) regarding websites.
3. Visit websites of companies recommended to help you. You will determine quickly if you think the site is professionally designed. Try to pick three companies with which you would consider working.
4. The front page of your website should look like the cover of a magazine or the front of a dressy store window. **You must entice!**
5. There are so many virtual options available now through web technology that you can provide sound, animation, and all kinds of alluring tactics to get your client to contact you.
6. SPECIALIZE! Make sure you let the visitor to your website know that you are a specialist in some area of real estate. Whether it is the first-time homebuyer or relocation, or "Seniors on the Move," tell them!
7. Provide valuable information! More than anything, people want to know about the city they live in or are going to live in. What would you want to read about quickly? Most recommended movie, most recommended restaurant, largest shopping mall...? Whatever it is, incorporate it within your webpage and promote yourself.
8. Give all the information about yourself! Make sure your website has: your full address, your e-mail, your fax number, your car phone, any additional numbers and information that gives you credibility.
9. Be sure to include a good quality photo of yourself. People like to see what someone looks like.
10. Add linking opportunities. People like to learn. Keep your site updated, changing, and linked to other informative real estate sites.
11. Include html formatting, online forms, e-mail access, a blog, internal and external links to other websites, website maintenance, logos, menu bars, image maps, and icons.

MAKE YOUR WEBSITE EXCITING!

Sample Web Page

| home pix | *Barbara Nash*
"sells homes" | **REAL ESTATE
COMPANY LOGO** |

(click ☐ button of interest)

☐ *MAIN PAGE*

☐ *TODAY'S PROPERTY*

☐ *FOR HOME BUYERS*

☐ *FOR HOME SELLERS*

☐ *MORTGAGE SOURCES*

☐ *SCHOOLS/DAYCARE*

☐ *CONTACT ME*

☐ **HOMES FOR SALE UNDERLINED DAILY*

"Your Real Estate Tour Guide"
From cities to suburbs . . . Barbara has spent thirty years selling homes to satisfied clients! My new website can help you fill ALL your housing needs today! I look forward to talking to you now. Simply pick up the phone or e-mail me at the following address.

Sincerely, Barbara Nash

Barbara Nash's Picture

ABC REAL ESTATE
MEETING ALL YOUR HOUSING NEEDS

☐

Million Dollar Mortgage Co.
The fastest, best mortgages in town!

☐

Latest Real Estate News
All the latest trends!

☐

Housing Advice
Everything on homes

CONTACT INFORMATION:

Barbara Nash

Phone:	612-885-7899	1-888-234-4500
Fax:	612-947-9869	
Website:	barbaranashome.com	
E-mail:	lifeaware@mac.com	

Address: 1234 Minneapolis Street
Minneapolis, Minnesota 44444

Recommended Reading
Twin Cities Touring
Refinancing Now
Best Home Features
Home Trends
Residential Remodel
Latest Appliances
Landscaping Layouts
Realistic Floor Plans

Hi.   Thinking of **selling** in the Twin Cities area?

Wondering **how much** your home may be worth?

Questioning how long it **would take** to sell?

Is this the **right time** to put your house on the market?

Barbara understands the Twin Cities real estate market. She has been helping people meet their housing needs for 30 years! Let her answer your questions and others . . . *with absolutely no obligation whatsoever.*

Just fill out the short form below and then CLICK on the SEND NOW button.

☑ Yes, please send me a free, no-strings-attached market evaluation today. I have provided information on myself below. Send the information to:

Name

Address

City

State/ZIP

Phone number

Fax number

E-mail address

I prefer to communicate by: phone ☐   e-mail ☐   fax ☐

I am describing my property for you so you can gather market data on similar properties and prepare a comparison for me when we connect.

Information on the home I am selling:

Address

City/State   Number of BRs   Number of baths

Type of property   Size of home   Year built

Condition of property: Excellent   Good   Fair   "Fixer upper"
    ☐   ☐   ☐   ☐

That's it! Now just CLICK the SEND NOW button. Thanks!! *Barbara*

Buyer's Registration Page

TO FIND YOUR PERFECT HOME,

please ...

1. Enter Guest Book   2. Submit Guest Book Entry

1. Guest book for **BARBARA NASH**

DATE: January 1, 2008 **ABC REAL ESTATE COMPANY**

GUEST: First [_____]

                    Last [_____]

CONTACT AT: E-mail [_____]

ENTER YOUR E-MAIL ADDRESS   Phone [____] [_____]   [____]
AND YOUR PHONE NUMBER   Area   Ext.

HOME/BUSINESS ADDRESS   Street [_____]   Unit [____]

                               City [_____]

                               State [_____]   ZIP [____]

2. NOW, LET'S FIND YOUR PERFECT HOME!

> CLICK
> submit GUEST BOOK ENTRY HERE

I get tons of business this way!

Website Linking

Once you have decided to start your own website, you will want to establish links with other companies or individuals who complement your own website. The most common linking is reciprocal linking, discussed next.

Reciprocal linking

Two individuals decide to put each others' website address on their own sites in order to cross-reference each others' business. Reciprocal linking is a standard practice on the Internet.

- Choose a link that has a lot of traffic.
- Make the address known: promote, advertise.
- List your website address on cards, letterhead, listing sign attachments, etc.
- Write a compelling lead line about yourself. Example: "Click here for free home design info" Example: "Visit the Nash Real Estate Hotline" Example: "Get latest housing and mortgage news."
- Perhaps include your own logo and symbol.
- Write an e-mail to website owners: "Hello, website partner." I very much like your website and have decided to add you as a favorite link. Please be so kind as to add me to your site in return.

Complementary websites

1. Mortgage lenders
2. Title companies
3. Real estate attorneys
4. Housing inspectors
5. Escrow companies
6. Moving companies
7. Interior designers
8. Furniture companies
9. Private schools/daycare
10. Doctors/dentists
11. Insurance companies
12. Social organizations
13. Local dry cleaners
14. Local grocers/health food stores
15. Local florists/landscaping companies

Conduct searches frequently on google.com or Yahoo.com. See what buyers/sellers are requesting in relocation.

Advertise the Best Website

- Check your web page(s) for spelling errors. People will want to see a professional job!
- Use a font that is easy to read. Type in lowercase.
- Remember, your audience asks these three questions:
  1. What do you have to offer?
  2. When is it available?
  3. What are the terms?
- Your pictures must be scanned before loading them onto your website. All text must be carefully, methodically typed in.
- If possible, hire a website designer to create your website. Try to listen to ideas and select carefully from background.
- Remember, your designer is not necessarily in the real estate business! Do not assume that certain words and phrases known only to agents will be understood by your designer or your audience. Make everything an easy read.
- When using your digital camera, be sure the date feature is turned off! You don't want dated photos.
- Send information to your designer via e-mail. Keep your copy short and to the point.
- Sending pictures to your designer is so easy! With the use of your digital camera and your scanner, it can be done immediately. Be sure the quality of your pictures is good.
- When working with a designer and sending information back and forth via e-mail, avoid abbreviations. Spell out the name of the files you are sending, for example: pfpb7.doc (pictures for personal brochure 7).
- Be sure your e-mail address and full name, address, and phone number and blog are on each page of your website!

Real Estate Website Addresses

Adobe, Photo Deluxe Business Edition: www.adobe.com

Agent soft: Live agent professional: www.agentsoft.com

Bookmarks: Traveling bookmarks: www.briefcase.com

Broad vision: One-to-one relationship: www.broadvision.com

Commercial invest: Hook up with agents: www.recyber.com/consumerinvestor

Commercial real estate: Business/brokers: www.comps.com

Company profiles: Leads on companies: http://www.harrisinfoonline.com

Computers to purchase: http://www.onsale.com

Computer updates: Examines your computer and suggests software: http://oilchange.mcafee.com/oilchange/

Consumer property: Loan finder: www.loopnet.com

Consumer Reports: Ratings/reports: http://www.consumerreports.org

Dell computer: Laptop computers: www.dell.com

Dragon systems: Speech recognition software: www.nuance.com

Earthlink: Internet service provider: www.earthlink.net

E-Bay: World's largest online trading: www.ebay.com

E-fax: Hooks up e-mail to fax: http://www.efax.com

E-letter: Handles bulk mailings: www.zairmail.com

E-mail: E-mail at your fingertips: http://www.mailstart.com

E-mail, Remove junk mail: http://eremover.bizhosting.com

E-mail Encyclopedia: All you want to know: www.emailaddresses.com

Entrust: Security digital tool certificates: www.entrust.com

E-stamp: Download postage: www.stamps.com

Express copy: Full-color creation overnight: www.expresscopy.com

FSBO Central: For sale by owner site: http://www.fsbocentral.com

Geocities: Creates free home pages: www.geocities.com

Home owners info: Listings available: www.homeowners.com

Homefair: Real estate information, meetings: www.homefair.com

Homegain: Sellers choose a real estate agent: www.homegain.com

Homestead: Creates free home pages: www.homestead.com

Hotoffice: Everything-in-one-place office: www.hotoffice.com

House price index: Housing appreciation: www.ofheo.gov

IBM: Voice recognition software: www.ibm.com

ICQ: Virtual office assistant: http://www.icq.com

Information: On everything: www.CIA.gov

Inmedia: Multimedia slideshows: www.inmediapresents.com

Intel: Create and share: www.intel.com

Intel: Desktop information: www.intel.com

Intel: Laptops and servers: www.dell.com

Internet public library: http://www.ipl.org

Internet voice messages: http://www.rockettalk.com

Iprint: Moving kit information: www.iprint.com

IRED: International real estate directory: http://www.ired.com

Kodak: All Kodak digital cameras: www.kodak.com

Mortgage needs: One-stop shop: http://www.Rate1st.com

Mortgage rates: http://www.priceline.com/newfinance

Office Information: www.mrofficespace.com

On sale at cost: Wholesale computers: www.onsale.com

Priceline: Name your mortgage rate: www.priceline.com/newfinance

Problem sales: Analyzing sales: http://www.SalesAutopsy.com

Public records: Billions of public records: www.knowx.com

Real estate: Anywhere, best information: http://burns.dcb.du.edu

Real estate: Around the world: http://www.realestateol.com

Real estate: Enhance your image: www.RealEstate.com

Real estate: Latest Internet technology: www.recyber.com/expo

Real estate: Sale and marketing on the Internet, help: www.recyber.com/
reintelligence/selling8.html

Real estate cyberspace: Seller hookup with agents: www.recyber.com

Real estate cybertips: Ideas, miscellaneous information: www.recyber.com

Real estate directory: Realtors to appraisers: http://aree.net

Real estate help: Investment tips: www.inetworks.com/revest

Real estate info: www.Realtor.com

Real estate news: Articles and real estate information: www.successeditor@ired.com/
news/industry/981229.htm

Research: News releases, Wall Street Journal: http://online.wsj.com

Research: Secretary's home page: www.sec.gov/edaux/searches.htm

Search engines:

- Alta Vista: http://www.altavista.com
- Excite: http://www.excite.com
- Google: www.Google.com
- HotBot: http://www.hotbot.com
- InfoSeek: http://go.com
- Lycos: http://www.lycos.com
- WebCrawler: http://www.webcrawler.com
- Yahoo: http://www.yahoo.com
- Goto: http://www.go2.com
- Snap: http://www.snap.com

Selling real estate: List your real estate: http://www.internet-real-estate.com Service providers:

- http://www.aol.com
- http://www.earthlink.com
- http://www.netscape.com

Spot remover: Keep real estate clothing clean: www.wackyuses.com

Statistics for real estate people: http://www.realestatestatistics.com

Switchboard on the web: Find anybody: www.switchboard.com

Voice messaging: Send your own voice: www.rockettalk.com

Website: Create your domain: www.tabnet.com

Add your own website addresses:

_____

_____

_____

_____

Benefits of Real Estate Websites

- Agents make online home searches and evaluations available to prospective clients immediately.
- Informational newsletters with continuously changing formats make a visitor want to keep in touch.
- Website links (information about related websites) are available through the click of a button. Examples include mortgage sources, moving sources, map and city information, restaurant and movie information.
- Real estate agents with websites today earn 70 percent more than those who do not have a website.
- Top-producing agents list a website and e-mail address on all literature they send out.
- Real estate agents today network with other agents around the country and e-mail to one another.
- Information on cities throughout the country is now available at the click of a button: a newspaper from any city can be viewed by a potential client immediately!
- Agents can access agent online discussion chat rooms all over the country to discuss real estate situations and network with each other.
- Virtual tours enable clients to view homes all over the country, in a matter of minutes!
- Promotion of yourself on your website is now possible all over the WORLD! *There are millions of webpayes in existence today.*

*Real estate agents now must **distinguish** themselves by consistently updating their computer skills and daily striving for professionalism!*

Computerized Real Estate

The real estate industry has been greatly affected by the Internet. Advanced technology is part of an agent's daily life.

There are so many intelligent agent programs available today that a person can go to his or her computer and find out just the right agent or just the right house, anywhere in the country, in a matter of minutes.

Buyers can go to the computer, search websites, and find homes that meet their requirements. This means that today's real estate agent must have a computer.

- A laptop computer and/or desktop computer is **essential.**
- A real estate agent needs a unique website—one that sets that agent apart from all the other competition.
- A real estate agent needs to be well versed in computer skills and must develop hands-on knowledge of important programs.
- Designing a creative and professional home page on your agent website is a key to potential growth and success with future real estate clients.
- Continually updating your site keeps you current with the competition of real estate agents around the country.
- Inserting newsworthy information on the real estate market makes people want to work with you, the professional!
- Search the Internet for relocation contacts.
- Search the Internet for real estate continuing education classes.
- Search the Internet for real estate mortgage information.
- Know how to operate scanners and digital cameras to make picture taking and the creation of personal brochures easier.
- Connect with an international online-broker for a referral.
- Connect via blogging and/or various other real estate agents.
- Stay current through your local MLS board and "tour" new/existing properties.
- E-mail clients the latest/newest properties for sale.
- E-mail/attachments (i.e. listings/purchase agreements).
- "Ichat" with clients worldwide.
- Send "iphoto's" instantly—also virtual tours.

Desktop Computers Handling

Your Real Estate

Once you get the right computer that works for you, the next part is getting your Internet connection. There are a variety of real estate sites on the Internet that can help you take care of all your real estate transactions, put together your real estate tours, manage your listings and of course online blogging. Following is a partial list of providers and what they do:

- RELAY transaction management
  RE FormsNet, www.rebt.com
  866-736-7328
  Allows real estate agents to continuously track documents and activities and contact information as the transaction gets closer to closing. Supports cross-brokerage access.

- TourFactory Unlimited

  www.tourfactory.com

  888-458-3943

  This is a virtual-tour creation that is a host and distribution solution. It provides online tools for uploading images and listing information into virtual tour templates that link to a subscriber website. Tours have 360° images, maps and a mortgage calculator, plus professional voice narration.

- Top Producer 7i

  www.topproducer.com

  888-821-3657

  This company captures contact data from web forms and/or email and then schedules correspondence and marketing campaigns. Also contains school reports, community updates, and a marketing campaign with customized letters for communication via e-mail.

- Agent ValuePak

  www.realtysoft.com

  This company boasts a host of web-based real estate productivity tools. Creates site with five e-mail accounts and their domain name registration. Document preparation and online advertising. A wonderful technology is the VOICE RECOGNITION SYSTEM. This system not only talks to you, but can understand voice commands that enable you to access your listing data, phone numbers and just about any other real estate information.

The following are some hardware and software companies that contribute to the real estate industry.

- Blackberry 8830 Smart Phone

  www.sprint.com

  888-253-1315

  This smart phone allows the agent to look up phone numbers, access real estate information, and make calls with voice-activated control calling. There is increased storage capacity and memory cards. Color screen with key pad.

- Windows Speech Recognition

  www.microsoft.com

  800-642-7676

  This is a Microsoft operating system for all types of personal computers. Voice recognition built into Vista gives voice activation commands and speech-to-text dictation for composing contracts for real estate agents.

- Maestro 4050 GPS Navigation System

  www.magellangps.com

  909-394-5000

  This is a portable GPS unit with voice recognition features. It is compatible with a Bluetooth-enabled phone. Comes pre-loaded with street-level maps for all 50 states and an AAA TourBook. Functions are controlled and directions are received via spoken commands.

- iListen 1.7

  www.macspeech.com

  Voice recognition for the Apple Macintosh. Provides voice-command operation of computer and speech-to-text dictation. Users can create custom commands. Several people can use the software installed on same computer. Optional module available.

Real Estate Blogging...

The real estate blog became very popular in 2006. What exactly is a REAL ESTATE BLOG? A real estate blog is similar to a website. The biggest difference is the fact that you can include a "chat room" where you can communicate daily with total strangers!

A Real estate blog is like a "real estate platform for every REALTOR®."

How is a real estate blog different from a website? Basically it revolves around YOU! Your opinion, your latest and greatest of places to go to for meals, vacations, restaurants and so on. A real estate blog seems to give you the latest and the greatest news on the inside dirt of just about anything—in real estate—and beyond!

Before all this blogging and personal website information, a client found it necessary to go only to the real estate agent for all of their needs. Not so anymore. Now the client can surf the Web and go just about anywhere on their computer and find anything they need. If you don't supply it, some real estate agent that is techno-savy will. The real estate information that is available through websites and specific real estate blogs is extremely consolidated, organized, and to the point.

Lets say you are wondering about the price of a house that has been sitting on the market. Well, just go to your neighborhood real estate blogger and she or he might very well have the latest scoop. There is actually a site now that rates real estate agents. It is called www.homethinking.com.

How does blogging affect real estate today?

So what does this do to the average consumer and real estate client today? It enables them to be far more savvy on pricing of homes and what to expect to pay for the next home they are buying or selling. Because of this, it is essential to consider having your own blog. Agents are considering whether they want to have a separate blog from their own website or merge them all together. There is a service provider out there that will manage all your real estate from your website to leads, contacts, reviews, drip campaigns, e-mails and of course, your blog. They are called "Incredible Agents" and they are located online. They claim to be able to set you up and be "live on line" in just a couple of days. One agent that tried blogging for the first time said in the last couple of years they did over $10 million in real estate business, 95 percent of which was attributed to blogging.

Real Estate blogging is the quickest and newest way to create new customers online. As a real estate professional, you now have an opportunity to write about your favorite niche marketing your latest solds and your newest listings. And don't forget your very own chat room!

What does it take to set up a blog?

If you have no experience in setting up a blog, the best places to consider are the following:

Blogger.com—a very easy platform to use.

Wordpress.com—this will help you all the way to an advanced level with lots of downloads to plug into.

Typepad.com—small monthly fee for the use of this; lots of outside plug-ins, but one step installation.

Be sure to find a good title for yourself and incorporate it with a catchy phrase. Examples might be: "Real Estate Shoppe," "Real Estate Gal," "Minnesota Real Estate Nice," "Barbara's Blooming Real Estate Corner." Take a paragraph and outline what you are all about. Where do you FARM in your day-to-day real estate business? It is important to target your blog in this direction! Make sure once you have set up your blog and added various organizations, you keep current every day. Also, don't forget that you need to be part of as many directories as possible. This is how your blog will get out there! Some directories that are important to check out are as follows:

MyBlogLog.com—basic blogging community center

ActiveRain.com—posts community information

GetBlogs.com

Zillow Local Real Estate Blogs

BlogExplosion.com

Real Estate Voices

Real Estate www.blogdirectory.com

Be sure to send e-mails to all your client lists so they can visit your blog. You may want to spend a minimum of one half hour every day to update your blog with current and useful real estate information and any/all new information about the areas that you are farming. For example: new listings, price changes on current listing, easements, road closings, new restaurants, new store openings . . . anything that is community, newsworthy information!

Don't forget about linking to other blogs and keeping the integrity of your blog real-estate friendly. You might want to set up an account with bloglines.com—which will give you a subscription to different blogs all over the Internet. You might want to consider giving away a free market analysis of a potential client's home! This is a great way to get inside the door of a potential customer and get them to e-mail and/or call you as well!

Whatever you do . . . make your blog exciting!! Create a blog that has character and lots of newsworthy, up-to-date, current information. Most people want to read something that they DON'T ALREADY KNOW. Keep current with real estate rates and the market ups and downs. Lastly, network, network, network . . . meet other real estate bloggers!

Chapter Summary

A real estate agent must take time out each day to develop computer skills and spend a minimum of ONE HOUR a day learning new computer programs. More and more transactions are being completed over the Internet. New PIM (Personal Information Management) programs allow you to contact up to hundreds of people a day. A good computer financial program will create a CMA, qualify a buyer, and show buyers the monthly cost breakdown. A good word-processing program will produce a letter/postcard quickly and produce a listing presentation book quickly. When buying a computer, always find out what the purchase price does not include. A laptop computer can save you endless hours by helping you to figure your net sheets instantly. E-mail allows you to get your message out instantly. Business over the Internet allows for virtual real estate tours of homes all over the world! When creating your website, be sure to make the front page of your website look like the cover of a magazine or the front of a dressy window—you must entice! Include e-mail/blog, and internal and external links to other website menu bars. Once you have established your own website, you will want to establish links with other companies/individuals who complement your website. If possible, hire a website designer to create your website. Real estate agents must distinguish themselves by consistently updating their computer skills and daily striving for professionalism!

CHAPTER 7

DAILY SCHEDULE

- Time Management

big deal by Lorayne n' Neil

Daily Schedule

> **Definition:** daily = every day
> schedule = a plan describing work to be done and specifying deadlines
>
> **My definition:** A daily schedule is imperative for successful time management in the real estate profession.

A **daily schedule** is essential to success in real estate.

There is no such thing as keeping it all in your head. You must be able to function at a moment's notice, rearrange your schedule, and change appointments depending on your calls. Sometimes the schedule will be totally changed if there is an offer to present or a listing to go on.

A daily planner and/or computer planner/BlackBerry is imperative.

A real estate salesperson must be able to function completely out of a daily planner with all of his or her current needs and inventory in one book. Whether I am in the car, at an appointment, or out of town, my daily planner goes with me. I formerly used the 5" × 7", which appeared to be adequate. I chose the larger size only when I became aware of time management and the importance of carrying certain items with me *at all times*. I advise using the *larger* one for real estate business. The larger version will hold one set of contract listings.

In setting up the daily planner, I prefer to keep the following items:

Inside front cover:

- extra personal brochures
- business cards
- amortization schedule

Inside back cover:

- two copies of purchase agreements and buyer information sheets
- two copies of blank listings and seller net sheets

Arrange your daily planner as follows:

1. Yearly appointment book tabbed with each month
2. Month-in-view calendar
3. Performance report, including business origination and cost of promotion
4. Buyer section

5. Seller section
6. FSBOs
7. Listings
8. Current and past five years' transaction sheets
9. Plastic business card holder
10. Address section

You are ready to begin planning your schedule. Let's assume that your daily schedule starts out with a *blank week*.

Start with Monday morning:

My Monday schedule

8:00–9:00 A.M.	Check the newspapers for FSBOs. **Circle the ads and call for appointments.** If you get an answering machine, don't worry. Leave your name and your company's name. Explain that you are interested in knowing how they are handling appointments with real estate agents and that you would like them to call you back. **Seventy-five percent will call you back!**
9:00–10:00 A.M.	**Call at least 10** of the expired and canceled listings. Try to get at least three or four appointments. Give your name and your company's name and ask how they are handling appointments with real estate agents. If they want to talk, listen. They usually have a long, sad story as to why their house hasn't sold and why the agent didn't sell it. Be compassionate and try not to sell yourself too strongly over the telephone. **Just get the appointment and go from there.**
10:00–11:00 A.M.	**Contact at least five companies** that are relatively new in the area. Sunday papers usually list these companies in the business section. Ask for the personnel office and see if they would be interested in working with you. Ask to stop by and drop off your personal brochure and/or additional information.
*11:00 A.M.–12:00 P.M.	**Call at least five friends, acquaintances, or relatives** and see if they know of anyone who may be interested in buying and/or selling. I usually choose a property that is reasonably priced and that I really like, and often I refer to this property first in calling friends. I might say, "There's a new listing that just came up in our area, and it has a super floor plan. Do you know anyone who might be interested in it?" **Remember that everyone loves to hear about a house.**
12:00 A.M.–1:00 P.M.	Go to lunch. **Try to have lunch with a potential client** or someone who could assist you in the real estate business. If I don't have a client, **I might bring my lunch back to the office** or order at a drive-thru; then while eating, I will preview areas and new homes on the market.
1:00–2:00 P.M.	**Set up appointments on good candidates to hold open the next Sunday.** Call and ask the agent if you can hold an open house on their property. Set up appointments at other homes in the same neighborhood.

My daily planner keeps me totally organized!

*Get some lunch! *(Continued)*

2:00–4:00 P.M.	Photocopy each property that you are looking at with the **lock-box combination in the upper corner** and any added information regarding locking doors or animals. **Drive by and go to appointments on at least six properties.** Take notes and keep track of these homes that you have seen in a special folder marked *Properties Viewed*. Rate the home as you would for yourself, and make notes in the margins of the paper on **each** home. When calling friends or relatives, it is a plus to be able to tell them about a property that you have seen yourself.
4:00–5:30 P.M.	**Go back to the office to return calls** and messages that have come in. If you made at least 25 calls today, you should have at least a few returned calls. Schedule appointments for the evening hours, and remember to bring your personal brochure and personal promotion book as selling tools when going to clients' homes.
*5:00–6:30 P.M.	**Take a break to go home,** have dinner, relax, unwind, and freshen up. Hopefully you have one appointment for tonight to preview a property for a buyer. Perhaps you have an appointment to talk to a FSBO. Remember that on the first appointment, just walk through and come back to present the CMA and list the home.
7:00–9:00 P.M.	**Appointment with FSBO to preview** home for a potential listing. This is the best time to catch owners at home, whether expireds, canceleds, or referrals. They usually are free in the evenings. This is the best time to sit down and talk real estate, or if you are not going on a listing appointment, try to arrange to have buyers meet you at the office. Prequalify them and have them look at the MLS properties that they may want to visit.
9:30–10:00 P.M.	**Highlight for tomorrow** what is important, what is first on the agenda, and what you don't want to forget. Record all information, keeping a separate legal pad just for **phone numbers.** I sometimes keep these legal pads for years.

*Get some dinner!

My Tuesday schedule

8:30–10:00 A.M.	**Office meeting** to share knowledge of new properties.
10:00–12:00 P.M.	**Tour all new properties** in at least two main areas that you are willing to work exclusively. Try to preview six to eight homes.
12:00–1:00 P.M.	**Take a break,** but keep track of time. Perhaps wash your car, shop, do errands, have a bit of lunch. Never spend too much time at lunch unless with a prospect or potential client. Take different people to lunch. *Going to lunch with fellow real estate people is great for networking!*

(Continued)

1:00–3:00 P.M.	**Can I show a buyer?** Do office work; contact FSBOs to make appointments for later in week. Try to schedule two open houses for this weekend. Send out letters to clients from Sunday's open houses. Send out other letters to potential clients. Try to send out at least five letters to future clients, and perhaps include computer printout material. Include the day on which you will call them back. *Make a note* to call on that day.
3:00–5:00 P.M.	Leave this two-hour interval for some kind of **business outside of the office.** Visit a FSBO. Show properties. Meet with any other appointments in this time slot. Take a short walk. If possible, get some exercise.
5:00–7:00 P.M.	Family time, dinner, your own time.

Divide a call into two-hour intervals. These schedules may vary. Yours may be completely different. What I am trying to show is how important balance is.

You must work hard.

Relax.

Work hard.

Relax.

Find social time with family and friends **each and every day.** I personally favor 7:00 to 9:00 P.M. with my children. Frequently I read to them, do school projects, help with homework, drive to piano or violin lessons, and enjoy quiet time that is just for my family. I try to see that this is done *at least three of the five school days*. It is very rewarding for me and helps me function at my best for my clients and overall business.

You cannot do all things, be everywhere, and expect your days to fall into place unless you have set up a *specific schedule* each and every day of the week. If 7:00 to 9:00 does not work, stick with 5:00 to 7:00 and do update work from 8:00 to 10:00.

My Wednesday schedule

8:30–10:30 A.M.	**Write ads for Sunday open houses.** Make sure you have selected open houses that you feel comfortable with. When writing your ad, try to have three headlines in two caps (see Chapter 3).
10:30–12:30 P.M.	**Make appointments with buyers to look at houses.** Preview six to eight properties in two favored areas. Show houses to a buyer who can look midweek. Make an appointment with a FSBO to bring back competitive market analysis.
12:30–1:20 P.M.	**Take a break!** Wash your car and have lunch.
2:00–4:00 P.M.	**Office work. Send out letters and other mailings to buyers.** Check computer for buyers. Make weekly updates. Check computer and send sheets for sellers' comparative listings. Make appointments for Thursday and Saturday.
5:00–7:00 P.M.	**Family or personal time.** Dinner time too!
7:00–9:00 P.M.	**Family time or call clients for appointments.** Contact buyer with computer information. Set up appointments for weekend showings and other sellers' appointments.

My Thursday schedule

8:30–9:30 A.M.	**Set up appointments** for showings. If not showing, preview four to six homes before noon.
10:30–12:30 P.M.	**Show properties. Preview properties.** Keep a list of properties that you see in your daily log book along with prices so you always have a reference of reviewed homes. Rate the homes that you see on a scale of 1 to 10 so you can reference the best deals for the current market price.
12:30–1:30 P.M.	Take a break! Always take a lunch break somewhere different, and wear a name tag showing that you are a real estate agent. I have met clients grocery shopping.
2:00–3:30 P.M.	On Thursdays, **I preview estate sales and moving sales that are in the paper.** These are usually good for a lead or two!
4:00–5:00 P.M.	**Contact a client for an appointment** tonight or Saturday to show homes and a potential listing. Call some expireds. Fill up the remainder of your daily log book.
5:00–7:00 P.M.	Dinner and quiet time alone or with family.
7:00–9:00 P.M.	**Return calls from today** to clients for showing. Contact some FSBOs. Meet with a potential seller to list his or her home. Meet with a buyer at the office. Listen to a positive CD about having a good attitude. An excellent CD is *Insight*, which can be ordered through Nightingale-Conant at 800-323-5552.

My weekend schedule

FRIDAY	**I try to take Fridays for myself**, especially because on Saturdays I show and Sundays are busy with *open houses*.
SATURDAY	**I divide the day in half**. I either show properties in the early part of the day, perhaps 10:00 A.M. to 2:00 P.M. or go after a listing in this time slot. I may also give myself the early part of the day and meet with a buyer in the afternoon (perhaps 1:00 P.M. to 5:00 P.M.). Or hold a open house.
SUNDAY	Mornings are for church and brunch with family.
12:00–2:00 P.M.	First open house.
2:30–4:30 P.M.	Second open house.

Sometimes on Sunday evenings I call on FSBOs from the paper. Also, if I cannot have two open houses on a Sunday, I preview FSBO homes, visit with the owners, and make sure that I leave with another appointment.

This is just a rough draft of my overall schedule, but basically it remains the same. *I continuously contact clients* and constantly preview homes.

That is our business. If we don't do it, another agent will.

It is our business to know our inventory and network too!

> **IT IS ESSENTIAL THAT WE CONTINUOUSLY ADD NEW PROPERTIES TO OUR INVENTORY.**

Daily Schedule Fill-ins

If you are at odds about what to do and when to do it, worry no more. After reading this chapter, you will have a firm understanding of what is expected of you in the real estate business.

You cannot avoid keeping records if you are to be successful. You must learn that the more records and charts you keep, the more you will see where you are going.

I've got two opens saturday and sunday and I'm showing houses all week...

It's the weekend soon...I'll think of something to do...

IF YOU DON'T KNOW WHERE YOU ARE GOING, YOU WILL END UP SOMEPLACE ELSE. DISIPLINE YOUR DAY!

Keep track of what you do daily with a chart.

Weekly Chart

	Mon.	Tues.	Wed.	Thur.	Fri.	Sat.	Sun.
Call FSBO							
Call expireds							
Call canceleds							
Send thank-you letters							
New listings							
Open houses held							
Open house contacts							
Showed houses							
Relocation referrals received/sent							
Phone canvassing (hours?)							
Door knocking in neighborhoods (hours?)							
Listen to positive motivational CDs							
Real estate education seminars							
Listings sold							
Price reductions							

Monday 1/25

7:45 A.M.	See children off to school/start crock pot
8:15 A.M.	Go to office
8:30 A.M.	Review day and start calling clients
8:45 A.M.	Call D. Vesttie, confirm appointment to walk through home at 4609 Beritage
9:00 A.M.	Call two FSBOs: J. Schmidt, 609 Edin Blvd. and T. Kent, 671 Samuel Rd.
9:30 A.M.	Send two letters to above FSBOs
10:00 A.M.	Walk-through on D. Vesttie, 4609 Beritage
10:30 A.M.	Appointments on three houses for D. Bronstrom: 9800 Richy, 9904 Toledo, 9807 Little (meet client at first house)
11:30 A.M.	Appointment on FSBO: 609 Edin Blvd.
12:15 P.M.	Stop for drive-thru lunch; take back to office
12:30 P.M.	Start CMA on FSBO on 609 Edin Blvd.
1:30 P.M.	Call buyers: G. Kent (130 + Edin only)
2:00 P.M.	Research houses to show G. Kent in Edin
3:30 P.M.	Finish appointments for G. Kent; make two copies; send letter to new buyer coming into town (referral friend); double-check computer and newspaper for new houses to show buyer tomorrow
4:15 P.M.	Walk-through on FSBO on 671 Samuel Road—T. Kent; bring book and personal brochure to show some houses in two areas of interest
5:30 P.M.	Office: check phone messages; call D. Marsh, 504 Arden (expired list) and G. Owens, 660 Gleason (expired list)
6:15 P.M.	Leave office; drive by two properties for Kent: 4400 Maple and 4600 Brown (new listing)
6:30 P.M.	Home for dinner
7:45 P.M.	Appointment with D. Sandstrom (church referral) to appraise their home at 6208 Highwood
9:00 P.M.	Home with family; review appointments for tomorrow

MAKE THE MOST OF EACH DAY
BY BACKTRACKING AS LITTLE AS POSSIBLE.

PLAN YOUR DAY. The time you spend driving by houses to preview is also the time to stop at the store, to drop off dry cleaning, or to stop by the post office.

When previewing homes, don't forget the estate sales and the garage sales! These people are often cleaning out because they are getting ready to move! Usually the best days for these sales are Thursday and Friday.

EACH DAY   *check the local and suburban newspapers.* Check also for job promotions and new companies.

CHECK   the area that you farm. Your farm area should be your special area of influence. Example: Send mortgage information, new properties for sale.

PLAN   your meals in advance. Try to plan for the evening meal. If you are eating out and entertaining clients, make sure all reservations are made early in the morning. Keep *your telephone daily legal pad with you at all times!* This enables you to remember which calls need to be returned and which calls haven't been returned. Also, by *keeping the sheets from each day* to the next (just turn one over the other and fasten with a paper clip), it is *easy to reference and double-check* for past numbers that have been misplaced or numbers that you have forgotten to record in your daily planner book.

What I Do Daily

8:30 A.M.   *Clip all the FSBO ads from Sunday* and start calling for appointments (see Chapter 8). *Contact at least four* good FSBOs.

9:30 A.M.   *Make at least two appointments* for this week.

11:30 A.M.   *Go to lunch only* if I have some appointments made!

1:00 P.M.   *Contact a buyer.*

2:00 P.M.   *Send five* letters to potential clients.

3:30 P.M.   *Contact another buyer* to show houses this weekend.
 Buyers may have come from opens from last weekend.
Or...
Check the computer printout of the area in which I live.
Check the computer printout of the farm area I work.
Check the computer printout of homes I want to see.
Or...
Preview homes for my buyer and/or my own portfolio. Do not look at more than seven or eight homes.
Or check my email/blog/faxes coming in.
Contact a FSBO. Contact an expired owner. Contact a potential buyer. Call clients who came through open houses.
Or...
Work on CMA (competitive market analysis) for future listing.

4:00 P.M.   *Send five letters* to potential clients.

5:00 P.M.   *Call a friend and ask for a referral.*

What I Do Daily

CHECK MY E-MAIL...
GO TO DRY CLEANER...
SORT MY MAIL...
CALL NEW CLIENTS...
MAIL OUT "FARMING"
STOP AND SEE FSBO...
AD FOR OPEN...
CALL FRIENDS FOR WEEKEND
    DINNER (ASK IF ANYONE'S
    MOVING)
UPDATE DAY TIMER...
EXERCISE AT HOME
MAKE HEALTHY DINNER...
RETURN MY CALLS...
WASH MY CAR...

What I Do Daily

...GO TO THE OFFICE...
SEE WHATS GOING ON...
GO TO LUNCH WITH ONE OF
    THE GUYS...
SEE IF ANYONE WILL LEND
    ME A FEW BUCKS...
PICK UP A SIX PACK AND
    A PACK OF CIGARETTES...
WATCH THE FOOTBALL
    GAME...
SEE IF BOB WILL GOLF
    SATURDAY...

Things to Do When the Phone Doesn't Ring

1. *Plan* another open house.
2. *Call someone* you know to say business is appreciated.
3. *Write* a schedule for tomorrow's activities.
4. *Call to qualify a new buyer.*
5. *Check the newspaper* ads for estate sales.
6. *Drive around* areas that are foreign to you or that you want to know better.
7. *Write a new ad.*
8. *Try to get a price adjustment* on an unsold listing.
9. *Read a good book* that is positive.
10. *Review your last appointment* with a buyer or seller to determine what went right or wrong.
11. *Contact a company* for relocation.
12. *Call a new buyer to suggest homes* as a tax shelter.
13. *Visit the city hall* planning commission to find out what's new in the area.
14. *Call a FSBO.*
15. *Call the owners of pour current listings* and give an update on the activity on the property.
16. *Call fellow agents* who have shown your listings to get feedback.
17. *Try a new idea* that you've been putting off until you had time.
18. *Review your sales volume* in the past months and replan.
19. *Send out notes or postcards* to FSBOs and expireds.
20. *Clean out your desk* drawers and files. *Throw away anything that isn't absolutely necessary to keep.*

I like to send my personal brochures to FSBOs with a short note!

Agent Activity Monthly Chart

I don't mind an open house once in a while

- *See* where the majority of your business is coming from.
- What do you like to *do the most* and the least?
- Where do you *need strength?*
- Disipline each day!

Real Estate Agent Activity Monthly Chart

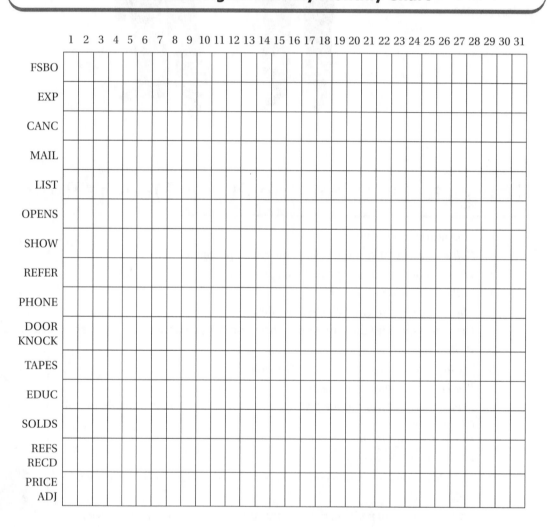

	1	2	3	4	5	6	7	8	9	10	11	12	13	14	15	16	17	18	19	20	21	22	23	24	25	26	27	28	29	30	31
FSBO																															
EXP																															
CANC																															
MAIL																															
LIST																															
OPENS																															
SHOW																															
REFER																															
PHONE																															
DOOR KNOCK																															
TAPES																															
EDUC																															
SOLDS																															
REFS RECD																															
PRICE ADJ																															

FSBOS	SEND REFERRAL
EXPIREDS	CANVASS BY PHONE
CANCELEDS	KNOCK ON DOORS
MAIL THANK-YOUS	LISTEN TO TAPES/VIDEOS
NEW LISTINGS	EDUCATION/SEMINAR
OPENS	SOLD HOMES
CONTACT BUYER FROM OPENS	RECEIVE REFERRAL
AND SHOWINGS	REDUCE PRICE

Ten Business Sources

	Mon.	Tues.	Wed.	Thur.	Fri.	Sat.	Sun.
Personal reference							
Business reference							
Neighbor							
Family							
FSBO/Expired							
Ad call							
Church							
Political							
Social							
Volunteer							

Weekly Tracking

	7 A.M.	8 A.M.	10 A.M.	12 P.M.	1 P.M.	2 P.M.	3 P.M.	4 P.M.	6 P.M.
Monday									
Tuesday									
Wednesday									
Thursday									
Friday									
Saturday									
Sunday									
Misc.									

Homes Viewed Pad

*Client	Client Rated	Address	Lockbox Comments	Date

*NO CLIENT NAME IF VIEWING ALONE.

1. When looking at homes with your client, have two sets of info sheets.
2. Ask your client to rate each property from 1 to 10 (1 = worst, 10 = best).
3. After viewing each home, add additional likes and dislikes about the property.
4. At the end of the day, ask your client, "If you had to pick the best…"
5. Place the client "homes view pad" sheet on top of the pile of homes you looked at. This will be a ready reference and will help you narrow down and determine which home is best and what styles to eliminate!
6. Eliminate and identify "best one(s)"

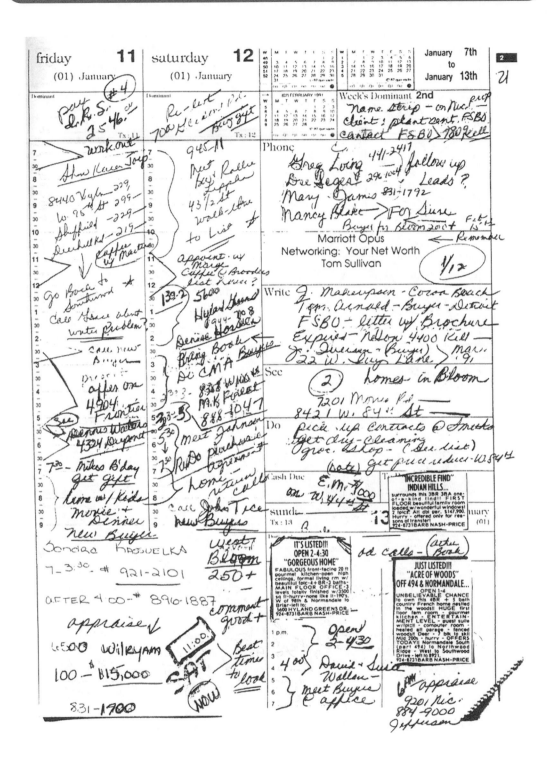

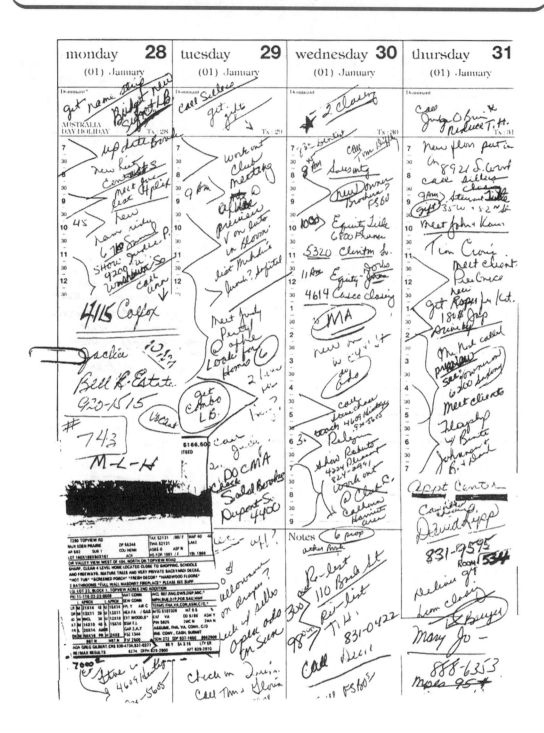

Sample Week's Schedule

Time	MONDAY	TUESDAY	WEDNESDAY
8:00	CALL OWNERS	NETWORK W/AGENTS	CALL CLIENTS
9:00	CALL EXPIRED	TOUR NEW PROP.	COMPUTER TIME
10:00	SET UP OPEN'S	TOUR HOMES	MAILING (EXPIRED)
11:00	PREVIEW HOMES	COMPUTER REFERRALS	WALK THRU
12:00	LUNCH	LUNCH	LUNCH
1:00	CALL BUYERS ↓	CALL ON FSBO	WRITE ADS
2:00	↓	MAIL ↑	SHOW ↑ (PREVIEW)
3:00	MAILINGS ↓	FARM MAILINGS	
4:00	↓	SHOW ↑	HOUSES ↓
5:00	CALLING	HOUSES ↓	WALK RE-GROUP
6:00	DINNER	DINNER	DINNER
7:00	CALL ON	CALL ON	GO ON LISTING
8:00	FSBO	EXPIRED	PRESENTATION

Time	THURSDAY	FRIDAY	SATURDAY	SUNDAY
8:00	CALL CLIENTS	CALL CLIENTS		
9:00	COMPUTER TIME	CHECK COMPUTER		
10:00	MAILING	PREVIEW	OFFICE CALLS	CHURCH
11:00	CALL REFERRAL	HOMES CALLS	+ COMPUTER	↓
12:00	LUNCH	LUNCH	LUNCH	CHECK ADS / LUNCH
1:00	CMA FSBO →	PREVIEW HOMES	SHOW	OPEN
2:00	↓	CMA FOR ←	← HOLD OPENS →	← (SHOW HOUSES) →
3:00	SEND RELO'S	FSBO ↓	↓	
4:00	CALL ON ←	MAILINGS ↓	HOUSES	HOUSE
5:00	FSBO ↓	↓	CALL CLIENTS	STOP BY FSBO'S
6:00	DINNER	DINNER	DINNER	DINNER
7:00	MEET BUYER ↑	EXERCISE		FOLLOW-UP CALLS
8:00	BUYERS ↓			CALLS

Chapter Summary

A daily schedule is essential to success in real estate. Call at least 10 of the expired and canceled listings—at least 75 percent of them will call you back! Call at least five friends or relatives and ask for a referral. Remember: Everyone loves to hear about a house! Always highlight for tomorrow what is first on the agenda. Tour all the homes that are for sale in two of the areas that you are willing to work exclusively. Try to preview at least six to eight homes. Divide your day into two-hour intervals. It is essential that we continuously add new properties to our inventory. You must learn that the more records and charts that you keep, the more you will see where you are going. Send five letters to potential clients. When the phone doesn't ring, plan another open house, call a FSBO, write an ad, or contact a company for relocation. Make a *Homes Viewed Pad* for your buyer and have them rate, on a scale of 1 to 10, homes they have seen from. Be sure to give your client copies of all homes looked at and keep separate copies for yourself. Keep large legal pads with pens by all your telephones for all incoming calls.

CHAPTER 8

FSBO

- For Sale by Owner

big deal by Lorayne n' Neil

FSBO—For Sale by Owner

What? call the FSBO?

I started in the real estate business almost 30 years ago. I had no particular contacts and no real source of referrals. *There was really only one* way to bring myself business in a manner that would be profitable for me in a short amount of time:

Call people who want to sell **NOW!**

FSBOs (FSBOs) very much want to sell **right now.**

Contrary to what you may think, FSBOs do list.

Consider these statistics:

> 95 percent of FSBOs list their home.
> Almost 90 percent of FSBOs are interviewing agents to list their home.
> Almost 80 percent of FSBOs like to have agents call them.

Nine out of ten FSBOs have business to refer to you later. Every Sunday, FSBOs wait to be called by agents. FSBOs usually have more than enough information already prepared for you before you come to the home. Working on FSBOs can increase your business 75 to 100 percent!

Now note this statistic: I have consistently increased my business over 50 percent by calling on FSBOs.

Why not make one phone call to them? *You can't lose anything by trying.*

Almost all FSBOs really are *nice guys.* Just make one call and change your income for the better.

Ten Best Ways to Get an Appointment with FSBOs

Call them on the phone and say:

> *"Hi, I'm _____, and I'm from _____ Realty. I'm calling to see how you are handling appointments with agents in regard to looking at your property."*

If they say "No thank you, I'm not interested," you may want to select one of the following foot-in-the-door statements:

Ten best ways to get an appointment

1. *I prefer to concentrate in your area* and like to keep up on *any* property that comes up for sale.
2. *Every day I work with different buyers* and try to keep up on new inventory whether listed through Multiple Listing Services or *FSBOs*. They are all *important* to me.
3. *I try to actively pursue relocation clients*—clients transferring in from out of town—and they don't always know about *your specific* neighborhood.
4. *I'd like to compare your home to others* that our company has sold in your neighborhood and, of course, give you my professional, qualified opinion.
5. *I pride myself on being successful* with other clients *in your* lovely *area*.
6. *I would like to stop over tomorrow* and see your home because I will be in the area looking at another piece of property. I can stop by between the hours of 1:00 and 3:00. When would you prefer?
7. *I feel my enthusiasm and experience* helps me sell more homes, especially in your area, which is where I prefer to work.
8. I feel that my *unique method of marketing* will most definitely appeal to you. I can show you this method either at 1:00 or 3:00. Which would you prefer?
9. *I will be previewing homes* for clients in your area between 5:00 and 7:00 tomorrow. I can stop by between these hours. When would you prefer?
10. *I am enthusiastic about another home* I have seen in your area, and it would be ideal to compare properties. I will be over near your home tomorrow or Wednesday after 3:00. What timeframe would work out best for you?

These methods work.

BE ENTHUSIASTIC AND GENTLE.

PICK ANY ONE OF THEM.

I HAVE USED THEM ALL.

THEY WILL NOT FAIL!

Calling the FSBOs

1. *Get the Sunday paper* and circle the owner ads.
2. On Sunday afternoon or night, call the FSBO's number.
3. When the owner answers, say the following:

> *"Hi, I'm _____ from _____ Realty. I saw your ad in the paper, and I was interested in knowing how you are handling appointments with real estate agents."*

4. The owner will do one of the following three things:
    a. *Ask you* why you want the appointment. See "Ten Best Ways to Get an Appointment."
    b. *Set up an appointment for* you to see the house.
    c. *Act genuinely not interested* in you and attempt to hang up. (These owners are a minority and not worth pursuing. *Don't worry.*)

Getting the Appointment

After you have said:	"Hi, I'm _____ from _____ Realty and I was calling to see how you are handling appointments on your property."
The owner may say:	"What do you mean?"
At which point you:	Tell them you are available for an appointment. (Never ask them, "May I come over?")
Tell them:	You would like an appointment between (certain hours) and you will be in their area.
Always offer choices:	*"Which time frame is best suited for you?"*

DON'T BE AFRAID OF REJECTION

Owners don't bite!

THEY USUALLY SAY YES!!

Be enthusiastic but gentle.

Be curious but kind.

Be professional and polite.

And, most of all, be interested in knowing what their situation really is. Find out!

TALK to the *FSBO.*

LISTEN to the *FSBO.*

After calling four FSBOs...I really have an appointment! It does work.

Become a *friend* to the FSBO.

Be curious but *kind*.

> One FSBO who listed with me had already
> interviewed over 45 other real estate agents!

Following is a recap of why an owner decided to list with me:

1. "She wasn't overly complex and her CMA was *clear* and to the *point*."
2. He was impressed with the fact that I *did* my homework.
3. He said two of the other agents who came in promised to get back with him. *They didn't*.
4. The owner had no intention of listing the night I presented the CMA, *but he listed that evening because*, first, the presentation was *thorough* and complete, and, second, *I had sold him on me*!

HE FELT THAT I WAS VERY PROFESSIONAL.

He said that one of the agents from a well-known company came with nothing! She had no figures about the house, no history on when it had been sold, nothing. She just walked in as if off the street. He said he had an appointment set up with her. He thought they had a good rapport with her, and she had worked with him many times, showing him properties for rehab possibilities. However, she walked in totally cold! She said, "I would really like to list this house for you!" She expected the listing without doing any work. She did not *appear professional*.

SHE HAD NOT DONE HER HOMEWORK!

The owner was asked if I seemed pushy or if I made him feel uncomfortable in trying to get him to list immediately with me after I presented the CMA. He replied, "*Her genuine enthusiasm* and the fact *she had done all her homework* on our house made us feel comfortable. The fact that she had everything right there made us decide simply to sign and *get it over with*."

Remember that when you bring your CMA back to the seller for the second appointment, always bring your full-size legal book with:

I just keep talking if
the seller says no...
I remind them how great
the open house could be...
I serve food...

1. Listing agreement
2. Seller's statement of condition
3. Lockbox
4. Net sheet
   Be honest.
   Be enthusiastic.
   Be careful with figures.

ASK THE SELLER IF YOU CAN SHOW HIM OR HER HOW THE LOCKBOX WORKS.

After all is explained say, "It's important that we get started right away to give you the maximum exposure time on the market. If you would sign right here, I'll explain the tour (other agents who will be coming through next week) to you."

Don't forget:
- Try to find a *common interest*.
- Try to *get to know* the seller a little.
- Try to employ your *sense of humor*.
- Try *not to be dull*.

I ask the owners to write down why they like their home. I take those comments back to my office, *rewrite* them on my letterhead, and bring them back to the seller. He insists on having an open house on his own home first, so then *I make my second appointment to come back.*

Calling on For Sale by Owners

Pick up the telephone. "Hello, I'm _____ from _____ real estate. I was wondering how you are handling appointments with real estate people?"

Ask the owners for an appointment to come over and look at their home.

Almost every owner wants the agent to come over and tell them what price they think the home should sell for!

The majority of FSBOs do list their homes and sell with a real estate company.

To get a listing with a FSBO, you must do the following:

1. Make the phone call,
2. Get the appointment, and
3. Do a CMA (competitive market analysis)

   Never talk to a seller in a *negative* tone.

   Never ask a question that they can answer *no* to.

   If a seller says that she is going to try for one more week to sell her home on her own, say,

   "Why don't I stop by next Monday, after 5:00 or maybe 7:30 would be better, because I am listing a home earlier. How would later in the evening be?"

Okay, okay . . . I can make some phone calls! I guess it's not that hard when you think of it as "my next listing."

If a seller says that he wants a couple of weeks to try it on his own, say:

"I understand. After my two open houses next week, and when I finish working with my buyer who is coming into town, why don't we set up an appointment for, say, 15 days from now? That would make it September 20. I'll call you right before that."

Never leave the house of a FSBO *without another appointment* or something settled regarding a signed listing.

There are a few people who are ornery! If so, you will find it out the first time you meet with them! Don't be upset. Those people would go out and beat up a brick wall. Leave them alone.

GO ON TO THE NEXT CLIENT!

Remember that on a $100,000 home there could be a 7 percent commission ($7,000). Do not think that you can just walk into a house and list it *without* doing your homework and without any questions. You have not convinced the seller that *you are worth it!*

DID YOU TAKE A LOT OF NOTES?

DID YOU ASK A LOT OF QUESTIONS?

Did you prove to them *beyond the shadow of a doubt* that you are worth it?

Did you show them *beyond a shadow of a doubt* that you did your homework on their house?

If you study this manual completely, you can dedicate less than two hours per client and have a complete knowledge of the property and a 100 percent better chance of winning the listing.

For Sale By Owners usually list with a Realtor!

FSBO Costs

Other expenses in selling your own home

Will someone always be able to answer the phone?

Will you know about the latest financing methods?

Will the prospects confide in you about their financial status?

Can you get buyers to sign the purchase agreement? (Remember, once they sleep on it, they seldom sleep in it.)

Who will draft the purchase agreement?

Will you really save money selling your own home?

DESPERATE OWNER NEEDS TO SELL

THIS TYPE OF ADVERTISING STEERS WOULD-BE BUYERS AWAY FROM OWNERS LIKE YOURSELF!

FSBOS HAVE PROBLEMS PRICING!

Dangers of overpricing:

Takes longer to sell
Has fewer showings
Receives low, low offers
Helps other properties sell by comparison

Three of my listings this month were FSBOs...they really want help!

Remind the FSBO

A home must have a good location,
Good terms, good price, and good condition.

> ### Remind the owner where buyers come from:
>
> 40   percent from real estate company or real estate contact
> 20   percent from the for sale sign (real estate company)
> 18   percent from a real estate company ad call
> 8   percent from an open house ad or sign
> 7   percent from a relocation service
> 3   percent from an advertised property
> 1   percent buy an open house they saw
> 3   percent buy for a combination of reasons

Other FSBOs weaken the seller's position

Other owners advertise:

"Bail us out"
"Foreclosure"
"Owner says, must sell"
"Divorce; must sell"
"Desperate owner needs to sell"

The more prepared I was...the more the FSBO respected me. He signed the listing on the first visit!

This type of advertising steers would-be buyers away from owners like yourself!

Ask the owner:

Are you familiar with contracts?
Recording the deed?
Notarizing documents?
Filling out forms?
Closing costs?
Lien waivers?
Title searches?
Tax certificates?
Warranty deeds?
Earnest money deposits?

Tell the FSBO:

Getting you a buyer is just a third of what my job entails. (See Chapter 10.)

Besides marketing your home,

listing your home,

advertising your home, and

promoting your home.

I also:

Show your home,

arrange the financing on your home,

get an appraiser for your home,

call for the inspection of your home,

get a Truth-in-Housing Inspection on your home (if required),

follow up on all the mortgage arrangements on your home,

take part in the closing of your home,

and, finally, help you with any last-minute arrangements on your sale!

Example FSBO dialog

Door knocking:	"Hi. I saw your sign (ad). May I ask how you are handling appointments with real estate people?"
By phone:	"Good (day/afternoon/evening). This is _____ from _____ Realty. I saw your ad (sign). May I ask how you are handling appointments with real estate people?"
If FSBO says:	"What do you mean?"
	or
	"We are not."
You say:	"May I ask one quick question? If we had a qualified buyer willing to pay a price acceptable to you, would you accept an offer through our company?"
If FSBO says:	"No."
You say:	"May I ask why?" (or repeat the question)
If FSBO says:	"Yes" to the first or second question.
You say:	"Fine. It will take just a few minutes to see enough of your home so I can tell potential buyers about it. May I do that now?" or "Will 6:30 tonight be okay, or would 8:00 be better?"

6-2-6 System

This system is specifically for *"FSBOS."*

1. Make the initial call to the FSBO.
2. Write down the name, address, and phone number.
3. *Call them at least two times a week!*
4. Do this for six weeks.
5. You should get the FSBO *in one month.*
6. If not converted, replace with another FSBO.

The average agent calls the first week, and the FSBO lists in the fourth week! Average FSBOs say no four times before saying yes.

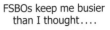

FSBOs keep me busier than I thought....

> REMEMBER:
>
> 1. WORK WITH SIX OWNERS AT A TIME.
> 2. CALL THEM TWO TIMES A WEEK.
> 3. DO THIS FOR SIX WEEKS.

IF YOU KEEP REPLACING FSBOs, YOU WILL ADD SIX TO EIGHT NEW LISTINGS TO YOUR INVENTORY MONTHLY!

Four things to say to the FSBO:

1. "I can certainly understand that."
2. "I would love to see your house!"
3. "May I come over today?"
4. "I'm in your area . . . when's a good time?"

In our city there are thousands of real estate agents, and if 14 other agents called a FSBO today, *my job is to eliminate the 14 so the sellers pick me!* I work with only six *FSBOs at a time. I call them twice a week for six weeks. After that I take them out of my file!*

FSBO Six-Week Follow-Up

1. It is now your job to stay in touch with the FSBO for *at least six weeks*—until they list, sell, or give up.
2. Stop by and drop off some information on today's market, such as rates, point sheet, a pertinent article out of one of our trade magazines.
3. Call and ask how their open house went on Sunday.
4. By selecting only two or three FSBOs to keep in touch with *each week*, you maintain a consistent influx of potential new listings—two one week, four the next, then six, and so on.

Establish a legal-size notebook

1. Set up your index by district.
2. File your cards by phone number. Most FSBO ads have phone numbers; not all have addresses.
3. Place the phone number in the upper right-hand corner with name and address directly below.
4. Down the left-hand side, tape their ads to the card and *date the ads*.
5. In the space to the right of the ads, record your conversations.

When the time is right

1. In your conversations with the FSBO, mention things that *get listings sold* for you:
   a. Many agents in a large office try to sell the same listing
   b. *Homes* magazine will advertise for you
   c. MLS (Multiple Listing Service)
   d. Referrals from past clients
   e. Corporate referrals
   f. Any others you can think of, including your market plan (but do not show the plan until you get a commitment)
2. An excellent conversation closer is, "If you felt that you could actually get more money, a quicker sale, and fewer problems by doing business with our company, would you do so? If the FSBO says no," say, "May I ask why?" To the FSBO's typical response, "Because I want to try it myself for awhile," say, "Fine, I'll check with you after my open house this next Sunday. I'll stop by to walk through, OK?"
3. That will be *appointment number one!*

Three keys to listing FSBOs

1. Be persistent.
2. Build trust.
3. Be professional. Show them you can get the job done.

The third time I called my FSBO back, I got an appointment and listed their house!

Why selling by FSBOs is difficult

1. Most buyers are just *window shopping.*
2. People will *stop at all hours* of the day and night.
3. A seller *cannot qualify* the buyers comfortably.
4. A seller is letting complete *strangers into his or her home.*
5. It is *difficult for the seller to negotiate* with the buyer.
6. The *seller misses opportunities* to sell when away from home.
7. Buyers will also want to *save commission,* even from an owner.
8. Sellers have only *three ways to attract buyers:* ads, opens, and a for sale sign.
9. Sellers *have to give potential buyers the address:* they can *drive by* and not look inside the house!
10. Buyers do not like to *deal directly with the owner!* Many sellers price their home according to the price of a home down the street that hasn't yet sold.
11. Some agents will *promise anything* to get the listing.
12. There are *60 different financing methods* that usually require a real estate agent's help, including FHAs, VAs, discounted notes, amortizations, ARMs, wrap mortgages, points, interest rates, balloons, graduated payment mortgages, and so on.
13. *A seller's lack of familiarity with all real estate contracts* may scare a buyer.
14. *Does* the *seller* know that the *four things that make a property sell are* location, price, terms, and condition?
15. Does the seller know the *grave danger of overpricing a listing?*

    a. **takes four times as long to sell**

    b. **fewer showings**

    c. **receives lowball offers**

    d. **only helps other homes to sell**

I took the listing too high…now It's six months later…

> Sellers should know that other FSBOs weaken their position with ads such as "foreclosure," "divorce, must sell," "bail us out," "desperate to sell." *Tell them!*

Letter to a FSBO

It's very hard to sell your home by yourself because most people have their life savings tied up in their home, and buyers and sellers usually want to work with a professional who not only knows the financing aspect of selling the home but is willing to personally represent them.

Most of the buyers calling For Sale by Owners think they can save money because they don't have to pay a commission. They think they can knock the commission off the sale price! It's impossible for the buyer and the seller to save the same commission at the same time. Somebody has to give. If you come down in the price, you lose. Remember, there will be buyers who will give you ridiculous offers. Don't get angry.

Nationally, it's been shown that the seller will make far more money after the commission is subtracted than if they try to sell the home on their own. There is no standard commission set in the industry, but you really get what you pay for.

What do we do for our commission that you can't do? Most importantly, we have more buyers coming to us! We also act as the third party. This is very important when you begin to negotiate. People will be more candid with a real estate agent than they will with the owner. You may become offended from the beginning by something the buyer says.

We will use all professional tools and utilize the Multiple Listing Service system, which helps establish the highest market value possible for you.

Probably a real estate agent's most important function is that we can qualify the buyers. This will be very uncomfortable for you to do! Can you ask them about their income, whether they have declared bankruptcy, and their level of indebtedness without feeling uneasy?

The only reason that properties fail to sell is either overpricing or poor marketing. After looking at a good Competitive Market Analysis, you would know exactly what range your homefalls into. I would provide a CMA for you at no extra charge.

I want to caution you, however, that many agents will tell you what they think you want to hear just to get your listing. I won't do that. I am a professional with many years' experience and referrals. Please call me for additional information.

And, good luck!

Twenty Questions to Ask the FSBO

1. Do I have the time to sell my house by myself?
2. Do I know where my buyers come from?
3. Do I know how to make my home show the best?
4. If I list with a real estate company, will I be bothered by people all the time?
5. Do I know the questions I should ask buyers?
6. Do I know the information to give buyers?
7. Do I know what to say when I show my home?
8. Do I know how to qualify my buyers?
9. Do I know the latest financing methods?

10. Do I have ways of attracting buyers other than an ad and a for sale sign?
11. Do I know what my closing costs and obligations are?
12. Do I know how to write a contract on the spot?
13. Do I know how to negotiate and compromise with a buyer?
14. Do I know what to do during the showings?
15. Do I have the time to invest in follow-up on a buyer?
16. Do I know what is involved in title examination?
17. Do I know different and unique marketing techniques?
18. Do I know how to "read" my buyer?
19. Do I know how to close?
20. Do I know if FSBOs list with agents? (Yes—88%)

If you answered no to most of the questions, you probably should be seeking competent real estate advice!

> 90 percent of expired listings re-list too!

> I WANT YOU TO KNOW THAT GIVING YOU THE SECRETS I'M GIVING YOU TODAY IS SIMILAR TO GIVING YOU THE RECIPE FOR COCA COLA!

I've been selling real estate for 30 years and I credit at least a third of my business to FSBOs.

In the beginning I did not have referral business, nor did I have any solid leads. I tried expired listings and found them somewhat successful. However, it was harder to convince sellers who were already soured in one way or another by other agents. So I decided most FSBOs wanted to move, and if I could list their home, it would mean three things:

1. *automatic buyers*
2. *a secured listing, and*
3. *if sold, money in my pocket!*

I also decided to go after a goal that I knew I could fulfill within a 6- to 12-month time period, such as a new stove, a trip to Florida, a new car. Every owner I listed would put me that much closer to my goal. Before I called each one, I would focus first on my goal, which always gave me the confidence to get through the phone call, whether positive or negative. I discovered something very interesting: *Most FSBOs really wanted to talk and talk and talk!* I'd call FSBOs when idle, while sitting in the sun or waiting at the club, before working out, from a friend's home, and in front of the TV! I found it really fun to take a moment and feel as though I had accomplished something. A day that seemed somewhat unproductive became *a day with an appointment made.*

In one of my first years in real estate, I earned $62,752. I attribute $25,104 of that to FSBOs. In a 12-month period, I took a month off in the summer to be with my children at our lake home, and I took a winter vacation. That leaves ten and a half months of actively working the real estate market. I discovered that in order to maintain the lifestyle that I was accustomed to:

I HAD TO CALL ON FSBOs!

I'll walk you through some individual FSBOs that I have called on in one year to let you see how I handled the situations.

Whenever you call on a FSBO, try to remember not to deviate from the initial statement and question:

BN:	"Hi I'm Barbara Nash from _____ Realty. I follow the ads closely in the paper and just noticed your home for sale. Could I make an appointment to see it?"
Seller:	"No!"
BN:	"Oh, I see. I was wondering if you could tell me how you are handling appointments with agents on the property?"
Seller:	"Well, I guess just setting up an appointment with us, why?"
BN:	I then go on to secure the appointment and go to the house.

Case Study 1

Audrey and Bud Gallahanly 650 Farm Dr.—$179,500

BN:	"Hi, Mr. Gallahanly. This is Barbara Nash from _____ Realty."
Seller:	"I'm not interested in listing my house, and I'm sick of all the agents calling on me. I'm fed up to here with it!"
BN:	"Do you have a second to tell me what happened? I'm really curious to ask one thing. How could one real estate agent make you so upset?"
Seller:	"Do you have 10 or 15 minutes?"
BN:	"I certainly do!"
Seller:	"Agents have called to try to get the listing by bringing people over, getting here two to three hours late. They brought the people in, raced through the house, never called back to tell me if they liked it, took off ahead of me, talked too fast and too loud, woke up my wife who was napping, made promises that I never asked for, told me the decorating was tacky and to take out all the carpeting, and told me my ad was cheap-looking."

By the time Mr. Gallahanly finished talking, he felt much better because I agreed with him. He was also growing more curious to meet me. Mr. Gallahanly and I made an appointment for Friday at 2:00 P.M.

Case Study 2

Julie and Bill Dornfeld 740 Glea Rd.

BN: "Hi, I'm Barbara Nash from _____ Realty. May I ask how you are handling appointments to sell your home?"

Mrs. D: "Right now we're letting anyone come that wants to, but not real estate agents!"

BN: "Oh, not real estate agents? I see. How are you handling real estate agents then?"

Mrs. D: "No! no! We have a real estate agent if we want to use her, and that's who we will list with."

BN: "Oh, shall I call her for an appointment?"

Mrs. D: "No! no! We're not listed with anyone now! We are really trying to sell it ourselves! But, oh, I don't know how to handle it. It's so new and we do want to sell. Did you really want to look at it? Do you have someone?"

BN: "Not right now, but it's the area I work heavily! I could have a buyer tomorrow. I would very much like to compare it to others. I also work with relocation buyers and new clients every day."

Mrs. D: "Well, maybe. I guess you could come to see it. After all, we don't owe anything to anyone, and someone my husband knew told us to list with her. We really don't want to move for months, and it's such a bother already with calls, and we're leaving on a vacation in two weeks."

BN: "Oh, by the way, I haven't even asked your name."

Mrs. D: "Julie Dornfeld."

BN: "And what is your address?" (The ad was a blind ad, no address.)

Mrs. D: "It's 740 Glea Road. I've known June Black from Realty Company for a long time, but like I said, I haven't told her she'll gett the listing." (Owners are often contradictory.) "You can come over and look if you want."

BN: "Well, perhaps I could stop by since I'm already going to be over in that area tomorrow. What time do you think would be best? I have 11:00 or 2:00 open and 3:00 or after."

Mrs. D: "3:30 is perfect!"

Case Study 3

This owner was a young couple transferring out of the state. I was the first real estate agent to make an appointment. When I got there, all the lights were on, even in all the closets! The house had just been vacuumed, and Keith and Rhonda Smith asked me to come back Friday. They said that this was the first time they'd advertised, and they expected to get their real estate agent this way. Some friends had told them to pick one of the real estate agents that called from their ad if they got tired of advertising on their own!

My sunday ad got me three good clients!

Keith and Rhonda had me come back Thursday night at 7:00 P.M. I listed the home for $96,900.
IT TOOK 43 DAYS TO SELL THEIR HOME.
I spent $187 in advertising.
I had two open houses.
The buyer for their home came to my open house. This was the ad:

JUST LISTED
OPEN 2-4
"BEAUTIFUL ENGLISH…"
Bungalow…this 3 BR 1-3/4 bath beauty boasts hardwood floors—formal dining room—handsome brick hearth—full dormer—finished 2nd floor—amuse.rm.down—plus dbl. garage…2 blks. to Lake Harriet—hurry! Mid-90s—won't last!! 490 Morgan Rd—Barbara Nash 920-0000.

The buyers for the home paid $95,400 × 7% = $6,678.00

Commission:	$6,678	30 percent list: $2,003
List commission:	$2,003	30 percent sell: $2,003
Sell commission:	$2,003	
My share of total commission:	$4,006	

I MADE $4,006 FROM AN AD IN THE PAPER.

I BELIEVE FSBOs WANT TO SELL!

Calling the FSBO

1. Sunday night pick up the telephone and dial the number.
2. When the owner answers, say the following:

   "Hello, I'm _____ from _____ Realty. I saw your ad in the paper and I am interested in knowing how you are handling appointments with agents."
3. *The owner will do one of the following three things:*
   a. Say *"Not interested"* and hang up. (Note: this very, very, small minority is truly not interested and not worth pursuing!)
   b. Ask you why you want an appointment.
   c. *Set up an appointment* for you to see the house:

I do three things on the first appointment with the owner:

1. *Take* lots of *notes*
2. *Ask* lots of *questions*
3. *Don't leave without* asking for a listing or another appointment to bring back a CMA!

The easiest part and the *hardest* part is *picking up the telephone* and making yourself known!

Another favorite activity of mine is going to house sales and estate sales. One FSBO that I sold for $223,000 was having a moving sale! I stopped by early one morning. I started asking a lot of questions. After calling on FSBOs and before going to their home if you have not secured an appointment, you can drop a letter in the mail and make a note to send various newsworthy articles or just a handwritten note *twice weekly* as well as *phoning.*

Remember that 88 percent of all FSBOs list.

Uh…let's see, why do I want an appointment?

> When you call FSBOs, you must *follow up* as well. If they take a long time to decide, one thing is for sure: They won't forget you. Calling on FSBOs can be fun if you make up your mind not to *fear failing*.

FSBO on the Internet

Sellers can now enter the information highway and make all their real estate business available to anyone in the nation and more than 40 million people all over the world.

A source called www.fsbocentral.com/ caters to FSBOs

Another source, called www.salebyowner.com is an organization that lets people sell their house themselves and still advertise to millions of potential buyers over the Internet. Included are color photos of homes for sale everywhere as well as information on mortgages.

A recent survey showed "more and more households agree that the Internet is useful in finding information on services they need."

Many households use the Internet on a daily basis and the number is growing! Real estate agents need to be aware of what the Internet has to offer FSBOs.

Buyers can go directly to the World Wide Web, locate a city and state with homes for sale, and view them within seconds of turning on their computer!

Sellers can go directly to the World Wide Web and market properties. They are able to reach millions of people all over the world without utilizing the services of a real estate agent! They can get market evaluations and MLS data online. Some FSBO marketing companies charge a $20 one-time fee to list your property on the Internet. Still other companies charge a fee of $45 for a "deluxe property listing" and offer a "listing on the World Wide Web until it is sold or one year is up ... " They go on to offer "full contact information, e-mail links, and links to important sites, as well as free page updates and price changes, no commissions, and no hassles!"

It is becoming harder and harder to compete with some of these companies. Yet, at the end of the day—

PERSONAL SERVICE IS STILL FOREMOST IN EVERYONE'S MIND!!!

Chapter Summary

Calling on the FSBO is one way to bring business in a manner that can be profitable in a short amount of time. For Sale by Owners very much want to sell right now! Eighty-eight percent of FSBOs list their home. Nine out of ten FSBOs have business to refer to you later.

There are 10 good ways to get an appointment with a FSBO. One of them is to set up an appointment to preview their home. Get a Sunday paper and circle the FSBO ads. On Sunday afternoon, or night, call the FSBO. Ask the FSBO for an appointment. Once you're there keep the listing agreement right out in front of you on the table. Ask the seller if you can show him or her how the lockbox works. FSBOs have trouble pricing. A home must have good terms, a good price, and be in good condition. Tell the seller you will get a Truth-in-Housing Inspection on their home. Use the "6-2-6 System" on the FSBO and call them at least two times a week for 6 weeks. The average agent calls the first week and the FSBO lists the fourth week! Average FSBOs say no four times before saying yes.

There are three keys to listing FSBOs: Be persistent, build trust, and be professional (show them you can get the job done). Nationally it has been shown that a seller will make far more money after the commission is subtracted than if they try to sell the home on their own. Most FSBOs want to move and if you list their home, it means three things: automatic buyers, a secured listing and if sold, money in your pocket! On the first appointment with the owner: Take lots of notes, ask lots of questions, don't leave without asking for a listing or another appointment to bring back a CMA.

Many households use the Internet on a daily basis and the number is growing! Real estate agents need to be aware of what the Internet has to offer FSBOs. Buyers can go directly to the Internet and locate a city and state with homes for sale, and view them within seconds of turning on their computer! Help them find the right home for themselves.

CHAPTER 9

LETTERS FOR PROSPECTING

- Expired
- Prospecting
- Price Reduction
- Open House

big deal by Lorayne n' Neil

Prospective Buyer Letter

Mr. and Mrs. Jordan
500 Arthur Street
Minneapolis, Minnesota

Dear Mr. and Mrs. Jordan:

My name is Barbara Nash, and I am associated with _____ Realty.

Investment opportunities come and go. Most people these days have difficulty depending on any sure thing.

Real estate continues to outlast any long-term investment.

There has never been a better time to build a home than now.

I am a specialist in the metropolitan area. With our computer services, I can show you the latest properties for sale almost immediately.

I look forward to your call, and hopefully we can set up an appointment in the very near future to see some great homes!

Sincerely,

Barbara Nash

Expired Listing Letters

Mr. and Mrs. Jack James
3000 West Street
Minneapolis, Minnesota

Dear Mr. and Mrs. James:

My name is Barbara Nash, and I am associated with _____ Realty.

I have specialized in your area for a long time and have enjoyed helping with the marketing of many properties in your neighborhood.

I recently noticed that your property has been deleted from the active file in our multiple listing books and computer.

I drove by your property, and this puzzles me a great deal.

I am currently involved with a client, but I will try to arrange an appointment with you the first part of next week.

Looking forward to meeting and talking with you soon.

Sincerely,

Barbara Nash

Expired Listing Letter

Mr. and Mrs. Jack James
3000 West Street
Minneapolis, Minnesota

Dear Mr. and Mrs. James:

I understand from looking over the computer printout of current multiple listings that your home is not listed at this time.

I drove past your property today. This really puzzles me!

I would very much like to meet without and talk with you about what the problem may have been and how the right remedies could expedite a swift sale for you.

Looking forward to meeting with you soon.

    Sincerely,

    Barbara Nash

Letter to Seller When [Your] Listing is Ready to Expire

Mr. and Mrs. Grand
1005 North West Street
Minneapolis, Minnesota

Dear Mr. and Mrs. Grand:

I understand from looking at my records that your listing will expire in a few weeks.

It's time to yet together to go over a summary of all the activity on your property.

I have come up with an additional marketing strategy and feel that it would be beneficial to the sale.

I have enclosed a new listing contract. Please feel free to sign it and return it to me in the enclosed self-addressed envelope, and we will also set up an appointment to review the information that I am concerned about.

    Sincerely,

    Barbara Nash

Just-Listed Letter

Mr. and Mrs. North
400 West Avenue
Minneapolis, Minnesota

Dear Mr. and Mrs. North:

Thank you for the opportunity to market your home. Following are a few suggestions that would enhance the desirability of your property.

1. *Put yourself in the place of a prospective buyer. Look critically all around your home, both inside and out.*
2. *Make sure that every part of your home is clean and in top-notch condition. Replace light bulbs, clean closets, and do anything else you feel would help.*
3. *Do something extra to make the home look "homey." Buy some flowers, use air freshener, wash rugs . . . anything to spruce it up!*

Let's do our job together so we will make a swift sale on your home.

Thank you for giving me the opportunity to serve you.

Sincerely,

Barbara Nash

For Sale by Owner Letter

Mr. and Mrs. Johnson
300 State Street
Minneapolis, Minnesota

Dear Mr. and Mrs. Johnson:

My name is Barbara Nash, and I am associated with _____ Realty.

I have specialized in your area for a long time and have enjoyed participating in the marketing of many properties in your neighborhood.

I recently drove by your property for sale. I very much would like to have an appointment to walk through your home as soon as possible.

I am currently involved with a client, but I will try to set up an appointment with you the first part of next week.

I look forward to talking with you.

Sincerely,

Barbara Nash

For Sale by Owner Letter

Mr. and Mrs. Johnson
300 State Street
Minneapolis, Minnesota

Dear Mr. and Mrs. Johnson:

I understand and respect your decision not to use a real estate agent at this time.

During the time you are working on your property, though, you will need certain information in regard to the selling of your home. Please find enclosed a purchase agreement, a buyer information sheet, and information on financing and the costs you will be asked to pay. I hope this helps.

I will be contacting you in the near future to see how you are progressing. Meanwhile, good luck!

Sincerely,

Barbara Nash

For Sale by Owner Letter

Mr. and Mrs. Johnson
300 State Street
Minneapolis, Minnesota

Dear Mr. and Mrs. Johnson:

I drove past your home today. It is really a nice property.

I have enclosed my brochure and my business card.

I have done a lot of business in your neighborhood, but I will talk with you later when you have a moment.

I look forward to meeting with Lou. Good luck!

Sincerely,

Barbara Nash

Farming Letter

Mr. and Mrs. Johnson
300 State Street
Minneapolis, Minnesota

Dear Mr. and Mrs. Johnson:

I noticed your "For Sale by Owner" sign today, and I am curious about what activity it has penetrated for you.

Your home is a property I would like to have in my inventory to market. However, I pride myself on the fact that I personally maintain only twelve listings for sale at a time. I feel that is the maximum number any agent can handle if he or she is to be fair to, and is to do an effective job for, the home sellers she is representing.

Since I have an abundance of listings now, it is really premature for me to discuss representing you, but when one of my current listings sells, I will contact you. Good luck.

Sincerely,

Barbara Nash

Farming Letter

Mr. and Mrs. Smith
1000 South Street
Minneapolis, Minnesota

Dear Mr. and Mrs. Smith:

The following information is a market update for homes sold in your area from the following dates: _____ ,20__, _____ 20__, _____ 20__.

During this time, two-bedroom homes have sold for an average of $_____ . Three-bedroom homes have sold for an average of $_____ . Four-bedroom homes have sold for an average of $_____ .

Should you have any questions about the value of your home, I would be happy to give you a free market analysis.

If you have and other real estate questions, please feel free to call.

Sincerely,

Barbara Nash

Farming Letter

Mr. and Mrs. Olson
1000 South Street
Minneapolis, Minnesota

Dear Mr. and Mrs. Olson:

My name is Barbara Nash, and I am associated with _____ Realty.

I have been working with some buyers who prefer only the area of _____.

Currently there have been few properties to show them, and I am appealing to individual homeowners.

If you would consider selling your own home or know of anyone in your area or surrounding area who is thinking of selling, could you call me today? I would appreciate it very much.

Thank you for your time and attention to this matter. I look forward to hearing from you soon.

    Sincerely,

    Barbara Nash

Farming Letter

Mr. and Mrs. Smith
1000 South Street
Minneapolis, Minnesota

Dear Mr. and Mrs. Smith:

My name is Barbara Nash, and I am associated with _____ Realty.

I have enjoyed working and specializing in your particular area for quite some time.

I especially prefer to work with relocation clients and corporate referrals, clients who are particularly stable in today's market.

If you are considering a move in the near future, I very likely could have a buyer for your home and/or could help you with the marketing of your property.

Please feel free to contact me at your earliest convenience. I look forward to our getting together soon.

    Sincerely,

    Barbara Nash

Farming Letter

Mr. and Mrs. Smith
1000 South Street
Minneapolis, Minnesota

Dear Mr. and Mrs. Smith:

My name is Barbara Nash, and I am associated with _____ Realty.

I have specialized in your area for a long time and have enjoyed helping with the marketing of many properties in your neighborhood.

At the moment I am carrying more buyers than I have homes for. I would very much like to talk to you about the possibility of selling your home.

I am involved with a client for the remainder of this week, but I will try to contact you the first part of next week for an appointment.

If this does not work out, please feel free to call me, and we will arrange a time we can get together. I look forward to talking with you.

     Sincerely,

     Barbara Nash

Farming Letter

Mr. and Mrs. Smith
1000 South Street
Minneapolis, Minnesota

Dear Mr. and Mrs. Smith:

We pride ourselves in offering real estate services in all areas. Our company also concentrates on a few specific areas where we have been most successful: _____ and _____ .

Some of our recent sales in your area have been:

_____

_____

_____

Our company is constantly working in these areas. Should you be thinking of buying or selling, we would appreciate the opportunity to talk with you before you consider anyone else.

     Sincerely,

     Barbara Nash

Farming Letter

Dear Homeowner:

The exposure your home has to the market of buyers is unbelievable.

Did you know that nearly 70% of all homes sold are to out-of-town buyers? They never read or even get the local paper. They usually come into town over the weekend. They are pushed to look at homes for two or three days straight and then they must decide quickly!

Usually they seek out a real estate agent. They know that the agent can tell them about the market value in various areas, what the best interest rates are, what schools are available, and what lender to use.

Please feel free to call me. I would be happy to give you a free estimate on selling your home.

> Sincerely,
>
>
> Barbara Nash

Open House Letter to Potential Buyer

Dr. and Mrs. John Graham
5813 Harris Avenue
Minneapolis, Minnesota

Dear Dr. and Mrs. Graham:

It was so nice to meet you and talk with you at the listing I held open last Sunday located at _____. Thank you very much for taking the time to tell me of your real estate needs in the near future.

I have taken the liberty of enclosing a few listings of properties that I feel meet some of the qualifications we discussed.

If you have any interest in any of these properties or would like to look at additional homes, please feel free to contact me.

This week I am with a client. Next week I look forward to contacting you to arrange a time we can get together to review some properties.

> Sincerely,
>
>
> Barbara Nash

Open House to Potential Buyer

Dr. and Mrs. John Graham
5813 Harris Avenue
Minneapolis, Minnesota

Dear John and Karen:

Thank you for coming through my open house yesterday and looking at the property on 213 Duncraig. It was sold this morning, and we have a closing set for April 30, 20___.

I have enclosed various current listing sheets in the Edina area. I think it will help you to get a good feel for the market in Edina at the present time.

Please feel free to call me regarding an appointment on any of the enclosed listings. I look forward to hearing from you and would be happy to give you a free estimate on your own property and go over what I think you would be able to realize from it. I will wait to hear from you.

     Sincerely,

     Barbara Nash

Open House Letter to Potential Buyer

Dr. and Mrs. John Graham
5813 Harris Avenue
Minneapolis, Minnesota

Dear Dr. and Mrs. Graham:

Thank you for coming through my open house last Sunday. The property that I held open at _____ happens to be one of favorite homes in this price range.

I feel that the market is excellent now for investing in real estate. Interest rates are very competitive. I would very much like to work with you to service your real estate needs. My specialty is working with buyers in the metropolitan area.

I pride myself on keeping up to date on the new methods of computerization and would like to add you to my computerized mailing list featuring all the homes in the areas that you desire.

Please feel free to call me to set up an appointment to look at some properties. I will also contact you the first part of the week to arrange an appointment. Thank you for your time and consideration.

     Sincerely,

     Barbara Nash

Holiday Letter of Thanks

Dear Friends:

At this very special time of year, I like to look back and give thanks for all of the wonderful things that have happened to me over the past year.

I want to wish you and your family a very happy holiday season. May God bless you in the New Year.

I look forward to helping you with any of your future real estate needs and hopefully servicing you in the years ahead.

My very best wishes for happiness.

     Sincerely,

     Barbara Nash

Holiday Letter of Thanks

Mr. and Mrs. Cooper
4003 Oak Street
Minneapolis, Minnesota

Dear Mr. and Mrs. Cooper:

With the end of the year upon us and the dawn of a new one in sight, I want to express my gratitude to you for your business and having had the pleasure of representing you in the past.

Last year I had excellent results in my business, and I want to thank each of my valued clients. Referrals from you and other friends are the most important asset in my growth as a real estate salesperson. I really appreciate your thoughtfulness and your loyalty.

My responsibility to you goes beyond merely selling you a home. Please feel free to contact me at any time if I can be of service to you for any and all real estate needs. Have a wonderful New Year and feel free to call me anytime!

     Sincerely,

     Barbara Nash

Holiday Letter of Thanks

Mr. and Mrs. Cooper
4003 Oak Street
Minneapolis, Minnesota

Dear Mr. and Mrs. Cooper:

Somehow, during scurrying hustle and bustle of the year and through the holiday season, we just don't seem to find the time to call on our friends and clients as often as we would like to.

A new year has come again with all its hope and aspirations—a chance to look ahead and a chance to review the many things done and left undone over the past year. But most of all, it gives us a chance to pause and reflect.

As I look back over the past year, it occurs to me that I may not have expressed adequately my appreciation for our relationship and what you have done for me over the year. I would like to thank you, gratefully and sincerely!

My very best wishes for abundant health, happiness, and all the success possible in the coming year and the years ahead.

Sincerely,

Barbara Nash

Just-Listed Letter to a Neighbor

Mr. and Mrs. Peterson
1002 Sun Road
Minneapolis, Minnesota

Dear Mr. and Mrs. Peterson:

We have recently listed your neighbor's home. They have asked for our help in trying to sell their property. I am currently trying to find people who may know of someone who would be interested in viewing this property. It is located at _____.

Perhaps you have a friend or a relative who would be interested in seeing this lovely home. Please feel free to call me for the price and the particulars on the residence.

Should you have any specific real estate questions, I would be happy to help you with them.

Sincerely,

Barbara Nash

Neighborhood Letter

Mr. and Mrs. Peterson
1002 Sun Road
Minneapolis, Minnesota

Dear Mr. and Mrs. Peterson:

As you may have noticed, we have recently listed the property at
_____ with our company.

I pride myself on selling properties in your area and would welcome your visit to any of the open houses that I will be holding on the home. Feel free to call me with any questions that I may answer and to suggest any friends or relatives to whom you may care to recommend the property.

Looking forward to talking with you.

Sincerely,

Barbara Nash

Just-Sold-to-a-Neighbor Letter

Mr. and Mrs. Jacobs
1563 Trellis Road
Minneapolis, Minnesota

Dear Mr. and Mrs. Jacobs:

I am very happy to inform you that I have just sold the listing located at _____, and that Mr. and Mrs. _____ will be your new neighbors.

I have completed many successful sales in and around your vicinity.

During this year I am pleased to tell you that the real estate market has been excellent. Should you have any questions about your own property, please do not hesitate to call me. I would be happy to answer them.

Sincerely,

Barbara Nash

Price Reduction Letter

Mr. and Mrs. Hanby
247 Parley Street
Minneapolis, Minnesota

Dear Mr. and Mrs. Hanby:

We have now had your home listed for _____ days. There have been _____ showings on the property. The following agents have these responses:

_____

_____

_____

In your area there are presently _____ homes for sale.

A comparison of your home to others in your area with comparable square footage and amenities tells us your home should currently be listed at $_____.

If we continue to market the home at the current price, without a reduction, we will only help the others in your area to sell faster! Thank you for your immediate attention to this matter.

Sincerely,

Barbara Nash

Price Reduction Letter

Mr. and Mrs. Hanby
247 Parley Street
Minneapolis, Minnesota

Dear Mr. and Mrs. Hanby:

We have had _____ open houses on your property to date. There have been _____ offers on your property.

I feel that we should sit down and talk about a price reduction with which you are comfortable and some additional marketing tools that may be advisable at this point.

I look forward to meeting with you within the next few days to go over the information that I think is important in getting your home sold as soon as possible.

Sincerely,

Barbara Nash

Price Reduction Letter

Mr. and Mrs. Realistic
247 Parley Street
Minneapolis, Minnesota

Dear Mr. and Mrs. Realistic:

We currently have been marketing your home at a price and terms that you have decided upon. Since we have had it on the market for _____ days, there have been _____ offers on the property. This level of activity is not going to get us a fast sale.

It is important that we realize that a lender will not put a mortgage on a property that does not appraise for a certain price.

I think you have a good property, and with a realistic adjustment of $_____, we should be able to activate a swift sale for you.

I look forward to your response. I will call you in the next day or so to set up an appointment.

> Sincerely,

> Barbara Nash

Staying-in-Touch-with-Seller Letter

Mr. and Mrs. John Doe
3003 Windsor Avenue
Minneapolis, Minnesota

Dear Mr. and Mrs. Doe:

Now that I have had the opportunity to list your property for a while (actually _____ days), it has become apparent to me, based upon comments from various real estate agents and people who have come through the home, that we may want to consider dealing with the following points:

1. *The roof needs to be repaired.*
2. *The exterior should be touched up and painted.*
3. *The lawn should be mowed.*
4. *The kitchen should be completely cleaned out and all papers tacked to the refrigerator should be taken down.*
5. *The draperies should come off.*
6. *The old lawn furniture should be discarded and the stray items on the lawn should be picked up.*

Let's get together, or perhaps you could give me a call to discuss how many of these items are doable in the near future.

There is always some solution, and we do want to get the highest price possible for your home without letting small annoyances get in the way. I look forward to talking with you this week.

> Sincerely,

> Barbara Nash

Price Reduction Letter

Mr. and Mrs. John Doe
3003 Windsor Avenue
Minneapolis, Minnesota

Dear Mr. and Mrs. Doe:

Although it has been over six months from the date we listed your property, remember that because of the situation we initially addressed in regard to the fact that the home is located [on a busy street, high hill, close to freeway], we did take into consideration that it would be a bit longer for the property to sell.

Rest assured that we are using every conceivable marketing strategy and will keep you posted as soon as we get an offer.

Within the next 30 days, if no purchase agreement is presented, we will address a price reduction that will help us to realize an offer.

Sincerely,

Barbara Nash

Thank-You-to-the-Buyer Letter

Mr. and Mrs. Buyright
2006 Right Street
Minneapolis, Minnesota

Dear Mr. and Mrs. Buyright:

Thank you for the opportunity to help you relocate. I sincerely enjoyed working with you.

Now that you have moved and life is back to normal (almost), I hope that I can stop by to see how you are doing. Please keep in mind that I will be happy to help if you have any concerns about real estate or and questions or problems.

Thank you again for your business. Should you have any friends or acquaintances who may be looking for a home or may be interested in selling, feel free to give them my name.

Best wishes in your new home!

Sincerely,

Barbara Nash

Thank-You-to-the-Seller Letter

Mr. and Mrs. Sold
1005 Date Street
Minneapolis, Minnesota

Dear Mr. and Mrs. Sold:

Now that we finally have your home sold and all the details have been taken care of, I want to extend my sincere thanks for the opportunity to have been of service to you. I am most thankful for your satisfaction and hope that my service has met with your approval.

Feel free to call me regarding any and all future real estate questions you may have. Should you have any friends or relatives who may be thinking of buying or selling, have them give me a call. I always love getting a referral!

Sincerely,

Barbara Nash

Thank-You-to-the-Seller Letter

Mr. and Mrs. Sold
1008 Date Street
Minneapolis, Minnesota

Dear Mr. and Mrs. Sold:

I recently received word that all has progressed well on the transaction of your home. I thoroughly enjoyed working with you in the marketing of your property.

Be assured that I will keep you abreast of any news in the real estate industry that I feel you may wish to know of.

Should you have any friends or acquaintances that you feel I may be able to help, please give them my name.

My very best wishes to you, and congratulations on the sale of your home.

Sincerely,

Barbara Nash

Thank-You-for-the-Listing Letter

Mr. and Mrs. Tucker
47 Roper Street
Minneapolis, Minnesota

Dear Mr. and Mrs. Tucker:

I want to take the time to personally thank you for listing your home with _____ Realty and me. Be assured that we will make every conceivable effort to market the home to the best of our ability and bring you the best offer possible in the current market.

You will continue to be updated and notified as to the showings and comments that are given to us regarding your home.

Together, you and I will be able, with a meeting of the minds, to bring a swift and smooth sale of your home. Thank you for entrusting your property to us.

    Sincerely,

    Barbara Nash

Thank-You-for-the-Referral Letter

Mr. and Mrs. Smith
1234 State Street
Omaha, Nebraska

Dear Mr. and Mrs. Smith:

Thank you so much for referring me to your neighbors, Mr. and Mrs. Green. I have since met with them and they have listed their home and are moving to Kentucky.

I appreciate the great referral and hope we can get together soon for dinner. I will call you next week to see if we can put something on the calendar soon!

    Sincerely,

    Barbara Nash

P. S. A great new Mexican restaurant just opened and I'd like for us to try it!

CHAPTER 10

LISTINGS

- 12-Point Plan

big deal by Lorayne n' Neil

Listings

When I first started selling real estate, I quickly became aware that you are never really in the real estate business until you have your own listings.

THERE IS NO QUICK SHORTCUT.

> On your first visit to a client's home, *take three things with you:*
>
> 1. Large, legal-size notebook and pen,
> 2. Lockbox and blank listing (just in case), and
> 3. Your appointment book/calendar/ BlackBerry/camera
>
> Take a picture of their house!

IT IS IMPORTANT TO START OFF RIGHT.

Throughout this chapter I will give you an account of:

1. what I do to *get a listing*,
2. what I do to *service a listing*, and
3. what I do to *market a listing*.

Once a salesperson has a *format* down, knows what is expected of him or her, and realizes what his or her chances are, things always look better than starting out in the dark!

**GOOD LISTINGS ARE LIKE GOLD.
THEY ARE WORTH A LOT AND
THE BENEFITS LAST A LONG TIME.**

Whether you are new to the business or have been in the real estate business for a long time, I've found that in order to *simply make ends meet* you must:

> list minimum of two to four homes and sell two to four homes monthly.

This level of activity is extremely *CONSERVATIVE!*

If you are not doing *at least this much business*, something is wrong. Something is not working for you to become *successful* in selling real estate.

Only you (and your sales manager) knows the truth!

Start by trying to better yourself. Discipline each day.

> If you are listing two homes a month, try to list four homes!
> If you are selling one to two homes a month, try to sell three to five homes.

WATCH YOUR LISTINGS GROW USING THIS CHAPTER'S APPROACH, AND SEE HOW MUCH BETTER YOUR REAL ESTATE OUTLOOK BECOMES!

Just try one NEW way. Call a for Sale by Owner!

Try to do ONE more CMA for ONE more seller. Constantly check with new listings

Watch what happens to your business when you learn to apply DISCIPLINE.

What to Do to Get a Listing!

Whether it is a *for sale by owner*, a referral, an expired, or a canceled, *sellers are the same in three ways:*

1. They *want* to sell their home.
2. They are investigating different alternatives—one being you!
3. You'd better know what to do if you want the listing.

When visiting a seller's house

7 Items to bring to a new listing

1. A partially filled-out listing agreement
2. Your measuring tape
3. Your net sheet
4. Your promotional brochure
5. A lockbox
6. Your laptop for doing CMAs
7. Your camera

Three characteristics guarantee a listing:

1. honesty
2. enthusiasm
3. application—ASK FOR THE LISTING!

> **TAKE A PHOTO OF THE HOUSE WHEN YOU ARRIVE.**

Make the *first appointment* short. Use a nice notebook with a cover to take notes! Tour the property, *take lots of notes,* and *don't leave without the listing or an appointment* to come back!

Questions to ask the seller

1. *When did you purchase* the home and for how much?
2. What is the *remaining mortgage* on the property?
3. Has the city sent you a card with the *estimated market value?* If so, what is it?
4. What is the *amount of the taxes* assessed on the property?
5. Have you *made any improvements* to the property since you bought? What is the approximate dollar value of the improvements?
6. If you were to get an offer to buy your home today, *where would you want to move and when?*
7. Have you come up with a figure that *you think your home would sell for?*
8. *Do you have a floor plan* with the dimensions, room sizes, and so forth? Often a seller has already prepared extensive highlight sheets on his or her home, thereby saving the agent time in doing a CMA.
9. Is there anything in your home that you are *specifically including* or excluding in the sale? Let's sign now and get going!
10. What is the *best phone number* to reach you at during the day?
11. How do the next few days look to *schedule an appointment* for me to stop by with the information that I have formulated into a market analysis on your home? I have either the afternoon or the evening of _____. *Which is better for you?*

All of these questions are essential. Above all... "ARE YOU READY TO LIST NOW?"

These questions should be written down and answered while you are visiting the property for the first time! Try to get a listing the first time!

DON'T LEAVE THE SELLER'S HOUSE without scheduling an appointment to come back and present your competitive market analysis (CMA) to them. As you leave the first appointment, make sure that you have given the seller *a brochure on you and one on your company.*

During your tour of the home with the seller, make sure that you not only ask questions about the home, but remember to get to know the sellers. Notice as you tour through the rooms any plaques or trophies that might have been given for a certain hobby or merit. Also notice any unusual collections they might have acquired. Take an interest in them as people. *Become a friend. Ask lots of questions.*

Timeless tips

1. *Do your homework* on their house.
2. *Do your best* to learn about those who live in the house and their housing needs.
3. *Be sincere.*
4. *Look professional.*

If the client is ready to list at first appointment:

1. Do a CMA on your laptop.
2. Sign the listing.
3. Put the lockbox on the property.

When you leave the property after your first visit:

1. Go back to the office and pull more comparable properties for the home that you just saw.
2. *Finalize the homes* that you are comparing to the subject property by eliminating all but three.
3. *Do a computerized competitive market analysis* (CMA) of the subject home, including the neighborhood (*get map coordinates*), the solds, current actives, and all *homes that have expired*—if you have not already done so.
4. *Consolidate your notes* by completing a listing that is ready to go with the information that you obtained from the seller as well as the highlight part of the listing (the verbage that describes the home).
5. *Write an ad* on the home.
6. *Get a lockbox* ready to take back to the property.
7. *Start a legal-size folder* on the subject property with the listing, statement of condition, and any other pertinent data.
8. Partly fill out a seller net sheet to put into the above file.
9. Get a *glossy 8" × 11" file folder* and insert information about your company, yourself, moving information, school information, computer information, and your CMA.
10. *Insert three pictures* of the comparable sold properties into your CMA folder.

NOW YOU ARE READY TO BEGIN.

If you did not *make your next appointment with the seller*, do so as soon as possible (within the next few days).

Second appointment

1. Keep the listing agreement out in front of everyone!
2. The biggest hurdle to overcome with the sellers is *getting to know them. Have a sense of humor.* Go over your Marketing Plan (sample at the end of the chapter). Drop the topic of real estate talk for a while, and discuss something that will create a common bond.
3. The best way to break the ice with a seller is to Make them feel comfortable!

a. follow through and look sellers in the eye

b. be concise and accurate with the CMA

c. discuss the net sheet and dollar amounts carefully

d. take time with the seller and explain things thoroughly

e. spend a few minutes discussing the sellers interests, not real estate!

f. go back and ask for the listing!

g. open your last real estate sentence with, "May I show you how the lockbox works?"

Don't assume that, just because a potential client has a friend in the business, you don't have a chance. *You always a chance.* However, you must be a professional!

> One seller said that *40 agents* had been to his home *prior to me.* I said, "You have not met *me* yet, and you haven't seen how I work."

The majority of agents who come through a seller's house do not ask outright for the listing!

Listing Luggage

To get a listing the right way:

1. The *first appointment* must be made. *Call and ask for it.*
2. Go to the property and *walk through the home.*
   a. Take lots of notes.
   b. Ask lots of questions.
   c. Write down everything.
   d. Take a *photo* of the home.
   e. Ask for the listing!
3. Don't leave the property without making the *second appointment* to come back. (But first, ask for the listing!)
4. Go back to the office and start a CMA on the property while it is fresh in your mind. If you can't do the CMA right away, at least try to find three properties that compare to the home and jot down some added notes about the home. In this case, work on the CMA as soon as possible.

I was so prepared, they listed on the first appoinment!

5. To the *second appointment* bring the following:

   a. *legal-size listing folder* with seller's name typed on it. The folder includes:

     (1) seller's net sheet

     (2) partially filled out multiple listing form

     (3) home condition statement

     (4) written ad on the property

     (5) computer printout of solds, expireds, and currents

     (6) notes taken on the property/legal pad

     (7) any mortgage or tax information you've accumulated

     (8) latest thank-you letter from a former client

   b. seller's folder (see sample)

   c. personal presentation manual (manual on yourself with past listings, thank-you letters, information about your company, and your real estate achievements).

   d. laptop computer

   e. lockbox

   f. measuring tape

   g. calculator

   h. highlight sheet about the neighborhood

6. Sit down with the sellers and start your conversation with a smile. I tell them, "I have enjoyed spending *a great deal of time* preparing this market analysis for you on your property." Then carefully go through the listing folder.

7. *"I will start with the CMA* that I have prepared for you and explain how each of the three properties compares to your home."

8. *"Now that we have gone over the CMA* and the net sheet, you have a fair idea of what you can realize from the sale of this home. There's no reason why we can't start now!"

> 9. *"Thank you for signing this listing.* I am going to show you how the lockbox works on the front door and ask you what inclusions you will be leaving with the house."

10. *As you leave the home with the signed listing,* remember to give the seller a copy of everything that he or she has signed. If there is no lockbox, *get a key to the house.*

11. *You will probably have to come back to measure.* Don't get caught up in measuring before getting the listing signed; the seller may find ways to stall. Come back the next day if you have to, or at the end of the listing presentation.

12. Put your lockbox on the front door if it's not there already.

13. You have a signed listing agreement on the property! It's not as hard as you think. *You have done your homework.*

14. Call the listing in to the office *immediately,* go to the office and turn it in, or fax it in via computer.

15. Turn in the ad that you have already written for the home. Make sure that it is open *on the very next Sunday.*

How did it go, Neil?

I did it . . . I really did it! Every step, and they signed!

16. Make a *highlight* sheet on the property and have copies made up as soon as possible to leave at the home. Leave 30 photocopies of the listing at the house to use until the highlight sheet is finished.

17. Call any and all buyers you think may be interested in this property. Tell your friends about it. Tell your relatives.

18. Write many "just listed" cards to send to as many of the neighbors surrounding this new listing as possible.

Twelve Tough Questions before Seller Lists

1. **How long have you been in real estate?**

   In the beginning this was a very difficult question. I answer it by saying, "I've been selling real estate for quite some time now."

2. **What is the average number of days on the market for your listings?**

   Your listings also mean your company listings. I would take this information from computer under AMS (area market survey) or the front section of the MLS book.

3. **What is the average listing price to selling price ratio?**

   "It usually varies from a winter market to a spring market and depends on the condition of the property and the price compared to others like it that have sold."

4. **May I have a copy of your marketing plan?**

   "Yes, I have included one for you in the CMA that I have prepared along with some other pertinent information."

5. **What do you know about our area?**

   "I have researched all the homes in your area that have been sold, expired, or are currently on the market, and I have included them in my CMA brochure for you."

6. **What is your professional fee?**

   "I am pleased to tell you that, although home prices have gone up over the years, our fee has stayed extremely competitive and will help the majority of real estate agents looking in this area to show your home."

7. **Have you sold any homes in our area?**

   "I was hoping we could touch upon that point. I have included in my CMA brochure information on various homes that our company has sold in or around your area."

8. **What is the standard length of listing?**

   "I have seen agents take listings from 120 days to six months. I feel that, although we would market the home with these parameters, we would be happy to insert a clause stating that you could cancel within 24 hours if for any reason you were displeased with my service." (Remember that you can't make a seller sell if he doesn't want to.)

9. **Does our home need anything major that you can see?**

   "I have brought along a helpful hints sheet that agents like myself use in selling homes. Hopefully it will answer all of your questions."

10. **What price range would you market our home at, just off the top of your head?**

    You sell real estate, so you should know these things!

"I enjoy selling real estate, and I have always found that it's difficult to eat your words, so ... I always try to do my homework, and you will see, as we go over the CMA that I have prepared for you today, that I have arrived at a price range that I feel would best represent your type of home. I never like to guess."

11. Do you have any references?

"I have made a point of keeping records of all my past clients after their successful closings, and I stay in touch by word and mail. I would be happy to have you talk with any one of them." (Make sure that there are a couple of references that you really do feel comfortable using just for this situation. Call them before giving out their names. If you just started in the business, use a good friend.)

12. Why do you think that you could sell our home?

"I love working in your neighborhood and this area. I feel comfortable telling buyers about the various advantages of living here, and our company enjoys a great deal of success here." (Remember to say that only if you really do mean it.)

Masterpiece Market Plan

A detailed market plan has always been the finishing touch to getting any listing that I have gone after. Following is information included in my personal promotion book and my market plan.

1. Prepare an *in-depth* CMA on the property for solds, expireds, and current listings.
2. Take a *color photo* of the subject property from its best angle.
3. Prepare a professional-looking highlight sheet on the property with color photo. Leave 150 copies at the property.
4. Place a *for sale sign with name rider on the property* with a brochure box attached so that people driving by can familiarize themselves with the home.
5. Install *a lockbox* on the door to facilitate access for showings.
6. Enroll the property in the *multiple listing service* with an additional supplement sheet (if needed) with picture and exposure.
7. Hold an *open house* for agents of my company and multiple listing companies on the first Tuesday after the listing is initiated.
8. Place *special feature cards* at the property to point out highlights to prospects.
9. Send *highlight sheets* to surrounding *neighbors* who may have friends or relatives moving into the area.
10. *Place an ad* in the first Sunday paper with "just listed" and bold lettering to bring attention to the property.
11. Give sellers all *follow-ups on showings* with comments and suggestions.
12. Insert *a picture ad* in our company's exclusive magazine promoting the property.
13. *Review property biweekly* and suggest remedies for selling.
14. Offer continuous service and *follow-up* to ad calls by listing two separate home lines, home answering service, office secretary, and car phone.
15. Carefully calculate *seller's net* on all offer presentations.
16. Complete *follow-up on all buyers* applying for loans and prequalify if buyer origination is through listing agent.
17. *Promote property weekly* to other agents at meetings and office.
18. Complete new CMA if necessary after *30-day checkup*.

19. Provide the homeowner with a *helpful home-selling hints* brochure (sample at end of this chapter).

20. *Help sellers* locate a moving company and/or relocation company if out-of-state. Provide free out-of-state newspaper from city seller is moving to.

This specific marketing plan will give a real estate agent credibility, especially to sellers who think the real estate person does not accomplish much. It also adds professionalism and causes the seller to wonder when and how you will ever have the time to do all the things that you are promising.

ACTUALLY, IT'S NOT THAT HARD!

As you read through each chapter of this book, look at the samples and examples of how to do everything that I speak of in the listing presentation and in the individual marketing plan. See if you can incorporate this plan in each and every CMA that you prepare to present to your seller.

Checklist for a New Listing

1. *Make a seller's file.* Use legal size folder (8 1/2" × 14"). Type seller's name in capitals. Examples: JONES, JOHN E. 444-3333 555 ELM ST. Fax: _____ Listed: _____ Sold: _____

2. *Turn the listing* in at the office and enter it into the MLS.

3. *Install a brochure* box at the property.

4. Research and record the utility payments.

5. *Note* any exclusions on the outside of the file.

6. Put the property on *office tour.*

7. *Write an ad* for Sunday's newspaper.

8. *Place the ad* in local homes or city magazines.

9. Make sure the *lockbox* is on the property.

10. Make a *listing entry on the listing sheet* in your daily planner book: include the seller's name, address, phone (work and home), date listed, and lockbox combination.

11. *Take a color photo of the property.*

12. *Prepare a home highlight sheet* on the property (8 1/2" × 11"). Have 40–75 copies made and leave them at the home and in the brochure box outside the home.

13. *Type just-listed cards* for the neighbors around the subject property (100 to 300 families).

14. Find out *where the seller's mortgage* is and record the loan number and the amount owed at payoff on the outside of the file.

15. Find out *if the property is torrens or abstract* and where the deed to the home is. Make sure this information is written on the file!

Filling Out a Listing

1. There can be a *lawsuit!*
2. You can *lose large amounts* of money!
3. A fellow agent can cause you *tremendous problems!*

   Example   A particular agent listed a home for sale and turned the listing in at 6 percent, but the computer printout of the listing showed 7 percent. The listing was on the market for quite a few months. When it finally sold and the listing agent was filling out the closing information papers, she realized what had happened. She wound up having to make up the difference (well over $1,100) in order for the other agent to be paid, based on a 7 percent commission!

This was a sad situation that *could have been avoided* had the listing agent checked and double-checked her listing long before the offer came in from another company.

Many, many more problems can develop at the buyers' end if they feel they have been *grossly misrepresented* and seek legal advice.

Be very, very careful

Fill out the listing carefully, and when you have completely finished it, go back over it and check it all out again.

Try not to leave any part of the listing blank.

Filling out a listing

1. Keep a *reference guide* for local school numbers handy.
2. Check in advance for *tax information* and assessments.
3. Bring a checklist on *home information* with you the first time you visit the property.

1. When I turn the listing in, I:
   a. Put the listing on *tour* immediately.
   b. *Send copies* of the new listing to all of offices in the surrounding areas.
   c. *Type up a highlight sheet* and take a *color photo* of the home. (Use the best picture of the house; have 150 copies made.) Put one color picture on each highlight sheet. This is an economical way of having a professional-looking information sheet at the property almost immediately.

2. I inform the secretary on call that *I wish to be notified of all showings.* This allows me to immediately follow up on the showings. I contact the agent and put his or her comments on the back of the showing card. At the end of each week, I contact the sellers and inform them of the progress in showings and the positive and negative comments that have been made. *Never forget to call* a seller to tell him or her about *every single appointment.*

3. I keep a *30-60-90 chart of all my listings.* Every 30 days I review the listing price, condition, and terms with my seller, as well as keeping them abreast of competition in their neighborhood by giving them a computer printout of all the homes that are in a comparable price range in their 8- to 12-block radius.

4. I normally try to take a *six-month listing minimum.* I tell the seller that *if the home is priced correctly, it should sell within the first 30 days.* We continue to discuss the marketing weekly after that period. I also tell them that if the home has not sold after 30 days, there is a greater opportunity of selling the home with *a price reduction* and change of format to put the home out as a *new listing!* At this time, perhaps we extend the listing agreement, depending on whether 60 or 90 days has passed.

5. If there has been a price reduction, I make sure there are new highlight sheets at the property. I always try to give the impression that the home is not stale.

Highlight Sheet

I use an 8 1/2" × 11" sheet of paper (usually a piece of my real estate stationery) and *I always put my picture at the top corner.* I center the address of the property and list in short sentences the main attractions of the home. I start with the room dimensions, the year built, the square footage, the lot size, the taxes, and whether there is any assumable financing on the property. I then go on to highlight advantages of the neighborhood and proximity to schools and bus. I especially tell about fireplaces, finished lower level, extra family rooms, and special decorating or updating in major rooms such as the kitchen and bedrooms. I also include any special comments that the sellers made regarding why they chose the home to begin with. If I cannot or do not have access to a printer, I make photocopies after all of the above information has been typed.

> **SELLERS ESPECIALLY APPRECIATE HAVING HIGHLIGHTED SHEETS AT THE PROPERTY IMMEDIATELY.**

Helpful Home-Selling Hints

Tell the sellers you are pleased to help in the marketing of their home. Let the sellers know that the following suggestions may expedite a successful sale for them.

1. *First impressions are crucial!* Mow the lawn. Trim the hedges. Weed the garden and/or rake the leaves and shovel snow. Replace any burned-out outdoor lightbulbs, and polish brass door knobs and/or light fixtures.

2. *Try to replace* any missing tiles in the bathroom and any broken windows, railings, and/or leaking pipes.

3. If paint is peeling off the walls, a *room should be repainted;* if there are water spots from a roof repair, paint is needed.

4. *If carpeting is worn out,* it should be replaced if possible. Otherwise the marketing price should be adjusted.

5. *Clean out the garage and basement!* Getting rid of junk makes the house look much larger.

6. *Straighten closets* and storage spaces to create a larger overall look.

7. *Clean stains* off of sinks and replace faucet washers as necessary.

8. *Check all windows* for sticking and broken glass. Replace sash chords and remove old drapes or broken window shades.

9. *Clean the house from top to bottom!* Nothing is more offensive to a buyer than clutter. Polish the windows, scrub the floors, vacuum, and clean curtains.

10. *Straighten up the house!* Get rid of old newspapers and magazines. Put out the garbage. Make sure the litter box is emptied! Make sure the kitchen counters are as clear as possible.

11. *Make sure all pets are confined* to inconspicuous areas. Many buyers are afraid of or allergic to animals.

12. *Make sure the house looks cheerful and bright!* All the window shades should be up for showings. Put soft background music on. If nighttime, turn all the lights on. Have flowers on the table. Light a fire.

13. When showing the house, if possible *leave for awhile.* If not, you and the children should try to be in one room that is out of the way.

14. Make sure that you have left *written comments that you feel* explain why you have enjoyed living in the house and the area. Also consider leaving a list of children and babysitters in the neighborhood. Leave helpful hints regarding your neighbors.

    Sample buyer questions:

    What school will our kids attend?

    Where does the bus run from here?

    Who is a good dentist/doctor in this area?

    Are there babysitters around here?

    What are the neighbors like on either side of this house?

    How close is the grocery store?

15. *Try to be flexible* in your schedule. Some buyers can see the home only at certain times. If you can't be home to show the home, make arrangements for a lockbox. It is wise to have a lockbox on from the beginning.

Sellers Questions: Now We've Listed, What Happens Next?

1. *All appointments on your property* will come from our sales secretary. Real estate agents will be asked with whom they are affiliated, and a record of their showing your home will be kept at our office and given to the listing agent for follow-up.

2. There will also be times when sales agents will call to request an appointment to *preview the property.* You will be called in advance for these appointments also.

3. *Only our office will be making appointments on your home.* The appointments will always be for a specific time, and you will be asked if that time meets with your schedule.

4. *The secretary may call to make the appointment* for the same day or for a few days in advance. The secretary will always tell you who the agent is and what company the agent represents. A typical time frame could be between 3:00 and 4:00, for example.

5. In the event that you cannot be reached by the secretary to establish an appointment that is within a short period of time from the initial call, *we will use the lockbox* if you give your approval. If it is quite a few hours off, we will continue to try to reach you and/or the listing agent before showing the home.

6. If you are planning on being away for a period of more than a day and a night, it is wise to *let your listing agent know, and leave a key* (if no lockbox) and forwarding number that would enable him or her to reach you for an offer.

7. Inform your listing agent of *specific instructions regarding an animal* being confined, cards left by agents in specific places, or special notes of interest so he or she can make a note on the appointment book and on the listing agreement.

8. Most *real estate agents try to be punctual.* However, there will be times when, because of previous appointments running overtime, they may be late. We hope it will not happen, but we want to prepare you for the possibility.

9. Occasionally *an agent may have to cancel an appointment*—if a buyer is late or has changed appointments, it becomes necessary. We always request that our secretary call you and inform you as quickly as possible.

10. A *sales associate may preview your home* after calling for an appointment. The agent may have a client coming into town or may be working with him in the near future, and he or she wants to be prepared.

11. A *stranger may come to your door* and ask to see the home (either from an ad and/or the yard sign), I suggest that you not let anyone in and that you call your real estate agent and refer this person to him or her.

12. *All real estate agents should have business cards.* If a seller does not know if an agent has been there (at times they may forget), agents should leave a note on the back of their business card.

13. Most *real estate agents have cell phones.* Occasionally they may phone for an appointment and be right in front of your house! Try to be as accommodating as you can. The buyers may be from out of town and not able to come back to see your home.

14. *Give your agent special instructions* regarding security systems, lights left on, or pets left out; your listing agent will inform the secretary of these special instructions.

You have selected us so that we may obtain a sale for you as quickly as possible. *Our ultimate goal is a sold sign.* We ask for your patience and understanding as we attempt to accomplish this goal.

Monthly Listing Update

Dear Seller:

This is a monthly update to familiarize you with the market today.

There are currently _____ homes for sale in your area.

There are currently _____ homes sold in your area.

There are currently _____ homes expired in your area.

There have been _____ showings on your home.

Other agent comments:

Price high: _____   Number of agents: _____

Price low: _____   Number of agents: _____

Price OK: _____   Number of agents: _____

Agents' comments: (number of agents) _____

Interior condition: poor: _____ average: _____ excellent: _____

Exterior condition: poor: _____ average: _____ excellent: _____

Seller's comments:

_____

_____

_____

Please return in the self-addressed envelope as soon as possible.

Thank you for your cooperation.

Sincerely,

Barbara Nash

Real Estate Agent

Ten Best Ways to Secure a Price Reduction

1. Do an in-depth market analysis of the current solds that are most comparable to the subject property.
2. Tell your seller the truth about everything regarding the property.
3. Give the property a maximum of 30 days at one specific price.
4. Get a signed agreement for a price reduction (if home is overpriced at start) for 30 days from the start of the listing.
5. Meet with the sellers every 30 days regarding the pricing of the property.
6. Keep accurate records of phone discussions and meetings with the seller regarding lowering the price. Send copies to the seller with articles regarding overpricing.
7. Have a Realtors® open and invite your fellow agents to leave their card with a recommended price of the subject property.

> 8. Remind the seller of the three things that sell a property fastest:
>   a. **location**
>   b. **price**
>   c. **condition**

9. Keep records of all showings and comments and relate them to the seller along with recommendations regarding the price in 30 days. Statistics show that 65 percent of overpriced listings sell at reduced price.
10. If all else fails and seller STILL will not lower the price: Mail the seller a letter stating that you have included two forms. One is a price reduction and the other is a cancellation. An overpriced property is not going to sell. Time is of the utmost importance and no one benefits from a "stale listing." If they are not willing to sign the price reduction form, it is best they sign the cancellation.

Sixty-Day Listing Action Plan

Following is a plan of action to sell a home quickly. Have your client check either yes or no in the appropriate sections and return to you as soon as possible.

	YES	NO
Have we presented an offer in writing to you in the last 60 days?	☐	☐
Have homes sold in your area in the last 60 days that you are aware of?	☐	☐
If so, has your agent made you aware of these sales?	☐	☐
Do you know of, or has your agent made you aware of, any qualified buyers who can make an offer on your home at the present time?	☐	☐
In the last 60 days, have you made the terms or conditions to a buyer more favorable?	☐	☐
Have you changed the condition or the appearance of your home in any way in the last 60 days?	☐	☐
Have you lowered the price significantly in the last 60 days?	☐	☐

If you answer no to the majority of these questions, it is time for us to meet to make an appropriate adjustment in the marketing strategy for your property.

Please return this form to me in the *self-addressed enclosed envelope* with any additional comments you may have.

Thank you for your time in responding to my questions.

Seller Net Sheet

SELLER'S NAME: _____

Address of property: _____

Date of presented offer: _____

Offering price:	$ _____
Mortgage balance:	$ _____
Interest adjustment:	$ _____
Contract for deed balance:	$ _____
Interest adjustment on contract for deed:	$ _____
Home improvement loans:	$ _____
Taxes owed:	$ _____
Special assessments:	$ _____
Deed tax owed:	$ _____
Abstract extension:	$ _____
Recording fees:	$ _____
New mortgage points:	$ _____
Real estate fee:	$ _____
Water/sewage connection fee:	$ _____
VA/FHA fees:	$ _____
Soil test:	$ _____
Inspection fee:	$ _____
Approximate selling fees:	$ _____
Final equity to seller: TOTAL	$ _____

Fill this form out at listing presentation.

New Listing

Items to bring to listing presentation

1. Company brochure
2. Newsworthy information about your company
3. Your brochure
4. Your city map
5. School information in seller's area
6. Information from any moving company
7. Helpful home-selling hints sheet
8. Map book sheet of home location and other homes for sale marked with red X
9. Computer printout of CMA on property
10. Subject property's photo on folder exterior
11. Marketing plan for the seller
12. Promotional ad of yourself (from newspaper)

I tried this...and the seller was impressed!

Listing Service Record

Property Address:

_____

_____

Owner: _____ Phone: _____

Date	Time	Prev	Agent Name	Company	Office No	L.B. Given	Canc	Comments

Seller's Acknowledgment Statement of Home Condition

*Seller fills out this form.

Property Address: _____

Date Listed: _____

When did you buy the home? _____

How long have you lived here? _____

Have you ever had a fire, flood, or disaster at this property?   YES ☐   NO ☐

Comments: _____

Details: _____

What is the age and condition of your roof?

Age: _____ Condition: _____

Has there ever been ice buildup?   YES ☐   NO ☐

Have you ever replaced/repaired the roof?   YES ☐   NO ☐

Details: _____

Comments on heat, plumbing, electrical systems:

Are they and will they be in working order at closing?

	YES	NO		YES	NO		YES	NO
OVEN	☐	☐	ELEC. SYSTEM	☐	☐	VENT FANS	☐	☐
HOOD	☐	☐	HOT WATER HEAT	☐	☐	SUMP PUMP	☐	☐
MICROWAVE	☐	☐	GARBAGE DISPOSAL	☐	☐	PLUMBING SYSTEM	☐	☐
DISHWASHER	☐	☐	SPRINKLER SYSTEM	☐	☐	PRIVATE WELL	☐	☐
CENTRAL HEAT	☐	☐	FURNACE HUMIDIFIER	☐	☐	PRIVATE SEWER	☐	☐
SUPP HEAT	☐	☐	WATER SOFTENER	☐	☐	T.V. ANT.	☐	☐
CENTRAL AIR	☐	☐	ELECT PURIF	☐	☐	INTERCOM	☐	☐
WALL AIR	☐	☐	GARAGE OPENER	☐	☐	FIREPLACE	☐	☐
			ALL CONTROLS	☐	☐			

Comments: _____

Condition of trees (any infected, diseased, etc.)   YES ☐   NO ☐   Explain: _____

_____

Insulation:

Does insulation contain urea formaldehyde foam?   YES ☐   NO ☐

Date insulation installed: _____ Company: _____

Known defects in home: _____

_____

Seller's signature _____   Date: _____

Buyer's signature _____   Date: _____

New Listing Property Information

7326 west 14th street

Quail Ridge is an exceptionally quiet, quaint, and friendly neighborhood.

There is a neighborhood directory, neighborhood crime watch, neighborhood fun days, and picnics at the park for neighborhood children and parents.

There are outstanding schools, such as Olson Elementary, which was nominated as an honorary school of excellence, and Jefferson High School.

The home is nestled on a lot abundant with wildlife, ducks in the pond, and deer in the backyard. The home backs up to park and trails.

There are six neighborhood babysitters.

This home is on the Sedqwick Blue Plan and has the furnace and the air conditioning checked twice a year.

The exterior of the home is maintenance free, upgraded in dryvit outsulation. There is no fading, no staining, and no cracking.

There is a central vacuum system.

7326 west 14th street

The builder of this home was Ace Construction, a top builder in the metropolitan area.

The upgrades include beautiful Princeton trim on the door and windows.

The formal living room and dining room have sensational skylights.

There are many children of all ages, and several kids in college and high school.

Seldom is a home offered with so many upgrades, additional built-ins, and the best in quality workmanship available.

Photo of Listed Property

PHOTO

1. When creating a highlight sheet for a new listing:
   a. Be as descriptive as possible.
   b. Write about the home with enthusiasm.
   c. Show where the home is located.
   d. Tell about the highlights.
   e. Take a color photo of the property and have a printer to make the highlight sheets.
   f. Glue the rest of the color pictures you have developed (at least 75) on the highlight sheets.

2. a. Be sure *the top agents in the office get one of your highlight sheets on the home.*
   b. *Mail highlight sheets* to other top agents at competing companies.
   c. Mail highlight sheets to some good buyers who you think may like the home.

3. Put at least 40 to 50 highlight sheets at the property and in the brochure box outside of the house.

   Total personal expense should be approximately $50.

Home Profile

$269,900

Offered by _____

Barbara Nash
Bus. (612) # _____
Res. (612) # _____

Information deemed reliable
but not guaranteed.

PHOTO

Highlights

Exceptional townhome in
Cedar Trails with land included!
Wonderful floor plan with floor-
to-ceiling living room windows
accented by white brick
fireplace, new carpeting, and
wonderful window treatments.
New wallpaper in great kitchen
with planning desk and perfect
eating area. The second floor
has very large bedrooms with
huge walk-in closet in the
master bedroom, plus access
to full bathroom. Second floor
laundry room and additional
storage closets! A once-in-a-
lifetime opportunity for privacy
and maintenance-free living.

Home

Approximate room sizes in this
fine home include:

- Living Room 13×9
- Dining Room 9×11
- Master Bedroom 10×18
- Bedroom (2nd) 11×12
- Taxes: $583.00
- Square Footage: 1,232
- Assoc. Dues: $90.00/mo.
- BBQ: owned by seller

Property

This property is located in one
of the most sought-after areas
of St. Louis Park. It is within
close proximity of shopping,
restaurants, and is five minutes
from downtown exits. These
are exceptional homes, and
the townhome maintenance is
outstanding. The amenities are
too numerous to name, with a
lovely private deck accenting a
double garage. All appliances
convey with the property.
The current owner's care and
upgrading within the interior of
this fine townhome are evident.

Home Profile

$152,900

Offered by _____

Barbara Nash

Bus. (612) # _____

Res. (612) # _____

Information deemed reliable but not guaranteed.

PHOTO

Highlights

Welcome to this beautiful custom-built, split-foyer home at the foothills of Indian Hills. The property is adjacent to the most conveniently located area of Edina between Highway 18 and Gleason Road. The lovely floor plan flows from the moment you enter to view neutral decorator tones throughout and excellent carpeting. Absolutely perfect floor plan includes formal dining and eat-in kitchen with separate planning desk and all built-in appliances! A feeling of warmth and pride are reflected throughout every spacious room, showing care and concern for home ownership.

Home

Approximate room sizes in this fine home include:

- Living Room   22 × 13
- Dining Room   12 × 10
- Kitchen   12 × 8
- Eating Area   9 × 8
- Family Room   20 × 13
- Bedroom #1   13 × 12
- Bedroom #2   12 × 11
- Bedroom #3   11 × 10
- Fam. Rm. (lower)   18 × 12
- Addl. Room   13 × 12
- Taxes: $6,746.48 (1999 HS)
- Lot size: 132 × 130
- Year Built: 1965
- Total Square feet: 1,700
- Total interior square feet: 2,310

Property

Special features of this home include:

- Beautiful first-floor family room with lovely window treatment and walkout to delightful private rear yard.
- Two beautiful brick fireplaces. One is located in formal living room and one is located in lower-level family room.
- Lower level is ideal for entertaining, with separate area for small game table and additional area for larger furniture placement around beautiful brick fireplace. Lovely daylight windows perfect for children!
- A tremendous opportunity for fine family living at its best!

Home Profile

$279,900

Offered by _____

Barbara Nash
Bus. (612) # _____
Res. (612) # _____

Information deemed reliable
but not guaranteed.

PHOTO

Highlights

WELCOME TO AN
INCREDIBLE HOME! This
property is located in the heart
of the Braemar area near the
base of Indian Hills. THE BEST
LOCATION … The property
was originally custom built with
the finest quality and has been
COMPLETELY RENOVATED.
THERE IS A BRAND NEW
KITCHEN with custom
cabinetry, new ceramic floor,
new appliances, and beautiful
decorator wall coverings.
CLASSIC LINES prevail in the
extraordinary FAMILY ROOM,
with vaulted ceilings and floor-
to-ceiling glass accented by
oak-pegged floor completely
REFINISHED. EVERY bathroom
is COMPLETELY NEW.
The entire interior reflects
WONDERFUL WHITE tones
complemented by wonderful
window placement. There is a
gorgeous lower level featuring
upgraded OFFICE WITH BUILT-
INS galore and two BRs.

Home

Approximate room sizes in this
fine home include:

- Living Room 13×18
- Family Room 18×18
- Kitchen 12×9
- Formal DR 10×11
- Master Bedroom 12×18
- 2nd Bedroom 11×13
- 3rd Bedroom 10×11
- Office 12×14
- Amusement Room
                       16×31
- Lower BR 11×11
- Lower BR 11×15
- Built: 1987
- Taxes 1999: $4,347.00
- Fireplaces: 3

Property

This custom-built beautiful
home has been totally
renovated, including every
room on every floor! THERE
IS gorgeous new carpeting
throughout the main level
with upgraded NEW BERBER
CARPET IN THE LOWER
LEVEL. BRAND NEW CEDAR
SPLIT-SHAKE ROOF, BRAND
NEW FURNACE. ALL WALLS
HAVE BEEN FRESHLY
PAINTED OR COVERED.
The lower level also features
a beautiful eight-person
sauna, plus two additional
bedrooms and office, as well
as storage room, utility room,
and wonderful lower-level
entertainment room with
BRICK FIREPLACE. THERE IS
ALSO AN INTERCOM SYSTEM.
This unique property backs
up to SOLID WOODS and
is nestled on a prestigious,
quiet CUL-DE-SAC location.
It is a property that is TRULY
DISTINGUISHED, loaded with
amenities and class. THERE IS
ABSOLUTELY NOTHING TO
DO EXCEPT MOVE IN!

Home Profile

$389,000

Offered by _____

Barbara Nash
Bus. (612) # _____
Res. (612) # _____

Information deemed reliable
but not guaranteed.

PHOTO

Highlights

Welcome to this custom-built,
two-story executive home
adjacent to 1,000-acre Hyland
Park Preserve, Hyland Hills Ski
area, and Mt. Normandale Lake.
Enjoy the deer in your backyard
as they walk through the woods!

This home, located on a quiet
cul-de-sac, is within 15 minutes
of the airport and 20 minutes
of downtown, yet feels like a
country location with the park
that has walking and cross-
country ski trails, and the lake
with its public beach.

Enjoy the wooded backyard and
private setting with the 38 × 17
inground pool and 6-person hot
tub surrounded by 900 + sq. ft.
of decking and low-voltage
lighting. Extensive landscaping,
a security system, and
underground sprinkling system
add to the amenities of this fine
home. Also enjoy downtown
skyline views from the MASTER
BATH jacuzzi!

Home

Approximate room sizes in this
fine home include:

- Living Room   16.5 × 12.5
- Dining Room   14 × 11.6
- Kitchen   13.7 × 10.3
- Eating Area   15.7 × 9.6
- Family Room   20.7 × 15.5
- Screened Porch   16 × 12
- Master Bedroom   17 × 16
- Bedroom #2   14 × 11.7
- Bedroom #3   13.6 × 10.6
- Bedroom #4   16.6 × 13
- Game Room   32 × 13.6
- Amusement Room
    20.7 × 15.5
- 1999 Homestead Taxes:
  $6,746.48
- Lot size:
  81 × 155 × 120 × 173
- Year Built: 1999
- Main floor sq. footage:
  1,712 approx.
- Total finished sq. footage:
  4,000 approx.

Property

Special features of this home
include:

- Country kitchen with
  center island, Jenn Air, and
  large eating area
  overlooking pool.
- Master bedroom suite has
  remodeled bath with
  jacuzzi tub and the largest
  walk-in closet you have
  ever seen with maximum
  space organized!
- Family room with brick
  fireplace and built-in
  bookcases.
- Oak-pegged hardwood
  floor in dining room.
- Lower level ideal for
  entertaining with game
  room and 2nd family room
  with another fireplace and
  daylight windows—perfect
  for children!
- 4th bedroom on lower
  level ideal for live-in help
  with its own full bath.
- Large main-floor
  laundry—loads of storage
  throughout!
- Panoramic views of Hyland
  Hills ski area from many
  rooms!

Home Profile

$340,000

Offered by _____

Barbara Nash
Bus. (612) # _____
Res. (612) # _____

Information deemed reliable but not guaranteed.

PHOTO

Highlights

Absolutely exceptional New England Tudor loaded with charm and character throughout! There is a main floor family room with handsome hardwood floors off front foyer. Perfect breakfast room accents delightful kitchen with an abundance of cabinet space and work area. Huge formal living room boasts full-wall picture window and beautiful fireplace, plus quiet den is the highlight room adjacent to living room/dining room. The second floor features three lovely bedrooms, each with a character and flavor of its own. Two bathrooms and separate exit to huge full-size deck above the garage, which is double and attached to the property. This very unique home is situated on a quiet corner lot in prime country club location.

Home

Approximate room sizes in this fine home include:

- Living Room 14×27
- Dining Room   Included
- Kitchen 18×19
- Family Room 15×14
- Main Den 8×10
- Master Suite 14×19
- 2nd Bedroom 12×14
- 3rd Bedroom 12×13
- Amusement Room
                       13×26
- Lower Bedroom 12×14
- Taxes: $5,445
- Lot size: $81 \times 155 \times 120 \times 173$
- Year Built: 1978
- Main Square Feet: 1,115
- Total Square Feet: 2,078

Property

Special features of this home include:

This property is located in one of the most sought-after areas of the country club. It is within blocks of the Edina shopping, theater, and library. Exceptional upper-bracket quality homes surround the property. The home is nestled on a prestigious corner lot, exemplifying pride of ownership throughout. The amenities are too numerous to list, and extra quality improvements have been made by the current owners, reflecting definite care and upgrading within the interior of this fine home.

Monthly Review Listing Sheet

Agent's name: _____

Company: _____

Phone: _____

Property address: _____ Phone: _____

Date property listed: _____ Expires: _____

Today's date reviewed: _____

Summary of activity:

Toured by agents: _____

Agent's comments (tour):

_____

_____

Agent's feeling about price:

_____

_____

Listing agent's comments:

_____

_____

Price reductions:

_____

_____

Open Houses:

Date: _____ Date: _____

Date: _____ Date: _____

Showings: _____ _____

_____ _____

_____ _____

Feedback Fax on Showings

Agent photo

Company name: _____

Company # _____

Kindly inform us as to
your opinion and your
customer's opinion of
the home at:

_____

_____

Opinion:

_____

_____

Price: OK: _____ High: _____ Low: _____

Showing agent

Name and Phone _____

_____

_____

Listings on the Web

A lot has changed in the twenty-first century, and with these changes come new opportunities to list and sell property. A lot of people feel that the Internet has become the Multiple Listing Service with everyone being able to participate. Agents are now able to sell and promote their properties on their own websites.

The better designed the website is, the more opportunity an agent has to offer their skills to a prospective seller. Agents are competing more and more for listings by impressing the seller with various LINKS TO OTHER SITES than by just how INTERESTING THEIR OWN SITE IS.

A real estate agent's website should address:

- NEEDS OF THE BUYER—PURCHASE PROPERTY ON WEB
- NEEDS OF THE SELLER—LIST PROPERTY ON THE WEB
- LATEST MORTGAGE INFORMATION
- ACCESS TO CURRENT HOMES FOR SALE
- LATEST HOUSING TIPS
- LATEST REAL ESTATE ARTICLES
- VIRTUAL TOURS
- MOVING COMPANY INFORMATION
- SCHOOL INFORMATION
- NEWSPAPER LINK

Listing property has become a one-step process over the Internet. An agent should have a LISTING CONTRACT ON FILE IN HIS OR HER COMPUTER. At this point, should a prospective client wish to:

How to list a property on the internet

1. compose an e-mail to client
2. hit "Attach"
3. find LISTING file
4. click "Open"
5. send e-mail

Seller receives listing agreement via e-mail within minutes.

LISTING PROPERTY OVER THE INTERNET IS ESSENTIAL!

A recent study by the National Association of REALTORS® found that most REALTORS® use the Internet for business, and that their income is one-third higher than REALTORS® who don't use the Internet. Real estate agents with their OWN WEBPAGES have EVEN HIGHER incomes. It is estimated that 90 percent of home buyers use the Internet for house hunting to find a new listing.

An agent can LIST HOMES and sell homes over the Net by designing their own website for under $1,000.

Feedback Fax on Showings

Company Name

Company No.

Date

Time

Kindly inform us
of your opinion and your
customer's opinion of
the home at:

(555-5555)

My photo goes here!

_____

_____

Opinion: _____

_____

_____

Price: OK _____ High: _____ Low: _____

Showing Agent

Name and Phone: _____

_____

_____

Date Shown: _____

Time Shown: _____

Chapter Summary

You are never really in the real estate business until you have your own listings. In order to simply make ends meet, you must list two to four homes and sell two to four homes monthly. When visiting a seller's home, bring seven things with you for a new listing: a partially filled out listing agreement, your measuring tape, your net sheet, your promotional brochure, a lockbox, your laptop for doing CMAs and your camera. There are three characteristics that guarantee a listing: honesty, enthusiasm, and application.

Ask for the listing! Don't leave the seller's house without scheduling an appointment to come back. Above all, ask for the listing now! The majority of agents that come through a seller's house do not ask outright for the listing. Take lots of notes; ask lots of questions; write down everything. Take a photo of the home and ask for the listing! A detailed marketing plan has always been the finishing touch to getting any listing. A specific marketing plan gives the real estate agent credibility. Prepare an in-depth CMA and take a color photo. Fill out the listing carefully, and when you have completely finished it, go back over it and check it all out again. Try not to leave any part of the listing blank. Prepare a highlight sheet to be left at the property.

Be sure to give your seller a monthly update. Do an in-depth market analysis of the current solds that are most comparable for a price reduction. Keep records of all showings and comments. Follow a "60 Day Listing Action Plan." Carefully calculate the sellers net takeaway on all offers.

A lot of people feel that the Internet has become the Multiple Listing Service with everyone being able to participate. Listing Property over the Internet is essential! An agent can LIST HOMES and sell homes over the Net by designing their own website.

CHAPTER 11

SENIORS ON THE MOVE: THE NICHE MARKET

big deal by Lorayne n' Neil

The housing market is about to experience a gigantic boom in the senior market. There is no question that home buyers are changing in age and needs. Seniors are dominating the market today, and they will continue to do so. The real estate agent's primary customer listings are senior clients. For this reason, the real estate agent of today cannot continue in a business-as-usual mode.

However the senior market phenomenon will allow dynamic real estate agents an opportunity to capitalize and acquire new business if they learn to go after this important market.

Migration of Seniors

There is a migration of seniors who still wish to remain independent. They want to live in their own new homes. These seniors want to leave their long-time homes and move into new ones. Some seniors may choose to downsize due to smaller incomes or because they do not want to use up their children's inheritance. Some seniors choose to move to better-suited climates because the elements of the different seasons have become overwhelming for them. Still other seniors have lost many of their close friends and now desire to live closer to family members or in communities of other seniors with whom they can make friends.

The American Association of Homes and Services for the Aging has recently reported that more and more seniors are traveling great distances to locate themselves near family members. They want to be assured that in case things go awry, they are close to family members who will act as caregivers or help them arrange for care.

Over the next 25 years, the population of those over 65 years of age will soar. In just a few years, more than 20 percent of the population will be over 65. Furthermore, the Association reports that the number of seniors between the ages of 65 and 85 will double. This statistic is even more significant in light of the fact that the overall life expectancy continues to rise for both men and women. Millions of Americans are enjoying healthy and productive lives long after the age of 65 and upon retirement from full-time employment.

So if it is a fact that independent seniors are uprooting themselves, placing their homes up for sale, and sometimes moving across the country to other states, then a new market is blooming. Seniors are searching for new friendships, security, and peace of mind. These new migrants are earnestly seeking living options that fulfill their needs for happiness and joy within their shrinking means. There is no question that the senior market is attractive for the successful real estate agent of the future.

A More In-Depth Needs Assessment

The senior listings and the sale of long-standing dwellings is a brand new ballgame. The typical needs assessment of the home buyer and the seller of the past was simple compared to those of these new clients. It may not be enough to get a quick start by asking them, "How much do you want for your present home?" and "How much do you want to spend on your new residence?" For seniors a quick discussion of "How much" may only add to their anxiety and fears. The seniors' real estate specialist may want to ask many more pertinent questions before even getting into pricing issues. This is not to say that these criteria are insignificant, but more important issues may need to be considered first.

Need for specialized senior market agents (S.R.E.S.)

Elderly home owners and sellers need special help relocating and dealing with the emotional turmoil of this dramatic change. Some seniors agonize over the questions such as: "Where should I move?" "What should I do?" and "Who will help me?" Some agents describe seniors as "first-time buyers." Just recently a veteran broker from southern California reported that there is a growing need for agents to become members of the Seniors Real Estate Specialists (S.R.E.S.), which was first organized in 1997. Probably the main reason the seniors' specialized training is needed is due to the more intense counseling role of the agent-senior client relationship.

To obtain senior-specialist credentials, agents must complete a two-day training course given by the Senior Advantage Real Estate Counsel. This course covers tax laws, probate, estate planning, and senior counseling, and it teaches agents to work with a professional in each of these areas. It may also cover generation differences and ways to market to this senior population. Age-specific services such a finding second homes, turning them into primary residences, or using home equity to finance retirement are rapidly growing areas of concern. As the population matures and more and more baby boomers retire, real estate agents are wise to capitalize on servicing the needs of this special senior market.

Servicing the senior market needs

The following guidelines are essential for agents serving the senior buyer/seller market.

- Seniors should be enlightened to envision the future in order to get an idea of the kind of community they want to live in.
- Seniors should be made aware of "target towns" and visit those of interest—the grocery stores, places of religious worship, community centers, shopping centers, and so on. All of these places will help them meet new people. These are all the factors to be considered in the seniors search for new living options.
- Seniors should be encouraged to be selective regarding the possessions that they wish to move with them. An agent can suggest to their senior clients to begin the mental process of sorting out items for sale and items to leave behind. This process should be ongoing and begin before the actual selection of housing facilities and seniors services. The important issue is: "How can I downsize?"
- Seniors should be reminded constantly to look positively to their new future. They should shift their thinking away from what they are leaving behind to what they can look forward to in this new adventure.
- An agent for seniors should consider gently approaching the subjects of health issues, financial setbacks, mental deterioration, and other unanticipated situations.
- The seniors' real estate agent should learn to address and to expect client resistance. It will take some patience for the agent to allow the senior buyer/seller time to get used to the idea of moving. The agent's patience and consideration early in the relationship will only make the client's selection less random and more focused in the long run. Agents will benefit from such consideration.
- Discussing a detailed plan with each senior client is critical. The experienced S.R.E.S. demonstrates a professional counseling approach to the seniors' needs assessment. Senior clients (like all other buyers/sellers) have individual needs. The agent needs to help the senior verbalize those needs. To help seniors find a new place, secure movers, sort through and decide what to keep and what to discard—all are part of the seniors' buying and selling ball game. The agent becomes more and more endearing when the client receives the benefit of the agent's experience. The agent may make recommendations on sales, help them update records and plan the actual move. The wise agent does not try to rush the client. This move, later in life, is definitely a traumatic one.

- The real estate agent should not be afraid to ask the senior client some tough questions such as, "How long do you think your savings will last?" "Will your savings support your retirement lifestyle?" "Do you have a fall-back retirement plan in case you run out of money?" An S.R.E.S. can provide the senior client with recommendations for financial planning if need be. Also, suggesting other sources of help, such as doctors, dentists, churches, hospitals, insurance companies, and financial planners, can help the senior clients immensely.

In summary, it is important to note that the needs assessment phase of the senior buyer/seller client may be the most important factor in closing listings. The senior real estate specialist's biggest challenge is to help their client feel at ease and comfortable about this emotional move. A client who feels that the senior agent will help them with their real estate needs is valuable in itself. However, the agent who is attentive to the anxiety caused by the client's lifestyle change will be the agent chosen for the listing. The senior client is often nervous and has feelings of uncertainty. The senior client needs to trust this new professional entering his or her life.

Perhaps the biggest mistake an agent can make is to assume that all their senior clients have the same needs and only want to move into retirement housing, assisted living, or age-restricted communities.

Lumping all seniors' into the same needs category just because of their age is not any more practical than lumping any other age group's needs. All individuals have unique needs.

Why are senior citizens as new home buyers so important?

> Because the aging population is one of the most important demographic rising trends of this century!

- Over the next 25 years the population of those over 65 will soar!
- More than 20 percent of the population will soon be over 65 years old!
- Millions of Americans are enjoying healthy, productive lives after reaching retirement age.
- For most seniors, THEIR HOME IS THEIR PRIMARY ASSET, and it has appreciated dramatically over the past 20 years!
- Increasing numbers of seniors are now GOING BACK TO WORK!
- SENIORS are seeking to simplify their lifestyle in smaller homes, one-story homes, condos, retirement communities, or areas that are closer to their children.
- Seniors are likely to receive public and private pensions.

Attitudes that shape SENIORS' decisions in LIFE:

a. Personal responsibility to fulfill financial debt.
b. Traditional attitude towards saving, spending and investing.
c. Seniors value work over leisure and saving over spending.

AMERICANS ARE LIVING LONGER AND ENJOYING A MUCH HIGHER
STANDARD OF LIVING GOING INTO THEIR 60s, 70s AND 80s.

Fortunately for most Americans, the recent rise in national home ownership rates (which
has increased in the past few years over 66%) has been associated with the sharp appreciation
of home values.

Most SENIORS will rely on FOUR things to live into retirement years:

1. Social Security benefits
2. Bank savings and mutual funds/stocks, etc.
3. Pension retirement income
4. Part-time employment

NOTEWORTHY: THE VAST MAJORITY OF ALL
SENIORS HAVE NO MORTAGE TO PAY OFF!

What Are the Senior Client's Options?

Since the senior buyer/seller has a myriad of choices as they prepare for retirement, the
S.R.E.S. now has an even more important role in the senior's transitional period.

This new venture for senior clients needs to be viewed now as more than a financial
investment. Their long-standing home is now synonymous with years spent raising a family
and personal ties to community. The S.R.E.S. who has demonstrated the knowledge, patience,
and expertise in advising seniors is now ready to present the variety of options available to
them when making their life-changing decisions.

Types of Senior Housing Facilities
and Services

The S.R.E.S. can introduce the senior client to a list of the following choice options for
housing and services.

Adult day care

A cost-effective alternative to live-in care—this care offers a safe environment for adults
during daytime hours to participate in social activities, nutritional, nursing, and
rehabilitation services.

Independent living

This is an excellent choice for seniors who do not require personal or medical care and who would prefer to live alone or at home. Facilities are equipped with standard safety features. Seniors would be with others who have similar interests and needs. Community-planned recreational activities include day field trips, shopping excursions, and on-premise projects. Many facilities offer optional meal plans for their residents, and most of the apartments come equipped with a kitchen so seniors can prepare their own meals. Independent living facilities are also known as senior apartments, retirement communities, and congregate living.

Assisted living

People who choose not to live on their own, but do not necessarily require 24-hour care can choose an assisted-living option. Assisted-living facilities have a homelike atmosphere with trained professionals who are available to help residents with their daily routines. On-and-off premise activities are arranged for the seniors. This living option is also known as residential care, personal care, and also adult congregate.

Nursing homes

People who can no longer live independently and require 24-hour care may choose a nursing home. Nursing homes offer 24-hour-a-day care. They are equipped with medical professionals along with supplies. They are trained to offer specialized care for those with severe illnesses or injuries. Trained staff can assist seniors with personal and daily activities, such as getting out of bed, bathing, eating, using the restroom, and dispensing medications. Daily meal plans, laundry, housekeeping, medical services, and many planned recreational activities are offered by nursing homes. Following is a brief description of services provided to patients by nursing home staff.

Medical

Many facilities require residents to be treated by their own physicians. Every community should have a doctor who is available on a 24-hour emergency basis. If a nursing home has a staff doctor, the agent should find out how often he or she visits and monitors the seniors. If a staff doctor has access to the senior's medical records, he or she may set up a treatment plan for the resident. The nursing home usually upholds a legally competent resident's right to have the final say in any matter affecting his or her health.

Hospitalization

Each nursing home must have an arrangement and procedure with a nearby hospital to handle patients who become seriously ill. The agent should inform the senior as to how the nursing home will handle such emergencies, including transportation, paramedic first aid, etc.

Nursing services

A registered nurse (RN) should be directing nursing services. RNs are assisted by licensed practical or vocational nurses (LP/VN) who have at least one year of specialized training. Those who assist the seniors with bathing, eating, dressing, and so on are called nurse aids and assistants. They are supervised by licensed nurses.

Physical therapy

If a senior should need assistance in regaining lost abilities such as walking, talking, or dressing, the agent will find out whether the facility has adequate, qualified physical therapists on staff.

Grooming

The agent will inform the seniors as to the availability of to barbers, beauticians, and other grooming services, including hair washing, manicures and pedicures, and so on.

Activities

The agent may want to ask what types of activities are offered, such as games, movies, crafts, classes, field trips, and so on.

Social services

The agent should help with the adjustment process and provide community and financial resource information. A social worker or community staff may be on-site to help with this information.

Religious services

The specialist should help seniors arrange for an opportunity to attend the religious services of their choice and visit with the clergy of their respective faiths.

Continuing Care Retirement Communities

The seniors should be aware that people sometimes choose retirement communities comprised of an entire campus of living choices from private homes to assisted living and even skilled nursing facilities. This allows residents the opportunity to age in one community without having to relocate, since this type of facility provides a variety of housing, regardless of medical needs. To live in a CCRC, the senior may have to pay an entrance fee or "buy in." Also, monthly fees for rent, meals, and medical care may be assessed. Many times the community will have requirements to live there, such as age, income, health status, and/or financial assets. Types of residences that you may find at a CCRC include patio homes, apartments, studios, and a nursing facility.

Alzheimer's care

The agent should make their client aware that some facilities offer specialized care to those who suffer from memory-impairing diseases such as Alzheimer's and dementia. Some nursing homes and assisted-living facilities offer these specialized programs.

Active adult communities

Some seniors may want to consider active adult or senior rental communities where residents must be 55 years or older and sometimes 62 years or older to live there. Age-qualified adults who desire the maintenance-free lifestyle can enjoy an independent lifestyle in addition to social and recreational activities with older adults.

A Survey for Senior Housing Facilities

The S.R.E.S. may wish to use a short and simple senior survey instrument as a guide in getting the senior client to seriously consider choices of their progression and migration for senior living.

What are your choices for senior housing and services?

Independent living	Nursing homes
Assisted living	Retirement communities
Continuing care	Ranch home
Alzheimer's care	Townhome
Adult day care	Condominium
Active adult community	Ranch-style condominium
Apartment	Attached home
Senior Apartment	Ranch-style condominium
Real estate for sale	Detached home
Active adult community for age 55 and better	Master on the main two-story
Community for all ages	Basement home available
Manufactured home	Lake lots available
RV community	Golf course lots available

Closing in on the Senior Listing

Once the needs of the seniors have been thoroughly analyzed and they feel comfortable with their moving plan as well as their specialized real estate agent, the agent can now move ahead smoothly and close the listing. Of course, by this time in the process, the enlightened senior client recognizes that perhaps just any licensed agent could probably handle the actual real estate transaction. However, they also now know that the seniors' specialist who has the expertise in the 55+ marketplace is the best bet for their listing choice. The comfort level has been established. Because the senior buyer or seller may not have purchased a home for over 45 years, they now have confidence in making a purchase with an experienced real estate agent. Thirty-five years ago, when the senior purchased his or her first home, the actual listing may have been one page long. Today that contract is approximately 18 to 20 pages long.

The "prep" work of showing patience, consideration, and knowledge may well be the most important factor needed to close the senior listing. The senior feels comfortable as the real estate agent counsels them through the myriad of choices available to them. The anxiety diminishes and the buyer/seller is ready to sign the contract.

Chapter Summary

The real estate agent who specializes in the growing senior market will profit most in today's slow-moving housing market.

Business as usual is not the criteria for success for the real estate agent who decides to specialize in the over-55 age group.

- This agent thoroughly discusses and analyzes the over-all specific needs of the senior buyer/seller.
- This agent helps the senior client choose from the myriad of choices available to them.
- This agent is patient, thoughtful, and knowledgeable in the whole area of senior counseling.
- This agent knows that the choices in senior housing are attached closely to the senior's needs for services.
- This agent is willing to take the time necessary to prepare the over-55 age group for a dramatic life change.
- This agent is eager to get a listing, but knows that getting the senior listing demands rigorous prep work and lots of patience.

CHAPTER 12

OPEN HOUSES AND NEGOTIATING

big deal by Lorayne n' Neil

Here comes Lorayne! I'll pull the shades; she'll think no one's home. I'll sell this one myself!

The sellers just called. I told them no one was through...Next sunday I'll sell it myself!

This was the last sunday... The sellers took the home off the market.

Hi, Neil, I tried to show your "open house", but no one was home. We bought the one across the street.

How Important Are Open Houses?

OPEN HOUSES ARE A KEY FACTOR IN HAVING GREAT BUSINESS.

From the onset of my career to the present time, I have consistently tried to follow this rule:

TWO OPEN HOUSES EVERY WEEK
(unless a major holiday)

By keeping this type of schedule, I am able to maintain an active business that keeps giving me:

1. *adequate qualified buyers*
2. *my own listings to sell*
3. *fast safes*

I have appointments all week just from my two opens...

My Sunday *schedule* is usually similar to the following:

First open: 12:00 to 2:00 p.m.
Second open: 2:30 to 4:30 p.m.
or
First open: 1:00 to 3:00 p.m.
Second open: 3:30 to 5:30 p.m.

OPENS ARE BIG BUSINESS. Open houses are very big business if you know what to do.

You must have a *plan of action* before going to the house that is to be held open.

OPEN HOUSES REALLY DO KEEP YOU IN BUSINESS.

Open houses enable you to select good buyers and sellers to work with if you know how to qualify them!

I maintain that many of the people coming through open houses have an interest in relocating.

Choosing a good open house

How to pick a house to hold open:

1. Should be *PRICED TO SELL.*
2. Should be in an *AREA THAT YOU KNOW WELL.*
3. Should *GENERATE BUSINESS* automatically.
4. Should be in *GOOD CONDITION.*
5. Should be *EASILY ACCESSIBLE.*
6. Should be *FAIRLY NEW TO THE MARKET.*

Open houses will make you a lot of money only if you do your homework, preview the home before you hold it open, and know the area.

Open house plan of action

1. Preview the home.
2. Drive the neighborhood and look for other homes for sale.
3. Check the computer for solds in the neighborhood and expired listings that you may be able to call on.
4. Make highlight sheets from the computer listing if there are none at the property. Add a copy of your business card to the highlight sheet.
5. Bring 25 to 30 extra brochures about yourself to the home.
6. Bring your open house legal pad.
7. Make a computer printout Competitive Market Analysis (CMA) of the neighborhood using the map coordinates. This will give you all the active, sold, and expired listings in the area.
8. Do an AMS (Area Market Survey) of the neighborhood. This will tell you how long the properties take to sell and the average, high, and low selling prices in the neighborhood.
9. Decide where you will need to place signs ... you may need extras. Perhaps put out a sign saying the home will be open (example: "home will be open next Sunday afternoon").
10. Work on a good catchy ad—not too long, but specific and enthusiastic (example: just listed—1st open—no others like it).
11. Try to memorize what has sold in the neighborhood and know the home. People like to work with knowledgeable agents.
12. Go over the highlight sheet and the listing sheet on the subject property. Know pertinent information such as taxes, square footage, year built, lot size, and so on.
13. Wear a name tag.
14. Do not forget the names of people once they introduce themselves! Stand at the door with pen, pad, and home information in your left hand. When the people come, extend your right hand and say, "Hi, I'm from Real Estate Company and you are?" As they tell you their name, repeat it to them, "Oh, it's nice to meet you, Mr. and Mrs. _____." Now write it down; otherwise you will **forget** it.
15. Try to spend a short time showing them part of the house and give them some time to look alone.

HOLD OPEN HOUSES EVERY WEEKEND (SAT & SUN)

What to Do at an Open House

1. Make sure that *every light* in the house is *turned on.*
2. Make sure that all draperies, curtains, and blinds are *completely open.*
3. Make sure that the *kitchen is spotless*, dishes are out of sight, and towels are discreetly put away.
4. Perhaps put a *little vanilla* on the burner to give the hint of bread baking in the oven.
5. *Air freshener or potpourri* is refreshing. Cloves in an orange are also a nice twist.
6. *Some agents like to have cookies* and juice and some mints out on the table. This entices the people to spend a bit more time talking, and if there are children, it seems to appease them.
7. *Stay by the front door* and, *greet each person* as he or she enters; get their name and phone number.
8. *Do not have the television on.*
9. *Have some soft, soothing* background *music on.*
10. *Make sure your brochures are out* and visitors have to ask you for a highlight sheet on the property. I prefer to give them the information and then, if their interest persists, I hand them a highlight sheet.
11. *Ask all potential clients* if you can take a *look at their home.* Get their address.
12. *Ask them if you could meet them tomorrow* at your office to talk about other properties for sale in the area.
13. *Ask them if you could come over later* in the week to see their home and give them an idea of what it is worth.
14. *Try to make some kind of appointment* with potential clients who appear to be qualified buyers before they leave. Set an appointment in your day planner.
15. *Try to be relaxed*, friendly, professional, and interested in asking a few questions about their life in order to familiarize yourself with their particular situation.

Always bring your open house legal pad!

OPEN HOUSES WILL MAKE YOU A LOT OF MONEY IF YOU DO
YOUR HOMEWORK,
PREVIEW THE HOME BEFORE YOU HOLD IT OPEN,
AND KNOW THE AREA.
DO NOT FORGET THE NAMES OF PEOPLE ONCE THEY
INTRODUCE THEMSELVES!
WEAR A NAME TAG.

What to Do If an Open House Is Slow

What if no one comes through?

What if you have 2 ½ hours of just sitting and looking out of the window?

DON'T LET THAT HAPPEN!

How to make a slow open house work

1. *Work on your schedule* for the next week.
2. *Call and talk to a prospective buyer* while you are looking at the MLS book.
3. *Call and talk to a prospective seller* and set up an appointment to appraise his or her house.
4. *Go through the newspaper and clip the* FSBO ads.
5. *Call the FSBOs* closest to your open house. Try to make an appointment following your open.
6. *Call other FSBOs* and set up appointments for the rest of the week. (You should have your schedule in front of you.)
7. *Go through your daily planner* from the previous week or month and see if there are appointments or people you have forgotten or overlooked.
8. *Update* your *buyer list.*
9. *Update* your *seller list.*
10. *Work on a competitive market analysis* (CMA) for a seller.
11. *Balance* your *checkbook.*
12. *Pay* important *bills.*

…*And if you are in a real slump,* bring an inspirational book to read, such as *The Power of Positive Thinking.*

OTHER THINGS TO DO DURING SLOW OPENS

Check the computer for new listings in the area. Sold's Too!

- *Do not have the television on.*
- *Have some soft, soothing* background *music on.*
- *Review your sales volume* in the past months and replan.
- *Send out notes or postcards* to FSBOs and expireds.
- See how many appointments you can set up for the week.

Ways to Achieve the Best Open House

1. *Try to call the neighbors* ahead of time to invite them over to see the property and to introduce yourself.

2. *Distribute door-hangers* about the property being held open to neighbors in a four- to six-block radius three to five days before the open house.

3. *Put out at least four open house* signs.

4. *Have with you your MLS book,* your laptop computer, and a computer printout of the area's for sales and solds.

5. *Keep your legal pad for open houses* in your hand while greeting clients.

6. *Bring brochures* about yourself and your company with you to hand out to prospective clients.

7. *Know the properties that have sold* in the neighborhood of the home you are holding open.

8. *Know all the properties that are for sale* in the neighborhood of the home you are holding open.

9. *Be sincerely interested* in each and every client who comes through your open house by *asking them what their needs are.*

10. *Ask every person coming through* if you could stop by and see their home, or if they would prefer to come to your office to talk about their real estate needs.

Items to bring to an open house

a. calculator/camera/phone

b. amortization schedule

c. loan officer's name and work and home phone numbers

d. current mortgage rates

e. laptop computer

Look professional! Go to your open house dressed for success with a tailored, sleek, polished look that will give a new client a feeling of being with a professional.

Every open house has the potential for giving you a new listing and a new buyer or both in one client! Be prepared to acclimate yourself to whatever needs the potential client has.

REMEMBER: DON'T LET THEM LEAVE WITHOUT AN APPOINTMENT.

Ask *the client if you could come over* during the week to see their home and give them an idea of what it is worth. Get the appointment!

How to get the right names and numbers at open houses

1. *Keep your legal pad* with you at all times.

2. Try to get the names of all visitors, along with their address and phone number. As you are greeting the first arrivals, another couple may come right behind them. *Do not let the first couple pass by* without asking for and writing down their name. Then let them pass and go on to the next couple. (Get phone number if possible.)

3. When you are with the next couple, ask them the same question: *WHAT IS YOUR NAME, AND WHERE ARE YOU CURRENTLY LIVING?* Most people will give you this information without having to think about it. *I do not use a guest register sign-in* because many people do not write down their correct name.

4. Repeat their name as they give it to you so that you will have the spelling correct from the very start.

5. *Ask them up front* if they are just looking at homes and are really serious.

6. While people are walking through the home, try to catch up with them in the latter part of their tour. *ASK THEM THE FOLLOWING QUESTIONS:*

   a. How do you *like* the house so far?

   b. How does this home *compare* to your own home?

   c. Is this the *area* that you feel you would move to?

   d. Have you gotten an *estimate* on your own home?

   e. *How many* homes have you seen already?

   f. Would it work out if I were to *stop by* after my open house today to look at your property? Or, *I'll be in your area* tomorrow or Tuesday. Which would be a better time for me to stop by and see your home?

   g. Do you think you and your family could *enjoy living here?*

   h. Have you had anyone give you an idea of how you *would qualify?* Why don't we sit down for a minute so I could give you a brief idea of *how you qualify* for this property?

7. Always, always smile, be pleasant, and show that you enjoy selling real estate.

8. Use your laptop to e-mail clients and search the Web.

9. Use your laptop to send letters to clients.

10. Use your laptop to check updates for new listings.

Open House Dialogue

Now You Are Set . . .

The lights are on, the music is soft, there is a fresh clean aroma in the air, and your signs are strategically placed. *IT'S THAT TIME!*

A couple pulls up in front of the open house, and you watch as a man and a woman get out of the car and come up to the door.

1. You are standing at the door to *greet them.*
2. You have your *legal pad* in your left hand with a pen clipped to it.
3. The *highlight sheet* is on top of the legal pad for you to refer to.
4. You now *extend your right hand* and say to them:
   "Hi, I'm Barbara Nash from _____ Real Estate Company, and you are?"
5. As they tell you their name, *repeat it and write it down.*

Now tell them five brief facts about the property . . .

1. *The price of this home is _____.*
2. *It was built in _____ and has _____ square feet.*
3. *These owners are very motivated to sell because _____.*
4. *The taxes on this property are _____.*
5. *The improvements that have been made are _____. OR The improvements that need to be made are _____.*

   Why don't you look around a bit, and I will be right here to answer any questions you may have when you are finished.

The potential buyers will walk through the home, enabling you to do **two things:**

1. *Get ready for the next people* who are either coming to the door or have already arrived.
2. *Position yourself so you're available with the needed information* when they have finished looking.

Let's assume that these are the only potential clients at the property for the moment. They have finished walking through the home. Never go down to a basement with a client! Let them look on their own. Now they have come back and are about to . . .

...Walk out the front door!

You see that this is not the home for these people. Now what?

You walk over to them and ask them the ***following questions:***

1. *Is this the type of home that you are looking for?*
2. *Have YOU been looking* in this area for a long time?
3. *Do you know* of all the *good properties that are available* in this area?
4. *Which would be better for you*—tomorrow or the next day—for me to stop over to show you a few things and to take a look at your property?

OR

Why don't I stop over after my open house, to go through some numbers on which home could work for you?

OR

Why don't you come into my office either tomorrow after 5:00—or would after 7:00 be better for you?

OR

Let's get together at my office and we could see how you would qualify for a home that I think might be just perfect for both of you. Then we could run over and look at it.

Sometimes I forget their names!

At some point you will see just *how serious* these people are. Most people will not want you to come over or set up an appointment with them if they do not have any intention of buying. You will be able to sort out the good buyers early if you can determine *when to ask for an appointment* and how to narrow down whether or not the people you have just met really do want to buy a home *from you!*

How to "close" at an open house

Closing at an open house is asking for an appointment to:

1. get together to *qualify* potential buyers,
2. *look* at the buyer's existing property, and
3. obtain *loyalty* from the buyers.

I keep my open house legal pad with me as I meet people at the door. I write down the names...

On a busy open house day a potential client will go right from your open house to the next. Unless you have established some sort of relationship, you will lose these people to the next agent soliciting them.

ASK FOR AN APPOINTMENT BEFORE THEY LEAVE THE OPEN HOUSE!

Letter to Seller/Selling Agent

THANK YOU SO VERY MUCH!
IT WAS A PLEASURE SHOWING YOUR HOME TODAY!

_____ Held property open

_____ Showed client

_____ I previewed home

My feelings: _____

_____

My client's feelings: _____

_____

If my client decides to write an offer on your home, or if I have any questions, I will call your agent. Again, thank you.

Barbara Nash

Document Open House and Registration Form

Date:	Name:
Address:	Phone:
Time:	Combo:
Client #1	
Client #2	
Client #3	
Client #4	

4515 Morexal

Open 2:00 to 4:00 P.M.

65 people came through (five buyers, three sellers), five letters to send, three call-backs for Monday morning.

PHOTO

Opinions on house: priced right, should sell, "as is" condition, lovely decorating throughout.

Seven dialogues with clients. Passed out all brochures (ran out of highlight sheets), lots of neighbors through. Two people through listing with another agent. E. Doon will list on Chappel Lane 4/25—approx. $200,000 walkout rambler.

One lady, single—working with Mary H.

Open House: Sunday (2:00 to 4:00 P.M.)

4515 Morexal South

4BR-3 bath

2500 square feet

$339,900

People through the open: March 1

Lisa and Rod Benson live on Williamsburg, just like to look, bought a Cape Cod three years ago. (Not ready, just looking)

Andy and Ellen Tugar, N. Riverside Drive, apartment E, New York, NY 10020, phone: _____. Write to them. Husband just took job here, just sold apt. in New York, no children, highly motivated, send sheets immed. for + $325,000 suburbs. (A buyer)

Diane and John Pittapold renting, no home to sell, working with Babette B. of this company. Very interested, will probably write offer; call Babette.

Kathy Maertner, 500 Arden, 620-6493, likes house a lot, not quite right, call to look at her house. (A buyer)

Kent and Lyn Gregory, 450 Casco Rd. 920-0000, young couple renting. Told to drive by 532 Wood Drive. (Mildly interested: C buyer)

Everyone is welcome
to view this home!
However,
if you are currently
working with another
agent, please
notify me
as you enter.

Thank you.
Barbara Nash

Open House Profile

$324,900

Hosted by _____

Barbara Nash

Bus. (612) # _____
Res. (612) # _____

Information deemed reliable
but not guaranteed.

PHOTO

Highlights

Welcome to an incredible home! This property is located in the heart of QUAIL RIDGE WHICH IS AN UPPER-BRACKET EXCLUSIVE WOODED NEIGHBORHOOD KNOWN FOR FRIENDLY NEIGHBORS WHO SELDOM MOVE UNLESS TRANSFERRED! The owners have meticulously maintained this fine home from the fabulous family room on the first floor to the beautiful master bedroom suite on the second floor and throughout the entire decorator's interior boasting classic eclectic lines.

The home offers very private wooded views of nature, deer, and wildlife. Every window overlooks beauty and scenery not often viewed in home sites. This incredible QUAIL RIDGE location has easy access to both downtown Minneapolis as well as the airport, both of which are within 20 minutes driving time. Quail Ridge is an exclusive upper-bracket area boasting pride of ownership and upper-bracket properties.

Home

Approximate room sizes in this beautiful home:

- LIVING ROOM   16 × 18
- FAMILY ROOM   19 × 19
- KITCHEN   10 × 18
- INFORMAL DINING   9 × 13
- FORMAL DINING   11 × 13
- MASTER BED-ROOM SUITE   18 × 19
- BEDROOM #1   16 × 11
- BEDROOM #2   13 × 14
- LOWER BEDROOM   16 × 14
- OFFICE   15 × 15
- PORCH   15 × 15
- WALKOUT FAMILY ROOM   19 × 18
- Taxes: $6,000
- SQ. FEET: 1,500 main floor
- TOTAL SQ. FT.: 3,600
- YEAR BUILT: 1985
- LOT SIZE: APPROX. l/2 act

Property

Highlights of this fine home include: incredible first floor family room with corner brick fireplace and walkout to deck overlooking woods. Beautiful built-in wet bar with custom shelving. Wired for stereo. Wonderful window treatments. The classic kitchen is a Julia Child's delight with a sensational center island. Planning desk, inverted informal dining, and every conceivable appliance plus first-floor laundry room. Accented by perfect porch, full-length deck all overlooking wooded views plus beautiful parklands and tremendous trails!! The lower level is a paradise in pleasure. The accent is on four-person custom steam room with piped-in music, separate guest quarters, and fantastic walkout family room with adjacent library hall. It's a beauty.

Open House Registration Card

To help me serve you better, please fill in the information below and leave this card in the box provided. Thank you!

Name: _____

Address: _____

Phone: _____

Children: _____ Boys, ages: _____

Girls, ages: _____

Please give your comments on this home:

_____

_____

_____

_____

Are you:

☐ planning to move to this area?

☐ planning to buy a home soon?

☐ currently working with an agent?

Agent's name: _____

Agent's phone: _____

☐ looking for something in this price range?

Desired range: _____

Back

Please answer all that apply:

Is this the kind of home you are looking for? _____

_____

Are you selling your present home? _____

_____

How many homes have you seen already? _____

_____

Why are you moving at this time? _____

_____

When would be a good time to discuss your move in more detail? _____

_____

Comments: _____

_____

Thank you for your time!

Open House Register

Name	Address	Phone	Comments

Negotiating a New Client

When you meet a new client, you will want to acquire an in-depth knowledge of them. If you have no competition, add them to your customer base immediately. Your goal is to market yourself in the best, most honest way possible. Some obstacles to completion of a sale are as follows:

Obstacle one

Inability to move out of your comfort zone. Suggestion: This obstacle often surfaces when an agent lacks self confidence or knowledge about the subject property. Increasing communication with the client and giving them the opportunity to establish trust helps keep everyone in a comfort zone.

Obstacle two

Lack of knowledge. Suggestion: Initially new agents may not know certain information that is crucial to a subject property. After some time in the business, this knowledge comes quickly. A good way to help speed up the process is to do lots and lots of HOMEWORK regarding a property in question.

Obstacle three

Failure to interface with the proper decision maker. Suggestion: It is important for an agent to be able to distinguish a key decision maker from the key influencer. REMEMBER: The person who writes the check for the purchase may not leverage the most influence during the negotiating effort.

Obstacle four

Inability to solve problems relating to the property. Suggestion: Watch body language and ask lots of questions. Try to understand what it is that the client wants. Listen well.

Obstacle five

Misreading and underestimating your client. Suggestion: For any salesperson, knowledge is power! Reading all the trade journals and attending training sessions, following a self-study plan, and joining associations all will help you spot industry trends, stay ahead of them, and analyze your client's needs.

A brief analysis

Your success is based on an unwavering commitment to real estate excellence and unparalleled customer service. When you MARKET SOLUTIONS, you enhance your own presentation strategies by understanding your customer's limitations and strengths!

Negotiation rules

1. Consistently strive for high moral character.
2. Avoid offending the buyer or the seller.
3. Start out with a good plan-of-action outline!
4. Avoid trying to get either party on your side.
5. Handle the people you are working with honestly.
6. Continually ask "Why?"
7. Bring attention to the item or items that you are most concerned with.
8. Be prepared to start all over again, and again, and again!
9. Be a good LISTENER: LISTEN, LISTEN, LISTEN!
10. Stay informed on all issues governing contract negotiation.
11. Set deadlines involving all parts of the transaction.
12. Continuously give yourself and your clients alternatives.
13. Work with the issues that you KNOW YOU can resolve!
14. Consider changing your typical format. Try something new.
15. Avoid criticizing any other real estate agent!
16. Utilize time frames and remind clients how many homes sell fast!
17. Always look the seller and the buyer DIRECTLY IN THE EYES.
18. Give your word and STICK TO IT.
19. Shake hands firmly and confidently!
20. Set DEADLINES AND ACT ON THEM!

Chapter Summary

Open houses are a key factor in having great business. Try to follow a rule of having two open houses every week. Open houses enable you to select good buyers and sellers to work with if you know how to qualify them. In choosing a house to hold open, it should be in an area that you know well, is easily accessible, is fairly new to the market, and is priced to sell!

Stay focused with an "Open House Plan of Action." This is a 15-point plan that includes previewing the home, driving the neighborhood, and doing an area market survey (AMS). When holding an open house, always bring your open house notes. Ask potential clients for appointments to buy/sell a home.

Stay productive at the open house if it is slow. Work on your schedule for next week. Update your buyer/seller list. Call on a FSBO closest to your open house. See how many appointments you can set up for the week.

In order to have the best open house, try to call the neighbors ahead of time to invite them over to see the property and to introduce yourself. Distribute door-hangers about the property being held open to neighbors in a four- to six-block radius. Ask every person coming through your open house if you could talk to them about their real estate needs. Remember: Don't let a potential client leave without securing an appointment! In order for you to get the right names and numbers at your open house it is important for you to keep a register with you at all times. Repeat their name as they give it to you. Ask them the important questions talked about in the chapter. Try to give a potential client five brief facts about the property. It is very important to learn to close at an open house. Therefore, always ask for an appointment before the potential client leaves the open house!

SELF-MARKETING

- Promotion Ideas

big deal by Lorayne n' Neil

I should go to the office…it's almost noon.

I don't need sales meetings to sell houses, Lorayne.

Hi, Neil, you missed the sales meeting.

Did you find your buyers a house yet?

Nothing to it, I've got 20 lined up for them to see today.

Later…

They announced a new listing at the sales meeting. It's sold now and my buyers hated everything I showed them. I should get involved more!

_S_elf-marketing is extremely important. The way you sell yourself will be the deciding factor in how successful you will become.

> You should have a brochure, card, and mailing system that causes a total stranger to select you as their real estate agent just on the basis of your promotional items.

MANY REAL ESTATE AGENTS FEEL THAT A CARD IS ENOUGH. A REAL ESTATE CARD REPRESENTING AN AGENT IS NOT ENOUGH.

Just about everyone has a business card that tells who and what they represent. As fast as they are given away, they are thrown away!

MAKE YOURSELF STAND OUT AND BE SET APART!

Essential self-marketing items

1. Dignified business card with picture (dignified means NOT flashy)
2. Personal brochure (single-page or two-fold, depending on layout)
3. Personal logo (identification mark personalized to represent me)
4. Personalized stationery with envelopes
5. Personalized postcards
6. Personalized calendars
7. Personalized notepads
8. Personalized market plan (see Chapter 10 on listings)
9. Personalized pencils (could carry a slogan, such as: "JUST SAY NO TO DRUGS." Pencils are inexpensive and adults can use them or give them to their children.)
10. Personalized stamp for my map book, MLS books, files, folders, and other real estate transactions
11. Laptop computer with my own web page and e-mail
12. Cell phone with real estate messages answered in 24 hours
13. Laser printer for my highlight sheets
14. Personalized open house signs
15. Fax machine to receive faxes 24 hours a day

Have Everything Personalized

- Business cards
- Stationery
- Envelopes
- Newsletters
- Calendars
- Open house signs
- Name riders for signs
- Newspaper ads
- Mail-outs to farming areas
- Thank-you letters
- Expired listing letters
- For Sale by Owner letters
- Grocery list handouts
- Postcards
- Personal brochure
- Personal promotion book
- Just-listed cards
- Just-sold cards
- Closing gift thank-you cards
- Personal notepads
- Open house arrows

personalize...

brochures
personal promotional book
postcards
stationery
post-it notes
desk reminder notes
monthly mailers
large pencils
calendars
bus stop bench placards

The seller liked my personal brochure... and he listed!

Five Components of Self-Marketing

Self-promotion involves **five** things:

1. Your business *card*
2. Your personal *brochure*
3. Your *notepads*
4. Your *stationery* and envelopes
5. Your *logo*

Personalize all of these items!

IT IS VERY IMPORTANT THAT YOU DEVELOP A STYLE THAT SETS YOU APART FROM OTHER AGENTS.

You can find a niche that instantly tells others how good you are. Buyers and sellers will want to *seek you out*. Looking, reading, and surmising the information on one of the above items (1 through 4) and from the unique logo specifically designed for you will get you many buyers.

Twenty Ways to Promote Yourself

1. *Call neighbors* and tell them you have a client interested in their neighborhood. Ask if they happen to know of anyone selling.

2. *Promote your relocation service* by calling people and telling them that you have a free service to put people personally in touch with an agent in the neighboring state.

3. If you just listed a property, *call the neighbors* and tell them all about it. Ask if they know of anyone wishing to move into the neighborhood.

4. Pick a certain day of the week to *promote yourself* and make a certain number of *cold calls* in a select area of town. Tell them that you would be happy to come out to give them an idea of the value of their home at no charge whatsoever.

5. If you just sold a home, *call the neighbors* to tell them all about the property and ask them if they know of anyone wishing to move into the area.

6. *Hold an open house.* Call surrounding neighbors, using the reverse directory, to tell them the time you are going to be there, and ask if they know of anyone buying or selling.

7. *Call a FSBO.* Tell them that you work the area, specialize in their neighborhood, and would very much like to see their home.

8. *Call an expired listing.* Tell the owners that you are frustrated with trying to figure out why their home did not sell. Ask if you could come over to see their home and give them your price opinion at no charge.

9. *Create a newsletter* and send it to a designated area. Do this four times a year.

10. *Make use of the holidays* to express holiday wishes to people in areas where you want business.

11. *Cold-call tenants in apartment buildings,* explaining that their rent could be similar to the amount of a monthly mortgage payment.

12. *Call your church parsonage* and ask if any members are new or are thinking of leaving the area.

13. *Ask your mailperson* if there have been any requests for changes of address.

14. *Join a neighborhood* organization.

15. *Join a school* organization.

16. *Find a volunteer program* that would interest you. Always wear your name tag.

17. *Join a local health club* and ask if you could advertise in their newsletter.

18. *Join a church* and advertise in the roster.

19. *Advertise in your local neighborhood* newspaper.

20. *Send personal flyers out* to your neighbors.

> The more you promote yourself, the more one person will talk to another person, and so on and so on, ABOUT YOU!

It is imperative that you eat, sleep, and talk real estate to as many people as you meet.

Clues for Promoting Yourself

1. *MAKE A VIDEO OF YOURSELF.* Tell clients exactly what you are prepared to do for them and how you service your listings. Tell clients how you work with buyers. This is extremely effective in attracting both buyers and sellers.

2. *HAVE A HIGH LEVEL OF INVOLVEMENT* with the National Association of REALTORS®. Join various organizations. Better your education. Keep a loose-leaf notebook with a list of all the classes you have attended. This provides added credibility for your potential clients.

3. *SECURE AND KEEP TESTIMONIAL LETTERS* about yourself and the way you have done business. Use these letters to improve your image. Secure letters from clients who have enjoyed working with you. Keep them in an 8½" × 11" loose-leaf notebook.

4. *MAT AND FRAME ALL AWARDS AND CERTIFICATES* that you receive, and display them in your office. Alternatively, you may wish to put them in clear sheet protectors in a binder.

5. *COPY* promotional ads that you have run and keep in clear sheet protectors to use as listing tools.

6. *KEEP TRACK OF VARIOUS UNIQUE OPEN HOUSE DISPLAY ADS* and other tour ads that you have run. Keep in clear plastic in a separate loose-leaf binder.

7. *KEEP A SEPARATE PROMOTIONAL IDEAS BOOK* and include different ways that you have promoted properties, yourself, and your company.

8. *KEEP YOUR CAR WELL SUPPLIED* with all promotional items on yourself and your company at all times.

9. *Update your briefcase and DAILY SCHEDULE BOOK WEEKLY.* Include promotional tools on yourself, such as extra brochures, cards, and highlight sheets.

10. *ON COMPANY LETTERHEAD, COPY ANY NEWS ARTICLES* pertinent to your real estate area of expertise to use as a listing tool.

11. Stand at a mirror before you leave home each day and say *ONE NICE THING ABOUT YOURSELF.*

12. Plan a specific amount of money from your commissions to be used to *PROMOTE YOURSELF.* This is very important.

Self-promotion ideas

- Call five new companies in town. Ask for the relocation department. Offer to work with relocation clients. Bring your personal resume, brochure, and personal promotion book.

- Run a catchy personal advertisement in the weekend edition of your local newspaper.

- Watch the financial and business sections of your local newspaper. Look for newsworthy articles that may make a good point of reference in a monthly newsletter that you would consider sending out to a farm area.

By implementing *a total design* for yourself—choosing a logo and imprinting it on your business card, brochure, personal stationery, envelopes, and notepads—you will set yourself apart with distinction.

People don't care how much you know until they realize how much you care about yourself and your business.

SOME IDEAS FOR NOTEPADS:

1. Logo *at the top* with only your name and phone in block letters
2. Logo *centered* at top with block initials and phone only
3. Logo *off-centered* with your name and "to do today" slogan
4. Logo *off-right-center* and your name and phone with "must do" slogan
5. Name, logo, phone on *top three lines* and fourth line down, centered, "my personal list" slogan
6. Name, logo, phone, and "and so today…" slogan

Some agents like to have a slogan *on their business card.* This is fine if you specialize in a specific area that enhances your real estate image overall. Be careful, though, **not to limit yourself!**

SAMPLE:

BILL JONES
SPECIALIST IN LAKE PROPERTIES

JANE JONES
VINTAGE HOMES SPECIALIST

This can work for or against you. You must decide what *image* you want to create and convey to clients.

I choose to work five surrounding, close-in, areas. This enables me to have my office centrally located and near my home. When I receive business and referrals that bring me into an area that I normally do not work, I simply *call another office* with which I am associated, refer the client to another agent, and *ask for a referral fee.* In the long run, this saves much time, energy, and gas that would be expended learning an area that I am not comfortable with. The buyer can usually tell, as can a seller, if you are not familiar with convenient stores, parks, and other points of interest close to the seller's home—not to mention properties that have sold and are active. It is best to create a plan, work the plan, and refer business that you are not well versed in to another, more experienced agent. In the long run, you will receive *more referrals* and be able to continue to promote yourself in the areas of concentration that you know well.

Ways to Improve Yourself through Education

Once you have joined your local association, there are many **educational designations** that you can acquire through the National Association of Real Estate Agents.

By acquiring knowledge beyond the information that is needed to pass the real estate test, you become more and more professional and respected in the industry.

Following are a few of the titles you can acquire:

- *GRI (Graduate Real Estate Institute)*
  - concentrated four-day program
  - must pass an examination
  - completing the initial level of education in real estate (required by your state)

- *CCIM (Certified Commercial Investment Member)*
  - successful completion of 240 hours of graduate-level study
  - submission of a resume of qualified, consummated transactions and/or
  - completing eight hours of comprehensive examination

- *CRE (Counselor of Real Estate)*
  - best source of knowledge to give home owners, investment people, and those developing property
  - CRE designation recognizes good judgment in all real estate matters, including integrity, experience, and client service
  - membership must be sponsored or by invitation only

- *IREM (Institute of Real Estate Management)*
  - insures high standards of professional practice in property management
  - membership consists primarily of property managers and real estate managers
    The CPM designation is achieved by conforming to the specific code of ethics and meeting all requirements for property management. This organization offers two award designations
    1. AMO (Accredited Management Organization)
    2. ARM (Accredited Residential Manager Recognition)

- *SIOR (Society of Industrial and Office Real Estate Agents)*
  - for people specializing in all phases of industrial and office real estate
  - offers full range of courses in office, industrial, and marketing
  - must complete course work for designation
  - also offers PRE (professional real estate executive) designation

- *SRES (Seniors Real Estate Specialist)*
  - two-day program

Educational Organization

- *Real Estate Agents Land Institute*
  - helps members improve their image in marketing and all areas of land brokerage, agricultural, and urban and recreational properties
  - this institute offers two programs:
    1. The RLI (Land University), a designation program with monthly publications
    2. The ALC (Accredited Land Consultant) earned by members who meet the standards and complete the requirements

- *Women's Council of Real Estate Assents (WCR)*
  - has referral and relocation programs (RRC)
  - gives award of LTG (Leadership Training Graduate) after completing four training courses and meeting the requirements

- *Real Estate Appraisal Section*
  - for real estate appraisers
  - publishes newsletter and holds three national meetings annually
  - annual fee
  - CIPS (Certified International Property Specialist) for members with in international interests
  - must complete several courses
  - must submit a resume
  - must have at least 100 elective points
  - can take courses at reduced tuition through your Board of REALTORS®
  - listed in international directory
  - international newsletter

All of the "distinctions" listed above enable a real estate professional to show that he or she is constantly seeking to promote himself—or herself—not only through advertising and self-marketing, but through education as well.

> Once you have joined your local association, there are many *educational designations* that you can acquire through the National Association of Real Estate Agents.
>
> By acquiring knowledge beyond the information that is needed to pass the real estate test, you become more professional and respected in the industry.

Promotional Ideas via Postcard

"PEOPLE SPREAD GOOD RUMORS ABOUT ME"

(Put slogan under your photo on front.)

"OUTSTANDING IN HER/HIS FIELD"

(Photo of yourself standing in a corn field.)

"I LOVE TO SELL HOMES"

(Photo of yourself in front of a sold sign at the Capitol.)

"I MAKE THINGS HAPPEN"

(Photo of you and sold sign in front of a house.)

"TOPS IN HIS/HER FIELD"

(Photo of you standing in a corn field.)

"NOT JUST ANOTHER PRETTY FACE"

(Six to eight photos of yourself with various facial expressions. Shrink down and put on the front of the postcard with the caption off to the side. You could also take enough pictures for the months of the year. For example, for January you could hold a Happy New Year sign, for February hold a valentine, for March hold a four-leaf clover, for April hold an Easter egg, and so on.)

"BARBARA'S BACK AND BETTER THAN EVER"

(Photo of yourself looking over your shoulder and pointing to your back with caption below picture.)

"HOME IS WHERE THE HEART IS"

(Photo of a beautiful home and your picture with the caption below.)

"LET ME INTRODUCE MYSELF"

(Put caption below your photo.)

"EXPERIENCE = RESULTS!"

(Divide the postcard in half. Make half with you holding a for sale sign and the other half with you holding a sold sign. Back of postcard can say, "Is your house too big? Too small? Let me know." Or the back can say "Why isn't your For Sale by Owner home selling? Call me today!"

"GOOD AT HIS/HER GAME ... REAL ESTATE!"

(Photo of yourself on front of postcard and the above inscription on half of the back. Also say, "Whatever your game ... when it comes to real estate, call.")

"ALL-STAR SERVICE"

(Photo of yourself on front of postcard with five stars.)

"BARBARA SELLS SERVICE"

(Photo of yourself on front of postcard holding a for sale sign with a sold sign on it plus your name strip and phone numbers.)

"SPOUSES SELLING HOUSES"

(Slogan on the front of the card with both your pictures on half of the back. Also say, "Let us put a Sold sign in your yard!")

"WHY WAIT ANY LONGER TO SELL YOUR HOME?"

(Photo of yourselves in front of a home with a sold sign.)

"IF YOU'RE THINKING OF BUYING OR SELLING ... NOW IS THE TIME!"

(Photo of yourselves on front of postcard with slogan below.)

"MAKE THE RIGHT MOVE!"

(Photo of yourselves on front of postcard.)

"I FIND YOUR WAY HOME"

(Photo of yourselves on front of postcard with slogan below.)

"TOGETHER WE CAN DO IT"

(Photo of yourselves on front with a for sale sign and sold on it.)

"PEOPLE ARE TALKING ABOUT"

(Photo of yourselves with slogan below.)

Self-Marketing is extremely important- sell yourself and you will sell a home!

"THE REASON PEOPLE ARE SATISFIED WITH BARBARA'S SERVICE IS ... SHE IS CONSTANTLY IMPROVING!"

(Photo of yourself with above caption below it and next caption below that on the back.)

"BARBARA RISES TO EVERY REAL ESTATE OCCASION"

(Picture of yourself with above caption below.)

CHAPTER 13

"WHEN IT COMES TO SELLING REAL ESTATE . . . I MAKE A STATEMENT!"

(Picture of yourself with above caption below it.)

"YOUR SEARCH IS OVER"

(Photo of yourselves with slogan below.)

"I'M HERE FOR THE MOST IMPORTANT MOVE OF ALL . . . YOURS!"

(Picture of yourself with above caption below picture.)

"I'LL TEND TO DETAILS . . . YOU TEND TO PACKING"

(Picture of yourself with above caption below picture.)

"TO INCREASE YOUR HOME VALUE . . . MAY WE SUGGEST AN ATTRACTIVE LAWN ORNAMENT . . ."

(Photo of yourselves holding a for sale sign of your company.)

"TOP PRODUCERS ARE ALWAYS TOO BUSY TO POSE FOR PICTURES . . ."

(Photo of an empty chair with a sold sign and your name rider.)

Make a postcard with the "Take Time" poem (author unknown)

Take time to think;
* it is the source of power.*
Take time to play;
* it is the secret of perpetual youth.*
Take time to read;
* it is the fountain of wisdom.*
Take time to pray;
* it is the greatest power on earth.*
Take time to love and be loved;
* it is a God-given privilege.*
Take time to be friendly;
* it is the road to happiness.*
Take time to laugh;
* it is the music of the soul.*
Take time to give;
* it is too short a day to be selfish.*
TAKE TIME TO WORK;
* it is the PRICE OF SUCCESS.*

I put this poem on the back of all my business cards. Now people don't throw them away!

Self-Promotion with a Farm

Farming (selecting a specific area to send real estate mailings to on a regular basis) can be more profitable than most agents think and is often completely overlooked.

Once an agent sets up his or her farm and develops a newsletter, the farm pretty much runs on automatic pilot.

A farm consists of the following:

1. An area of homes that you would like to WORK
2. An area that has a consistent *turnover*
3. An area that contains 200 to 300 *homes*
4. An area that includes 50 of your *closest neighbors*
5. An area that is *convenient* to both office and home

Typical survey conversation of a geographical farm:

1. *"Hello Mr. Jones. I am from _____ Real Estate Company. I am doing a survey and am wondering if you plan on moving sometime within the next few years."*
2. *"May I ask where you are staying in the area?"*
3. Make specific notes to call back at a future time. This will give you *leads for later.*
4. You can *use the CMA function* on your computer to locate the actives, solds, and expireds in your farm area.

How to Set Up a Farm

1. *Narrow down the area* that you want to work in, get the names and addresses of 200 to 300 people, and phone them.
2. *Make up an introductory letter* to send out on your personalized stationery with your personalized logo.
3. *Make up a newsletter that contains:*
   - real estate information
   - garden and home information, or
   - food and recipe information
4. *Have cards made up for:*
   Happy New Year
   St. Patrick's Day
   Valentines Day
   Mother's Day
   Back to School

My farm is a big area around where I live.... I mail every month! (Real estate news)

Fourth of July
Halloween
Thanksgiving
Happy Holidays

5. *Start a farm book to:*
   - keep a list of all the *homes* in your farm
   - keep track of all the *mailers* that you send
   - keep track of every house you *list* in your farm
   - keep track of every house you *sell* in your farm
   - keep track of all *solds* in your farm
   - keep track of all *actives* in your farm
   - keep track of all *expireds* in your farm

6. *Send out mailers four to twelve times* a year to your farm.

7. *Send an update on the market* at least *three times* a year to your farm.

8. *Send out a community directory* to each homeowner in your farm with your picture on the front.

9. *Give grocery list pads* to homeowners in your farm.

10. *Give list of handy service organizations for* spring cleanup, carpet cleaning, winter cleanup, window washing, and so on.

Fantastic farming ideas

1. Find a farm where there is at least a 5 percent *turnover yearly.*
2. *Buy a bulk rate stamp.*
3. Send out *four to twelve mailings a year.*
4. *Use gum labels.*
5. Send at least 300 to 500 pieces each time you mail.
6. *Go door to door* only if you have to.
7. Deliver at least *four doorhangers a year.*
8. *Call every home* in your farm at least three times a year.
9. *Personalize every piece of information* you send out.
10. *Go to* the community association *meetings* in your farm.
11. *Sponsor* a holiday *event* for your farm area.
12. *Give* people *gifts* whenever possible.
13. *Mail* your farm *just listed* and *just sold* cards.
14. *Send an annual letter* about yourself to your farm.
15. Keep a complete and *up-to-date farm book.*

My farm is where
I grew up.... I know that
area the best!

Suggested promotions

January	calendars, pencils, pens
February	valentines, postcards
March	St. Patrick's day
April	Easter, spring, flower seeds
May	Mother's Day, carnations, flags, Memorial Day
June	doorhangers, Father's Day, pens
July	flags, balloons, coupons for free market analysis
August	labor day, back to school, memos, magnets
September	back to school, pencils, pens, notepads
October	pumpkins, Halloween, lawn bags
November	Thanksgiving, turkeys, drawings
December	fruit baskets, poinsettias, magnets

Suggestions for magnet messages

Trust your doctor: _____

      phone: _____

Confer with your lawyer: _____

      phone: _____

Rely on your accountant: _____

      phone: _____

Consult your
REAL ESTATE AGENT: _____

      phone: _____

Five-Star Promotional Ideas

1. *Send out color envelopes* with your photo imprinted in the top left-hand corner.
2. *Have a stamp made* with your signature.
3. *Use personal stationery* imprinted with odd-size envelopes.
4. *Type or write* short come-on statements such as:

   "Your home could be worth more than you know."

   "Are you sitting on a goldmine?"

   "You wouldn't believe the interest rates."

   "Do I have news for you!"
5. *Send out recipe postcards.*
6. *Have a sticky label made up* with your logo, name, address, and a catchy slogan.
7. After a buyer's purchase, *send a scrapbook* with a picture of the home, school information, neighbors, and other useful information.
8. During the holidays, *give clients a beautiful holiday music CD*, nicely wrapped.
9. On 8½" × 11" sheet with your picture and phone number, *list favorite restaurants*, including name, type of menu, and phone number.
10. Set up a five-star plan of action for yourself. Promote yourself in this fashion:

Five Stars:	super selling experience
Four Stars:	best value for your home
Three Stars:	accurate preparation of all documents
Two Stars:	perfectly professional
One Star:	unbelievable service
11. *Send out yearly giveaways such as:*

    refrigerator magnets

    telephone pens and pencils

    notepads

    thank-you notes

    litter bags

    lawn bags

    pumpkins, turkeys, fruits, nuts
12. Create *Unique mailers*

PUZZLE PIECES	Contact:	CHUCK BODE 16227 ELM ST. OMAHA, NE 68130 402-334-9156
BASEBALL CARDS	Contact:	B.L.C. ORDER FORMS P.O. BOX C TEANECK, NJ 07666 201-692-8228
SUPERSTAR PERSONAL *PROMOTION* *IDEAS* (hundreds of marketing ideas)	Contact:	MARKETING YOUR SCRAPBOOK HOWARD BRINTON SEMINARS 3013 NORTH 67TH PLACE DEPT. O SCOTTSDALE, AZ 85251 602-994-9874
MAGICARD (magnetic backing for cards)	Contact:	M.C. ENTERPRISES P.O. BOX 406 BUSINESS OWINGS MILLS, MD 21117 800-634-5523

Ways to Promote Yourself to Get Sellers

1. *Call your friends.*
2. *Give your business cards* and brochures out everywhere you go.
3. *Wear a lapel pin* with your name and company everywhere you go.
4. *Use a name rider* on all of your signs.
5. *Try to secure walk-in office business.*
6. *Hold opens* at new subdivisions of homes being built.
7. *Get referrals* from out-of-town companies.
8. *Get referrals* from business management.
9. *Get bank referrals* from foreclosures.
10. *Hold open houses.*
11. *Relist properties* that have expired with other companies.
12. *Ask other agents* if they want to split any business that they either can't keep up with or don't want to work.
13. *Call* on FSBOs.
14. *Create and work a farm* area.
15. *Start a referral service* through networking with friends, church members, organizations.
16. *Send newsletters*, postcards, and so on.

Ways to Promote Yourself to Get Buyers

1. *Call your friends.*
2. *Give your business cards* and brochures out everywhere you go.
3. *Wear a lapel pin* with your name and company everywhere you go.
4. *Call past clients* from any other business.
5. *Try to secure walk-in* business.
6. *Work with a new subdivision.*
7. *Get referrals* from personal contacts.
8. *Ask for referrals* from management.
9. *Utilize the multiple listing service* and know your inventory. Keep track of homes for sale.
10. *Hold open houses* and try to qualify good buyers to work with.
11. *Establish a farm area* and work it.
12. *Write your ads* with your name and phone, and the price of the property!
13. *Call tenants* in good apartment buildings.
14. *Send newsletters* and postcards.

"I'LL TEND TO DETAILS...YOU TEND TO PACKING"
(Photo of yourself with slogan below.)

"TO INCREASE YOUR HOME VALUE...
MAY I SUGGEST AN ATTRACTIVE LAWN
ORNAMENT..."
(Photo of yourself holding a for sale sign of your company.)

"A TOP PRODUCER IS ALWAYS TOO BUSY TO
POSE FOR PICTURES..."
(Photo of an empty chair with a sold sign and your name rider.)

Perfect Prospecting

REAL ESTATE IS PROSPECTING!

From the day you begin to sell to the day you stop selling, **you are always prospecting.** The ways to find prospects are endless. However, here is a short list of some great possibilities for obtaining clients.

1. **Family contacts:** classmates, classmates' parents and relatives, teachers at school, husband's or wife's friends and colleagues at work
2. **Business contacts:** customers, clients, past and current employees, competition
3. **Personal contacts:** friends and their friends, their friends, and so on
4. **School contacts:** classmates, teachers, past and current fraternity and sorority members

5. **Hobby contacts:** members of church clubs, men's and women's golf and other clubs, farm organizations, military organizations, bowling leagues, and hunting, fishing, and photography clubs

6. **Service contacts:** dry cleaner, grocer, butcher, druggist, mailman, newspaper delivery person, plumber, dentist, physician

7. **Neighbor contacts:** this person knows this person, who knows this person, who knows this person

> An important fact to remember is that *prospecting is a lot like building a bridge.* You need certain things before you can cross over. In this case, you need *good, qualified* clients who will stay with you, thereby *bridging the gap* between the lookers and the buyers.

Personal Logo

HOW IMPORTANT IS A PERSONAL LOGO?

IT MAY VERY WELL BE THE ONLY THING THAT SETS YOU APART!

Real estate has become extremely technological. With all the roles the computer plays and all the competition, sometimes you have only that 30- to 60-second contact with a buyer and/or future seller at your open house. Your brochure and business card may be the only way to convince them to call you rather than someone else.

PERSONAL LOGOS DO NOT HAVE TO BE EXPENSIVE.

EVERYONE HAS A FLAIR AND A WAY ABOUT THEM THAT WOULD APPEAL TO DIFFERENT PEOPLE.

> *LEARN TO MAKE A STATEMENT WITH A PERSONAL LOGO.*

If you golf, a golf logo may be the opener in a conversation with someone you've just met. If antique cars are your hobby, find a picture of an antique car that you like and take it to a printer. You would be surprised at how economically you can design your own brochure and card.

> *Put the logo in the corner of your business card,* brochure, and every mailer that you intend to send out.

Maybe, as a woman, you love fashion and design and clothing. Have a classic woman drawn by a print shop. The expense for this service is surprisingly minimal.

Perhaps you play a musical instrument or have a favorite sport. Even a caricature of yourself is very unique.

Choose something that is a conversation opener and allows another person to get an inside "peek" at you.

- *A chess knight is a great symbol for a "move ahead."*
- A top hat and gloves suggest "top drawer" service.
- A symbol of the sun shows that you have a sunny disposition.

You could use a pretty picture of your city or your own home or something that interests you and sets you apart. Or choose something that you have always wanted to have as a part of you.

REAL ESTATE IS PROSPECTING!
SEE IT
DESIGN IT
MAKE IT HAPPEN

Write your name differently, and let that be your signature.

Spend a little extra time *looking at yourself from outside of yourself.*

Would you buy a home from you based on your personal promotion?

Finally, *consider having your photo taken beside something that is meaningful to you—* perhaps an antique car, perhaps a favorite pet. You may want to have a photo taken of you all dressed up and then have a cartoon or caricature made from that image.

Logos leave lasting impressions

Look at department stores. Look around your city now. How many different companies, restaurants, and businesses have added logos to their identity?

It is important to try to incorporate a logo into your look as the best professional in real estate.

IT MAY WELL BE THE ONLY THING THAT SETS YOU APART!

A Promotion Idea...Important Numbers to Remember

Emergency _____

Drug information center _____

FBI _____

Poison control _____

Police department _____

Personal

Doctor _____

Dentist _____

Babysitter: Name: _____   Phone: _____

                Name: _____   Phone: _____

Neighbors: Name: _____   Phone: _____

                Name: _____   Phone: _____

Utility Service

Cable TV _____

Electric co. _____

Gas co. _____

Recycling _____

Water co. _____

Telephone _____

Garbage _____

County Numbers

Public schools _____

Public library _____

Animal shelter _____

Community colleg _____

State numbers

Government info _____

Travel & tour _____

Drivers license _____

Farmers market _____

Museum of art _____

Museum of history _____

Vehicle registration _____

Other

Weather bureau _____

Better Bus. Bureau _____

Goodwill Industries _____

Red Cross _____

Salvation Army _____

YMCA _____

YWCA _____

Real Estate Agent _____

Barbara Nash

SERVICE YOU CAN'T LIVE WITHOUT

PROPERTY INFORMATION FOR:

7326 WEST 114TH STREET

- The builder of this home was Lecy Construction, a top builder in the metropolitan area.

- Upgrades include beautiful Princeton trim on the doors and moldings.

- The formal living room and dining room have sensational skylights.

- Here's a summary of neighborhood children:

Boys	*Girls*
1 baby	2 six-year-olds
2 three-year-olds	2 seven-year-olds
1 four-year-old	1 eight-year-old
1 five-year-old	3 nine-year-olds
1 eight-year-old	2 thirteen-year-olds
1 ten-year-old	2 fourteen-year-olds
1 eleven-year-old	1 sixteen-year-old
2 fourteen-year-olds	1 nineteen-year-old

- Seldom has a home been offered with so many *upgrades, built-ins,* and the best in quality workmanship available.

Outside

Testimonials...

Lorayne

"Lorayne is tops in her field. She goes that extra mile every time..."

"We worked with Lorayne after talking to 20 other agents. She was able to sum it all up and show us results fast."

"We needed an agent who was the best all the way around Lorayne kept us up-to-date on everything; we had a great partnership. She's the best agent in the field."

Bus. (612) 555-0000
Res. (612) 555-0000
Car (612) 555-0000

ANY PRINTER CAN PRINT THIS BROCHURE ON GLOSSY OR FLAT HIGH-QUALITY PAPER.

BE SURE TO USE A BUSINESSLIKE PHOTO OF YOURSELF.

Lorayne

The Professional...

- Thirty years full-time experience
- Multi-million dollar producer
- Member of Minneapolis Board of REALTORS®
- Top Outgoing Referral Associate
- Specialist in Edina-Bloomington-Maples Lakes Areas

The Person...

- Empathetic/Understanding...Lorayne has experienced the drama/trauma of moving families and helping them establish a new life. She fully analyzes and shows how your home and neighborhood will meet your physical and emotional needs.

- Supportive...Lorayne was co-chairman of St. Joseph Home for Abused Children and received an award for community involvement. She volunteers at her childrens' schools and was the first woman to change legislation for victims' rights in the State of Minnesota. She has also been secretary of her homeowners' association in Forest Haven.

- Knowledgeable...Lorayne continually updates her skills through courses, seminars, and synergistic interaction with other REALTORS®. For 25 years she has been a Twin Cities' tour guide—she knows the cities.

The Company...

BN Realty has fantastic financial and legal resources. It is large enough yet small enough to respond to your needs now. Its new 4-color Photo Trieve will dramatically and quickly expose your home to hundreds of buyers.

And YOU...

PARTNERS...you and Lorayne share joint responsibility. Lorayne works only with qualified people throughout the year—in the joint decision to be client and agent, you and she agree to communicate honestly. Lorayne's success in selling has been marked in large part through what is known in the trade as **REFERRALS**...

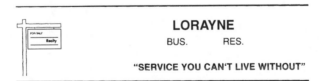

LORAYNE

BUS.   RES.

"SERVICE YOU CAN'T LIVE WITHOUT"

Chapter Summary

Self marketing is extremely important. The way that you sell yourself will be the deciding factor in how successful you will become. You should have a brochure, card and mailing system that causes a total stranger to select you as their real estate agent just on the basis of your promotional items.

Make yourself stand out and be set apart! Have everything personalized. There are five components to Self-Marketing: your business card, your personal brochure, your notepads, your stationery and envelopes and your logo. The more you promote yourself, the more one person will talk to another person about YOU! Make a video of yourself, have a high level of involvement with the National Association of Realtors. Join various organizations. Better your edication. Keep testimonial letters, keep track of your open-house ads, keep your car well supplied. On company letter-head; copy any news articles pertinent to your real estate area of expertise. Plan a specific amount of money from your commissions to be used to promote yourself. This is very important.

Promote yourself through educational designations. Promotional postcards are an outstanding way of self marketing. Setting up a "real estate farm" is an excellent way of self-promotion. Promote yourself with buyers and sellers. From the day you begin to sell, you are always prospecting. There are family contacts, business contacts, personal contacts, school contacts, hobby contacts, service contacts and neighbour contacts. Your personal "logo" sets you apart. Learn to make a statement with a personal logo. Logo's leave lasting impressions. There are samples of self-marketing ideas to include sample highlight sheets and self-marketing personal brochures.

TIME TO CLOSE

- Dialogues & Problems

big deal by Lorayne n' Neil

Time to Close

Three types of closings

1. Closing on a *buyer to buy*
2. Closing on a *seller to sell*
3. *Closing time* (close in escrow or settlement time)

I can't believe I asked for the listing at the first appointment and I got it!

All *three types of closings* require the agent to remember that:

1. the buyer needs a home,
2. the seller needs his money, and
3. the closing must go smoothly for the agent to get his or her money.

I have learned *three very important things* in the real estate business.

1. *Be ready to close* all the time.
2. Every person is *ready to buy* if they are looking.
3. *Be ready to list* and sell a house on any given day.

How many times have I been to my seller's house...I should ask for the listing....!

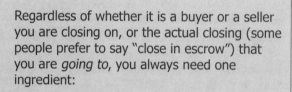

Regardless of whether it is a buyer or a seller you are closing on, or the actual closing (some people prefer to say "close in escrow") that you are *going to*, you always need one ingredient:

BALANCE.

You should strive to know when to "talk it up" and when to "clam up." No transaction is ever complete until the buyer and seller mutually agree to sign on the dotted line, the keys are exchanged, and everyone has shaken hands.

When they can't buy that house right now because
"THEY JUST HAVE TO THINK ABOUT IT A LITTLE WHILE
LONGER,"

KNOW WHEN TO CLOSE.

Thesaurus of Stall Phrases and How to Handle Them

CLOSING = OVERCOMING ALL OBJECTIONS

Closing on a listing

"WE DON'T LIKE SIGNS IN OUR FRONT YARD."

"That's fine. We can market the home through MLS and eliminate the sign for now." (Check in a few weeks for a sign.)

"WE DON'T WANT TO GIVE OUT A KEY."

"That's understandable. We can set up appointments for now if you are both home at different times, and I'll make a note to tell the secretary."

"WE HAVE SOMEONE OF OUR OWN WHO IS INTERESTED."

"Fine, let's put his or her name at the top of this listing contract as an exclusion for 10 days."

"WE DON'T JUMP INTO THINGS."

"I understand that, and I feel that we should spend a little more time discussing your objections and how important the timing is now."

"WE HAVE A FRIEND IN THE BUSINESS WHO IS GOING TO GIVE US SOME ADVICE."

"*I realize how easy it sounds sometimes*, however timing is everything, and when you have an interested buyer he or she needs an agent who will get the contract signed immediately."

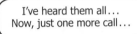

I've heard them all...
Now, just one more call...

"WE DON'T WANT TO PAY A BROKERAGE FEE."

"*I can see from your point of view* that it is a lot of money. However, when you are selling probably one of the most expensive investments in your life, you want a professional to help handle offers that are coming in. Most times the brokerage fee can be absorbed. Many buyers, knowing that the seller is marketing his own home, automatically take the commission off too."

"MY ATTORNEY WILL HANDLE THE PAPERWORK FOR US."

"*An attorney is a very valuable asset.* However, sometimes while getting all the paperwork to the attorney and waiting, you wind up waiting for the buyer to simply change his mind. Timing is everything in the real estate business. If a buyer sleeps on it, he may not sleep in it."

Closing on a buyer

**"WE DIDN'T PLAN ON BUYING A HOME SO FAST . . .
WE WANTED TO LOOK AROUND."**

"Rejection is just part of the business. I don't listen to no."

"I understand how you feel. Are you aware of the fact that most people find the home they like fairly quickly? Then they have a problem finding fault with it. I wouldn't want you to miss this one and then *compare it to all the others we continue to look at.*"

"WE DIDN'T BRING OUR CHECKBOOK WITH US."

"That is easy to remedy. We always have *blank notes* for just this situation. We can redeem your check upon acceptance of the offer."

"ONE OF THE BEDROOMS IS JUST TOO SMALL."

"*Let's take another look at the property* and see that overall, everything is workable. I think a few feet in the bedroom can probably be dealt with."

"IT'S $5,000 MORE THAN WE WANTED TO SPEND."

"If you consider the fact that most people take a vacation once a year and spend $5,000 . . . but whether you vacation or not, the difference amounts to about $1.50 a day. This way you can have the home you want and perhaps save the difference in another minor area."

> **"WE WANT TO KEEP LOOKING; THIS IS HAPPENING TOO FAST."**
> "*I understand the feeling.* Most buyers get a little jittery when they find a perfect home so quickly. The nice feature about finding a home right away is that you can start planning, placing your furniture, and making arrangements for moving now rather than having that worry in the future."

"WE WENT THROUGH THE HOME SO FAST THAT WE CAN'T REMEMBER . . ."

"*That can he easily remedied.* We can go back, look at the house again, and go through it slowly."

"WE WANT OUR FAMILY TO SEE IT BEFORE WE DO ANYTHING."

"That's understandable, and we can put a clause in the contract stating, 'this offer is subject to inspection and approval of buyer's parent on or before _____.'" (Try hard not to have this in writing though. It's best simply to say that you will *arrange to show the parents* the home within the next few days, as soon as everything is consummated.)

"IT'S EXACTLY WHAT WE WANT EXCEPT IT NEEDS DECORATING, AND WE DON'T REALLY WANT TO DO THAT."

"Sometimes it's important to see the value in a property 'before the after.' You can realize a greater profit by purchasing a property when you yourself can participate in the improvements rather than paying for them."

Closing on a seller

"WE HAVE A FRIEND IN THE BUSINESS WHO IS GIVING US SOME ADVICE."

"It's wonderful to have people who you can fall back on. However, when an offer is coming in from a buyer, there are many considerations that go into deciding if the buyer is even qualified to make an offer. An agent representing you knows, on the spot, how to handle difficult situations, while a friend would have to be called. In this time, the buyer might cool on the property."

"WE'RE NOT GOING AHEAD UNTIL WE TALK IT OVER TOGETHER TONIGHT."

"That is perfectly understandable. I meant to show you this ad that I have written up for this Sunday's open house if that agrees with you. And I would like to show you how this lockbox works on your front door." (At this point you try to change the subject, yet become more and more involved in getting the listing signed tonight.) "You see, Mr. and Mrs. Seller, if we get our ad in by tomorrow morning, we have a good chance of getting the best buyers who are in *the market today.*"

"WE CAN SELL THE HOME OURSELVES AND SAVE THE COMMISSION."
"Yes, it certainly appears that no one would better represent a home than the owners themselves, but sometimes it is likened to 'not seeing the forest for the trees.' You become too close to the situation. I know as an agent I tried to sell my own home and had to turn it over to another agent when I became incensed over a potential buyer's dislike for my kitchen wallpaper. The buyer wound up leaving my house in a huff. It is very difficult to put distance between the would-be buyer and yourself. It is also uncomfortable for you to ask a would-be buyer how much money he makes and if he has ever claimed bankruptcy."

"WE ENJOY TALKING WITH YOU, HOWEVER WE FEEL WE SHOULD GIVE ANOTHER COMPANY THE CHANCE TO SELL IT FIRST."

"I understand this completely and feel that they are a fine firm. I wanted to show you the highlight description that I am going to put on the supplement sheet. How do you feel about having a tour for all of our agents to come through? And I might serve a light lunch; this usually attracts many of the top producers in our company who have clients and relocation referrals coming up."

"WE DON'T WANT ANYTHING TO DO WITH REAL ESTATE PEOPLE!"

(*These people have probably been burned by a company before.* They need to talk it through.) "I understand completely how you feel and have had situations before in which the sellers have been hesitant until meeting with me and seeing how they can benefit from my presentation program and my techniques. Do you like the ad that I have written on your property?"

"I DON'T CARE IF THE HOUSE ISN'T WORTH IT. I NEED MORE MONEY."

"*It's important to realize all the dollars that we can save for you,* and in doing this we try to price the property for the best market price possible without overpricing it and helping other homes rather than yours sell. It's a fact that buyers are more likely to make full-price offers on homes priced right before making low offers on homes that are priced too high."

"WE DON'T WANT TO BE TIED UP WITH ANY REAL ESTATE COMPANY FOR A LONG TIME."

"*We understand this completely.* We could write into the listing agreement that the seller has the option of terminating this contract at any given time with 24 hours' notification."

> **"WE ARE THINKING OF LISTING WITH ANOTHER COMPANY THAT HAS A MUCH LOWER COMMISSION THAN YOUR COMPANY."**
> "*It's perfectly understandable* to think that way as a seller. However, in the real estate business, the homes that are sold from the multiple listing books are most often the ones with competitive commissions..."

"THERE IS NOTHING YOU CAN DO FOR ME THAT I CAN'T DO TO SELL THE HOUSE MYSELF."

"*I can see how most of it may appear to be simple.* However, getting a qualified buyer to pay top price for your home is a very hard part of the transaction, not to mention the tremendous amount of follow-up that it entails. Additionally, there is the fact that most prospects calling on owners are usually investors or bargain hunters."

"WE JUST WANT TO THINK IT OVER ANYWAY."

"*There really isn't anything that you would know differently tomorrow* than you know tonight. However, there might be that one buyer coming into town tomorrow that this home would be perfect for, and we would miss out. By letting me get started, you would get a good night's sleep."

"ANOTHER AGENT SAID WE CAN GET A LOT MORE FOR OUR HOME."

"*Whatever you do in regard to listing, make sure that you look at all the credentials* rather than just who will price your home highest. Too often in our industry an agent will 'buy a listing,' which means he or she will list an unrealistic price just to get the listing."

"I DON'T REALLY NEED YOUR SERVICES. I ALREADY HAVE A BUYER."

"Unless the buyer has given you an earnest money check and signed a purchase agreement, you still would want to market the home. *We can exclude that buyer for a period of ten days.*"

"LOTS OF AGENTS ARE WITH A MULTIPLE LISTING SERVICE. WHY SHOULD I LIST WITH YOU?"

"Because the chance for a successful sale relatively soon is determined, in large part, by the agent's know-how and success in the business, and *a successful company that knows and works your area.*"

"WE STILL PLAN ON LISTING WITH ANOTHER FIRM."

"That's fine. I want to take this opportunity to show you my *personal promotion book.* It has all the information about my successes in your area and surrounding areas. I also have some fine samples of my advertising here that I think would interest you."

"WE ARE TOO BUSY TO TALK WITH YOU ABOUT LISTING."

"*I would very much like to help you* in that area so that you can get on with your own interests, and I can absorb the real estate problems for you."

> **"YOUR COMMISSION IS WAY TOO HIGH!"**
> "*I want to be fair with you* and explain that, if there were two properties that I was showing and I had the opportunity to show either, I would show the one with the most competitive fee rather than a low-cut fee."

"THIS IS A BAD TIME TO SELL PROPERTY."

"*There really is no bad time to buy and sell property.* No one is inventing more land, so real estate will always be a steady, good investment. We need only one buyer."

"I KNOW AS MUCH ABOUT REAL ESTATE AS YOU DO."

"I DON'T TRUST REAL ESTATE PEOPLE."

"I agree with you that there are some unethical people in the real estate business. As in any profession, there is good and bad. However, I am sure you have heard of *our firm and the fine reputation we have.* I would be happy to acquaint you with clients who have been extremely happy with the service I provided."

"I WANT TO BUY A HOME FIRST BEFORE WE LIST."

"For most people not in real estate, that probably sounds like the best method. However, it is far easier to find a new home than it is to sell the old. We can achieve both objectives by *putting a clause in the listing* giving you the option of finding a property within the next 60 days while the listing is in effect. We call this a contingency clause."

"WHY DOESN'T YOUR COMPANY SHOW MY HOME AS MUCH AS OTHER COMPANIES?"

"I can see how you might be confused, however, I expect to give you overall marketing through listing with me rather than showings. I appeal to *all markets for total exposure.*"

Writing the Offer

Dialog from actual appointment

6:00 P.M.—arrived at 123 View Lane. Clients were interested in buying a home and selling their current residence.

Both clients seemed a bit nervous and said, "We don't think we will be doing anything tonight. We just wanted to talk to you and *not rush into things.* If we miss this one, it's OK. We just started looking."

I said,

> "I understand. I thought we would look at three or four homes that have sold in the neighborhood here and a couple more that are currently for sale."

I *knew that I would have to be easygoing*, not hurry too fast, yet *not* take the normal steps in walking through a home and coming back with a CMA. Tonight I would have to:

1. *list the home before I leave the property,*
2. *get a purchase agreement signed before leaving, and*
3. *present everything before everyone gets "cold feet."*

I *showed them the houses.* They agreed that these homes were certainly *similar to their own home.*

I *asked them what they paid two years ago*, and they said, "About $218,000." I told them the market had not appreciated much since that time. They probably would be looking at around $220. They told me that when they bought the home two years ago, it was listed at $225,000. I said that probably sounded about right for now. *They agreed.* I then did a *net sheet* for them based on a figure of $220,000.

> After I made them a "net sheet," we sat and talked about the home I met them at. "What would you want to offer on that home?" I said.

"Well, we were talking about it," said Ann, *"and we would want to offer, oh, I don't know. What do you think, honey?"* she said to her husband.

"Oh, I don't really think we talked much about that, did we? We might be rushing into these things."

"Let's do this." I said. *"Let's say you had an offer coming in on your own home right now. What would you consider an 'insulting beyond words' offer?"*

He said, "Something in the two hundred teen range."

"Oh," I said. "Then 10,000 less is insulting."

"*For our home, it is,*" they both said.

Turn the page...wait 'til you hear what she says next....

> *"Then we should keep that in mind when bidding the other home. We can't come in too low. That would be insulting. Yet, you still want to know that you got a good deal, right?"*

"Well," said Mrs. Buyer, "let's try an offer at $325,000. That's not a bad starting point, and if we get it, that's great! We will have to sign the listing in advance, though, because if they take a contingent offer, they will want to know that we have our house on the market. Isn't that right?" she asked me.

7:30—left buyers house (offer in hand!).

8:00—met at sellers' home at 452 Morexal for offer presentation.

Another offer had also just come in on seller's home, so seller had now received two offers.

1. One offer was $319,000 non-contingent
2. My offer was $325,000 contingent

They talked for one hour and **finally countered my offer** *at $335,000.*

10:10—*I called my buyers from seller's house.* My buyers came up to $333,000 and crossed out stove.

10:30—*sellers finally accepted,* but not before seller's agent suggested that they think about both offers overnight and let everyone know in the morning.

I said, "One offer should be countered."

10:45—sellers came back and countered my offer. They said, "*Your offer is cleaner-looking with stronger buyers who are prequalified.*"

11:00 P.M.—offer ended.

11:45—*secured all initials. Property was now "sold contingent" upon my buyer's home selling. My buyer's home sold two weeks later, and we removed the contingency.*

Closing gifts

ONE-MONTH MEMBERSHIP TO SATELLITE OR CABLE TV
ONE-YEAR MEMBERSHIP TO A DESSERT CLUB
ONE-YEAR SUPPLY OF CAR WASHES
DINNER ON MOVING DAY

Presenting the Offer

Most agents like to have an ideal setting. Some agents feel that it is best to have the sellers come to the office and conference table with both agents present. This gives the presentation a more professional feeling.

This is not always possible. Often the sellers want the agent or agents present at their own home and (as is the case for many sellers) they are set on a certain price. Then the scenario becomes more difficult from the outset.

Presenting a purchase agreement has always been the ultimate challenge for me. I prefer a good challenge, and I prefer to have all my bases covered from the beginning.

If I know the presentation will be difficult and I'll have to deal with a difficult seller and go to a home where I know there is a large family, a dog, and noise, *I try to do the following.*

I got an offer written because I stayed positive!

I ask if we could use a table that we could all sit around. I know there are little children at home before I come so I take coloring books and crayons, which our company gives away for promotion. I then proceed to tell the sellers that I know they would want all of us to be able to concentrate with our undivided attention to this matter and that it would be necessary to be uninterrupted for approximately 45 minutes to one hour. If possible, I try to call the seller ahead of time with this information, especially regarding the children and I tell them I will be bringing some coloring books. This gives the seller time to arrange for help with the children, or at least prepare the children so that we are not interrupted. Once the seller has made us comfortable and seated us around a table (even a coffee table works), one of the following three scenarios should occur:

1. **You have an offer on your OWN LISTING.**
2. **You have an offer from ANOTHER AGENT.**
3. **You have a CONTINGENT offer.**

Important information for purchase agreements

1. *Always put a time and date for final acceptance on your purchase agreements* so that the offer is accepted, rejected, or countered by a certain deadline, and neither party is left hanging.

2. The words "*subject to*" and "*contingent upon*" *are considered to have the same meaning.* For example, "This is subject to an inspection" would be the same as "contingent upon an inspection." The 48-hour contingency addendum stands apart, however, as a separate function.

3. *If a buyer gets an inspection report earlier than the stated time, the buyer's stated time to register objections begins then, not at the end of the time stated in the addendum.*

4. *A property may continue to be shown between final acceptance and removal of "subject-to," clauses, but the buyer and seller must agree to that in writing.*

5. If the buyer registers objections in writing within the stated timeline, a solution to the objections may well extend beyond the deadline.

6. When showing a home, try not to ask the seller anything directly about the real estate. *All inquiries should go through the listing agent.*

7. If the closing date should change, sign an addendum or an amendment showing the new date. *Be sure all changes are in writing.*

8. *When the property is sold, get a listing extension beyond the closing date.* This prevents situations in which the property does not close, but the buyer and seller then get together after the closing date.

(continued)

9. In some states, to file for homestead for the next year, the buyer must own and occupy the new home before June 1. *Set the closing date at the end of May.* If the closing must be delayed until June, determine *who will pay the homestead for the next year.*

10. *In order for a property to be considered sold, the delivery of an acceptable purchase agreement must be made to either agent.* Until the delivery is made, *another offer may be accepted.* A verbal acceptance or promise will not prevail. *Never wait overnight to deliver a copy of the accepted agreement.*

11. *If an offer has been presented and countered and another one is written, the seller must be told about the second one.* If the seller doesn't want to look at the second one until the first one is handled, this is all right. It is the seller's decision.

12. *Always notify a seller in writing with a list of names and addressee for your buyers within a certain timeframe.* Time frames vary from one state to another. *This list is in force only as long as the property is not listed with another broker.*

13. Make sure that both buyer and seller agree *on a date and time of possession*, before final acceptance is in effect. For example, if a buyer asks for possession on the same day as closing, it's best to put P.M. closing or A.M. closing in order to avoid overlapping with movers.

14. *Make sure there will be no surprises at the final walk-through*—such as a stove that does not work, lights that won't go on, or faucets that will not turn—*that could circumvent the closing and cause delays.*

Scenario 1
You Have an Offer on Your Own Listing

You have arrived at the seller's house and she invites you in to sit down. (Never accept an alcoholic beverage if offered.) They have cleared off their dining room table, and they ask you to present your offer. The people present are you and your sellers (husband and wife).

> You begin by putting the entire folder in front of you on the table, removing the earnest money check, and putting it in the center of the table.

You begin to explain to the sellers, "First I would like to tell you a little bit about the buyers." (You met them today at your open house, and it is important for you to establish some sort of rapport between the buyers and the sellers, something that will identify them with each other.) You tell Mr. Seller that Mr. Buyer, because he too enjoys fishing, noticed Mr. Seller's large Muskie hanging on the wall in the den. His job transfer has brought him here, and he is really looking forward to coming to the Twin Cities. He has heard so many good things about it. You go on to tell the sellers that you would like to explain what the buyers do, where they come from, and what line of work they are in. You also explain that you have spent some time *preapproving* them with a loan officer whom you called at home. The loan officer feels that these buyers appear to be pre-qualified.

You go on to say that the buyers said they *must buy this weekend.* Of all the homes that they have seen, *yours is the one they decided to write an offer on!*

Now it is time to proceed with the purchase agreement, and you ask the sellers if they would follow along. The agreement should be familiar to them because you gave them a "sample" purchase agreement to read over when you first listed the property.

You begin reviewing the document and take special note to mention the earnest money, which is sitting in the middle of the table. (*I do not take notes in place of a check.*) I read over the purchase agreement carefully and write down the points of interest that I feel the seller would like to discuss.

Points of Interest

1. *Earnest* money
2. *Contingent* or *non*contingent
3. *Price* of property
4. *Date* of closing
5. *Inclusions* in the contract
6. Division of the *taxes*

7. Type of *financing*
8. *Points* included, if any
9. *Tax* proration and special exclusions
10. Date of *possession*
11. *Additional* contingencies
12. Inspections

I go on to list the important points, and after reading over the entire offer **I ask the seller,**

"HOW DO YOU FEEL ABOUT THIS OFFER?"

(I *do not* offer my opinion until I hear what the seller has said. Sometimes even low offers, surprisingly, will be accepted. Learn when to keep quiet and when to offer an opinion.)

If the seller has a problem with the price and the terms, such as points, I list them opposite the offered terms. If there is a great deal of discrepancy, I say, "Mr. and Mrs. Seller, I feel that the buyer made an attempt at purchasing this property for *specific* reasons."

I list the reasons that the buyer has given me. Remember that if you have written a *low offer*, be prepared to back up the offer with good reasons substantiated by the buyer, such as *"comparable solds" in the area, internal condition, repairs and/ or additions.* All of these things will be crucial at the offer presentation if the offer is low and there is a wide gap.

They left before
I could ask them
to buy it!

> Go over the items in the purchase agreement that elicit the strongest objections.

Finish the purchase agreement by saying,

"You may do one of three things, Mr. and Mrs. Seller":

> 1. *ACCEPT* this purchase agreement,
> 2. *REJECT* this purchase agreement, or
> 3. *COUNTER* this purchase agreement.

It is considered to be in good taste to resolve this one way or another *before I leave* because the buyer has been good enough to put his offer *in writing.*

Scenario 2
You Are the Listing Agent and an Offer Is Made by Another Agent

You call your sellers and tell them that *from an appointment that was recently made*, a buyer came through with another agent and has written an offer with his or her *own agent.*

You first ask the sellers if it is convenient for them to come to your office. That is the most *neutral setting.* If this is agreeable, you proceed to reserve a conference room for the other agent, your sellers, and yourself.

When the other agent arrives, I usually:

1. Ask the other agent to *tell* us a little *about his or her buyers.*
2. Ask the other agent if he or she has *prequalified the buyer* and, if so, record on the file the name and phone number of the lender.
3. Ask the other agent to please put the *earnest money in the center* of the table.
4. Ask the other agent if he or she wants *me to present the purchase agreement* to the sellers (who are also present).
5. If he or she says it does not matter, I say that *I would be happy to present it,* and I take it from there.

6. If he or she wishes to present the purchase agreement, *I take out my legal-size notepad* and begin to list the items that are most important, including:

   a. Earnest *money*
   b. *Price* of property
   c. *Date* of closing
   d. *Inclusions* in the contract
   e. *Contingent* or noncontingent
   f. Division of the *taxes* and specials
   g. Type of *financing*
   h. *Points* included
   i. Date of *possession*
   j. *Exclusions*
   k. Any additional *contingencies*
   l. *Supplement* pages

7. When I have gone over the offer and clarified the points of agreement or conflict, I ask the other agent the following questions.

   a. How important is it for your buyer to *close on this date* (if there is a discrepancy in closing dates)?

   b. Does your buyer have the means to *put down more earnest money?*

   c. How did you and your buyer arrive at the *price of the contract?*

   d. Are certain items that you have written in *as inclusions very important?* I would like to add that these items may or may not have been on the listing agreement.

   e. If this is a *contingent offer* (subject to the sale of another property), I ask to see a picture of the property on which it is contingent, *a copy of the listing contract*, if it's *listed* at this time, and a list of any homes for sale in the immediate area of the contingent property. How marketable does that contingent home appear to be? Is it either a *48-* or *72-hour contingency*, so I can continue to market the listed property until this particular buyer can make his or her offer noncontingent?

   f. Are taxes prorated? I prefer to sell a home whose *taxes are prorated* from the date of closing. This means that a buyer pays from the time that he closes, and the seller pays up to closing.

   g. *What kind of financing* is involved? Has the buyer been qualified for the down payment, monthly payment, points, and so on?

   h. Are points included? If points are included, I look at the offer from all aspects. If the offer has come in full price, the buyer is conventional, and the seller is asked to pay a couple of points, it's *time to negotiate!* I try to remind the seller that the offer is extremely good and the buyer is well qualified. "If you do not want to pay all the points, is there a chance that you would be willing to *split the points?*" I also remind the seller that this buyer looks exceptionally well qualified and the contract is *noncontingent.*

   i. POSSESSION IS A MOOT POINT. Possession depends on two things: Where is the seller going or where has he gone? Does the buyer have a lease, or a closing date on his or her own house already? Try to remind the seller of the importance of an offer that is in hand, *noncontingent,* and the importance of the qualifying factor in the case. Try to show the seller, through the other agent, that the buyer truly wants to be accommodating!

I try to be as relaxed as possible. I smile and add casual comments....

j. Are there exclusions? I try to take care of exclusions ahead of time, but if at the last minute during an offer presentation the seller says, "I forgot to tell you I am going to exclude the fireplace screen because it was a gift and a very old antique, but we will replace it with another," I ask, "How important to the buyer is this exclusion?" *Remember that this must be in writing.*

k. Are there additional contingencies? Frequently the purchase agreement is subject to, or contingent upon, the attorney's opinion, the wife or husband, or results of the home inspection. Should the offer be contingent on an inspection first?

   In these cases, make sure the rest of the offer is favorable. Put a date in for the contingency removal. For example, "This offer is contingent upon the successful approval by buyer's attorney on or before (date)."

l. There may be supplements to the contract. If so, read them over carefully and make sure that any type of inspection report or survey report has a completion date. Should the offer be subject to a survey?

Scenario 3
You Have a Contingent Offer

CONTINGENT OFFERS are sometimes the best offers, if you can take care of all the loose ends and manage to represent the buyer successfully at the other end of the situation, too.

> An **offer** is often contingent upon the buyer having to sell his house first.
> Often that home is not even listed!

An *offer* may also be contingent upon approval by another individual, such as a husband, wife, partner, parent, appraiser, inspector, or someone who holds a vested interest.

Sometimes the offer is contingent upon the buyer getting approval for financing and/or securing the funds for the down payment by a particular date.

Often an offer is contingent upon the buyer being relinquished from a lease obligation.

Contingencies have one crucial requirement:

A *DATE* by which time they are *CANCELED* or *REMOVED*.

Should you have a *contingent offer* in which the buyer has a home to sell and you have not had the opportunity to develop much of a rapport yet, try to:

- *view the buyer's* home as quickly as possible,
- *do a CMA* on the buyer's home for your own satisfaction,
- *ask the buyer* what he or she expects to get from the sale of his or her home, or
- *have the buyer* list his or her home simultaneously with you as you prepare the purchase agreement.

Sample Offer Presentation

FOLLOWING IS A SUMMARY OF THE WAY AN ACTUAL OFFER WAS PRESENTED, FROM START TO FINISH. THE PROPERTY DISCUSSED HERE WAS A LARGE WALK-OUT RANCH STYLE.

(The owner came through an open house of mine.)

Background information

- I did a CMA for her and she insisted we *list the property high.*
- The home had currently been listed for over *three months.*
- There had been *39 showings* and *five open houses.*
- We had *three price reductions.*
- *Eight days* after the third price reduction, we received the following offer. Here is a summary of the *offer presentation* from start to finish, at which time it was finally *accepted.*

SATURDAY

3:00 P.M.	I checked my phone messages (which I do *every few hours*), and learned that an agent from another company had an offer on my property.
3:15 P.M.	I called the seller to ask *when we could present the offer*, and the seller, a single woman, asked if we could meet at her home at 5:00. I called the other agent to confirm.
4:50 P.M.	*I arrived at the seller's home to present the offer.* I asked to sit at the kitchen table and waited for the other agent to arrive. I brought the seller all of the appointment slips for the property and told her that the consensus of the agents showing the home thus far was that the home needed a lot of work, and if another agent were to write an offer on the home, the work needed would probably be reflected in the offer. The property was currently listed for $238,900.
5:00 P.M.	The other agent arrived. We all sat down at the table with the seller. Coffee, soda, and water were offered. I asked the other agent to tell us a little about the buyer. As she told us about the buyer, she put an earnest money check in the center of the table. The check was made out to the ***listing company*** in the amount of $3,000. I reviewed the offer for a moment and the agent asked if I would present the offer.
5:15 P.M.	I explained the offer to the seller and said the offering price was $215,000. I began **a "net sheet."**
5:25 P.M.	The seller asked to *talk with me alone.* The other agent waited in the living room.
5:40 P.M.	The seller said that the offer was *ridiculous.* She couldn't possibly make it with this amount, and she wanted to counter at full price. I explained that we had a much better chance of keeping this very good buyer if we *met the buyer in the middle.* I explained that the buyer looked excellent because:

1. Buyers offer was **NONCONTINGENT** and
2. Buyer had already been **prequalified** with good credit, and approved rating.

6:15 P.M.	*The seller listened,* and countered the offer at $228,000.
6:30 P.M.	*I telephoned the other agent* regarding the counter.
7:00 P.M.	*The agent called his buyer* back. They countered at $220,000.
7:15 P.M.	I spoke to the seller *who countered back again* at $224,000. *"I'm not giving the house away,"* she said.
7:30 P.M.	The agent felt the buyer stood firm on $220,000, but said she would let me know shortly.
7:45 P.M.	*The buyer's agent relayed that* the buyer came up to $221,000. "That's it," she said.
8:00 P.M.	*I told the seller,* "The buyer really likes your home. However, he has seen many properties now and feels that he is paying a good price for a home that needs a tremendous amount of interior work. Another issue we have to deal with is the *appraisal. Your home is the largest one on the block.* The appraiser will take this into consideration. Why not take a few minutes to reassess the situation. I know that the money is tight. *You could have a large estate sale* because you wanted to sell so many things. That would help a lot, too."
8:45	The seller said, *"I'll take $222,000 and not one penny less."*
9:00	*I told the other agent* that the counter now *stood firm* at $222,000.
9:30	After speaking to the buyer one more time, the buyer's agent told me, *"Congratulations, you have a deal.* I'm going to the buyer's home to get the changes signed, and I will drop the papers off at *your home mailbox shortly."*
9:45	I told the seller. The seller was nervous now. She didn't know why she accepted such a low offer, but she said "I guess it is all right."
10:50	1. *She signed the counter, and we had a deal at $222,000.* 2. *I left the seller with a copy of all papers she signed.* 3. *I took the highlight sheets I had made with me.* 4. *I left the lockbox on the door for the appraiser.*
11:30	I called the office message center to leave a message for the secretary that the property had been sold. (Some agents continue to show until the buyer's mortgage is approved.)
12:00	I turned out the lights and went to bed!

How's that new listing doin'? I should call my buyer and bring him over!

Oh! I sold that after tour last week, Neil. I left you a voicemail.

ANOTHER FINE DAY IN REAL ESTATE ADVENTURELAND!

Sample Problem Closings

1. **Seller didn't agree to leave the lamp in the living room.**

   It wasn't attached but it was on the wall, and the buyer thought it was staying. Buyer is visibly upset upon seeing this at the *final inspection* the day before closing. (Always make sure that you schedule a final inspection for your buyer before he or she closes on the home!)

   Agent tells buyer that he will contact the selling agent, and they will work out a compromise with which everyone will be satisfied.

   Agent calls listing agent and decides upon price of lamp, and asks whether seller would consider bringing it back. Would agent be interested in splitting the difference? If not, it becomes a case of whether or not you care about having the repeat business from that client based on how happy he was with you.

2. **Seller decided to stay an extra day, and everyone has already made arrangements with moving companies.**

   When it comes right down to it, there's not really a lot one can do. It's best to talk it over with the agents, and if there is still no compromise, volunteer your own time to help or to contribute a day's worth of food to help things go more smoothly. Always keep clients aware that you would do almost anything to keep the transaction running smoothly.

3. **Buyers want to bring things over and start putting them in the seller's garage.**

   Not a good idea. Seller is responsible until closing for anything stolen or damaged, even if buyer gets his or her own insurance. It complicates the situation. Best to wait until closing.

4. **There is a lien against the property which the closer failed to discover! Closing must be postponed and everyone must be notified.**

   Again, this is actually out of your hands. Remember, though, it is most important to *keep abreast of how the loan is progressing.* Stay close to the telephone and reconfirm to buyers and sellers the fact that you are willing to hand carry or deliver any documents necessary to consummate the transaction. You may have to reschedule times and dates. Stay calm and assured that all will go well. Never buy into anger or frustration. *A function of your job is to eliminate hassles that frustrate the buyer or seller.*

5. **The furnace broke the day before the closing.**

   Most contracts read that the seller is responsible for assuring that all mechanics of the home are in proper working order at time of closing. It will have to be fixed or replaced. Stay on top of everything, relating the status back and forth between buyer and seller.

6. **At the final walk-through, the buyer sees that the doorbell is not working. There was no mention of this problem before.**

   The seller will have to fix doorbell.

7. **The seller wants to close the day before the actual closing date, and the buyer wants to close two days later. No one wants to budge.**

   It's always best to leave the decision on which day is actually available *in the hands of the closer.* Sometimes it puts weight on a delicate balance between the buyer and the seller. The closer should really be in charge if the date has to be changed.

8. **The mortgage was paid off but not recorded. The closing is held up until proof of payoff is secured.**

   Not much you can do here except *make sure from the outset* (if you are the lister) that the mortgage satisfaction is intact and perhaps try to check with the other agent if it is not your listing. Keep the peace and, again, volunteer your time to get all documents transported as quickly as possible.

9. **Buyers and/or sellers were unhappy with settlement costs and feel that they were misrepresented.**

   This is so important because it involves their *trust in you. You must be sure the figures you gave them were accurate.* Also check with the loan officer to make sure the buyer's figures were what he expected at closing. Check with the closer beforehand and have him or her give you final payoff figures for the seller. (These figures should be given to the seller a day or two before closing.)

10. **Seller can't get his or her check at the closing.**

   Some attorneys feel no one should receive funds until all papers are recorded. Make sure you and your clients are aware of this.

11. **At final inspection the swimming pool did not seem to be in proper working order and it is too cold to check it.**

   If there is a discrepancy and the seller is aware of the fact that there might be a problem, funds can be held in escrow until the pool can be checked or fixed and then remaining funds can be returned to seller.

12. **Lender has stipulated that seller must repair a retaining wall before closing. The wall is submerged in snow.**

   Again, a contractor can be contacted and funds can be held in escrow for an approximate amount satisfactory to buyer and seller; remaining funds can be returned to seller when the job is finished.

13. **Buyer can't decide whether or not to take out an owner's title insurance policy before closing.**

   Explain to the buyer that the mortgage company has taken its own policy out on the property. However, if there were ever any undisclosed heirs, forged signatures, or errors in recording, an owner's policy would *protect him or her.*

14. **Seller left the draperies as specified in the purchase agreement, but took the drapery rods.**

   Seller must return them or make concessions for them at the closing. If all else fails, agents should try to compromise the best they can.

15. **The sale fell through. Who will pay for the abstract, survey, or termite inspection?**

   The person to whom it is *charged!*

16. **There is a sewer line on the property. Nothing is mentioned in the contract and neither buyer nor seller will budge.**

   It usually comes out of the commission. This is a case in which the seller feels he is already losing money, and the buyer says he was never told about it. The agent should stay on top of everything.

17. **It's two days before the closing. The appraisal came in late and low.**

   The first thing to do is contact the lender and tell them you want an independent appraisal done. This is permitted in most states. Go to your office and pull your own comparables. Fax them to the lender to make sure they are given to the appraiser.

18. **The attorney for the buyer makes unreasonable requests just three days before the closing.**

   It is imperative from the start that you maintain a good rapport with everyone involved with the closing, *especially the attorneys.* Try to stay abreast of the situation and work with the other agent and attorney, keeping the buyers and sellers removed from it. If a stalemate continues, talk with your own company attorney or a good real estate attorney with whom you have developed a relationship. (All agents should have contact with a good real estate attorney for legal advice.)

19. **The seller's agent was new and is not doing follow-up before the closing. Things have been left undone.**

   Some new agents are not comfortable with all the work that must be done in order to have the closing run smoothly. *Work closely with the other agent from the outset. Make yourself available* if they seek your help.

20. **The sellers are divorcing and don't want to see each other at the closing!**

   Usually this can be handled with a little tact and finesse. Simply explain the situation to the closer ahead of time and ask if it would be convenient for the sellers to sign off separately ahead of time. This saves much time and unnecessary embarrassment. Alternatively, they may choose separate rooms.

What to do if you are the listing agent and an offer is made by another agent

1. *ACCEPT* this purchase agreement,
2. *REJECT* this purchase agreement, or
3. *COUNTER* this purchase agreement.

Checklist for purchase agreement

1. Original purchase agreement completely signed
   a. Attached
   b. Out for signatures
2. Copy of purchase agreement
3. Supplements to purchase agreement
4. Earnest money check
5. Note to be redeemed
6. Copy of earnest money check
7. Interest-bearing account for earnest money
8. Listing agreement and computer sheet
9. Housing disclosure report
10. Seller's disclosure report
11. Well disclosure report
12. Seller's net sheet
13. Buyer's worksheet
14. Condo/townhouse bylaws
15. Contingency removal sheet
16. Lender information
17. Is/is not subject to contingency
18. Photo of subject property
19. Remarks
20. Date purchase agreement sent to title company
21. Follow up (weekly)

With a checklist I don't forget anything!

Worksheet for Purchase Agreement Final Closing

File Number _____

Seller's Name _____

Single _____ Married _____ Divorced _____ Widowed _____

Forwarding Address _____

Current Address _____ Phone _____

City/State _____ Zip _____

Buyer's Name _____

Address _____ Phone _____

City/State _____ Zip _____

Earnest Money: Check Attached _____ Amount _____

Interest-Bearing Account _____ Noninterest-Bearing _____

Date Deposited _____

Buyer's Attorney _____ Phone _____

Seller's Attorney _____ Phone _____

Condo _____ Association Name _____

Townhouse _____ Address _____

Present First Mortgage at _____

Phone Number _____ Balance _____

Assumption Approval Necessary _____ Date Received _____

Contract for Deed Holder _____

Home Improvements _____

New Financing _____

Lender Branch _____

Loan Officer _____ Phone _____

Type of Loan _____ Points _____

Purchase Agreement Date _____

Selling Price _____

Closing Date _____

Commission _____

Other Agent _____

Anatomy of a Closing Transaction

1. Final acceptance of offer by buyer and seller
2. Signed purchase agreements delivered to both buyer and seller
3. Real estate office notified that property is sold
4. Sold sign put on the property
5. Completion of all necessary papers sent to closing departments and title company
6. Mortgage payoff notice sent to lender
7. Home retracted from computer and marked sold
8. Loan application made by buyers; fees collected for appraisal and credit report
9. Earnest money deposited by listing company
10. Verification and credit report on buyer requested by lender for buyer appraisal and title policy also ordered

11. Credit report and appraisal received by mortgage company; documents reviewed for evidence of clear title; final application signed by buyer; loan file sent to the underwriter for his or her review
12. All payoffs on loans against the property ordered; fee owner contacted if seller has contract for deed; seller contacted to settle any title problems
13. Loan file of buyer approved, suspended for needed information, or rejected outright
14. All figures for payoffs against property received by closing department for seller; documents prepared; gets all tax information gathered; assessments verified
15. Loan approved; selling agent notified; buyers notified

16. Closing date set; all parties notified by mail
17. Loan package ordered from lender
18. Closing documents forwarded to title company
19. Final search done; final figures entered on closing statement
20. Lockbox and highlight information on home retrieved
21. **Closing day!** Mortgage documents and seller's documents signed; funds collected and dispersed
22. Package prepared for lender, recording, accounting, and title insurance
23. Loan payment book issued by lender's servicing department
24. Documents filed with county; final title insurance policy issued

Settlement Day

What buyers need to bring to closing

1. Photo ID of self and driver's license
2. One year's paid homeowner's insurance premium
3. Certified funds made out to self for exact amount
4. Decision to buy or not to buy a separate owners policy for title insurance
5. Verification that all utilities are in buyer's name as of closing date

What sellers need to bring to closing

1. Photo ID of self and driver's lincense
2. Proof of paid utility bills (a water bill becomes a lien on the property if not paid off)
3. Proof of payoff on tax lien, tax assessment, late taxes due, and late penalty due
4. All keys to all doors to property
5. Garage door openers
6. Warranties on appliances left at the home
7. Abstract on property or owner's duplicate if torrens property
8. Payoff notes or mortgages not recorded (shows as a lien against the property)
9. Rent adjustment with seller (if lease-back situation)
10. Servicing contracts (such as heating or air conditioning) that buyer may be assuming or taking over
11. Townhouse or swimming pool membership that has yet to be assigned to buyer
12. Termite inspection certification (also sent to attorneys and/or closing department)
13. Itemized list of personal property left with house (in accordance with contract)
14. Accumulated taxes or insurance funds, which go to seller unless otherwise designated
15. Survey copy if ordered

Closing Gifts

I brought a big basket of gourmet goodies to the closing. They loved it....

Monogrammed towels

Monogrammed door knocker

Monogrammed stationery with new address

Large wicker fruit basket

Large perennial plant/tree

Monogrammed picture frame

Subscription to *House Beautiful* (give card and inscription at closing)

Juice machine

Old-fashioned malted milk mixer (an all-time favorite)

Monogrammed pen and pencil set

Personalized letter opener

Personalized desk set

Subscription to *National Geographic* (for the buyer's children)

Year's supply of bottled water (looks impressive, yet still inexpensive)

Ipod

Monogrammed glasses

Answering machine

Picture of new home in charcoal

Dinner reservations at a renowned restaurant

Reservations for an upcoming play

Gift certificate on one-year anniversary in house

Theater tickets

One-month membership at a local health club

One-month membership to cable TV

One-year membership to a dessert club

One-year supply of car washes

Dinner on moving day

Uh...I went with that year's supply of water...I can check up on them monthly!

Address	Date Sold	Home Price	My Commission	Comments Closer/ Agents	Date Closed

CHAPTER 14

Chapter Summary

There are three types of closings: closing on a buyer to buy, closing on a seller to sell, and closing time. No transaction is ever complete until the buyer and seller mutually agree to sign on the dotted line, the keys are exchanged and everyone has shaken hands.

Know when to close. There are a variety of "stall phrases" and a ways to handle objections. Learn to close and overcome these.

When you call a seller to present a purchase agreement, the presentations is the key to a successful closing. Avoid telling the seller what the offer is over the phone if you can. Always put a time and a date for final acceptance on your purchase agreements, so the offer is accepted, rejected, or countered by a certain deadline, and neither party is left hanging. Make sure there are no surprises at the final walk-through—this could circumvent the closing and cause delays. When presenting your offer, make sure that the buyers have been prequalified. Read over the purchase agreement very slowly when presenting an offer to the sellers. Make notes and list the important points. After reading the entire offer, ask the sellers how they feel about the offer. Go over the purchase agreement and discuss the points that elicit the strongest objections. Finish the purchase agreement by telling the sellers that they may accept, reject, or counter the purchase agreement.

Before closing on a purchase agreement, go over a checklist to make sure all points are covered. Make sure the worksheet is complete when closing on a purchase agreement with the sellers. Go through the "Anatomy of a Closing Transaction" and cover all 24 points thoroughly. On settlement day make sure that the buyers know to bring 5 specified items to closing. Make sure the sellers know to bring 15 specified items to closing (if appropriate). Send a closing gift.

CHAPTER 15

PROFESSIONALISM

- Deceptive Trade Act
- Disclosure
- Ethics

big deal by Lorayne n' Neil

Weeks Later . . .

Your Guide to Professionalism

Everything is changing fast now. We are in the twenty-first century!

However, PROFESSIONALISM NEVER CHANGES.

Across the country, managers were asked; "How many agents would lie?"

34 percent would tell the truth

22 percent make unreal promises

22 percent sell the wrong information

30 percent say customer demand is "kickback"—no big deal to exaggerate

54 percent say a "drive to meet goals" does disservice to the customer

Actions that demonstrate a lack of professionalism

1. Putting homes on MLS that are not available for showing
2. Not taking homes off MLS when they have sold
3. Stating a property is "on the lake" when it is not
4. Not filling out a disclosure of problems with the property
5. Not canceling old listing before new listing is put into effect
6. Forgetting to lock doors after showing a property
7. Failing to put new listing on MLS within 3 business days

In a market where there is a SHORTAGE O F GOOD LISTINGS,

Never *OVERPRICE* a property.

If you are asked about another agent, ALWAYS be kind and fair.

Why does a CLIENT decide to do business with you?

1. What are you doing that is different?
2. How did you fulfill their expectations?
3. What did you promise them in the beginning?

Companies are starting to add EXCEPTIONAL SERVICE

1. Some companies pay to have the carpets cleaned.
2. Some agents/companies add home warranty services.
3. Some companies/agents paint/repair home or give allowance.
4. Give professional looking handouts listing schools, shopping, bonus information about the neighborhood and subject property.
5. Many companies furnish "information boxes"—talking stations that give additional information regarding the listing.

I always dress up to show houses!

Communication Is the Greatest Concern

If buyers or sellers have a problem, they want to know they can talk it over with their real estate agent. They want to see HOW their agent deals with the problem. Keep everything documented and keep records of all conversations with clients.

Since 1913, when it was adopted by the National Association of REALTORS®, there has been a *code of ethics.*

This chapter on PROFESSIONALISM is designed to help agents with ideas and suggestions for dealing with clients on a day-to-day basis.

Keys to success with sellers

- Be concise and fair in providing the seller disclosure forms at the outset.
- Be sure to comply with fair housing laws and equal opportunity in housing.
- Be sure the sellers receive an in-depth and well-researched market analysis on their property.
- Try to give the seller suggestions on home improvements *before* listing the property.
- Be sure sellers remove wall fixtures or items that are attached that are not included with sale. Wall must be repaired and, if necessary, fixture must be replaced.
- Check to be sure the seller is in compliance with all the housing ordinances.
- Take special precaution regarding open house signs for marketing townhomes and various condominium associations. (Association bylaws usually prohibit signs.)
- Carefully explain to sellers the arbitration program, if it applies.
- When advertising a property, never exaggerate or misrepresent the home.
- If multiple offers exist, present them as soon as possible.
- If you, the agent, are purchasing property for yourself, identify yourself in the purchase agreement as a licensed real estate agent.
- Attend closings of buyers and sellers and, if possible, give them a token of your appreciation at the closing.
- Always give *all copies* of purchase agreements, addenda, and supplements to buyers and sellers. Make sure you keep copies as well.
- A home cannot be put back on the market until a cancellation agreement is signed by the original buyer. *All parties must sign.*
- When advertising a property, identify yourself as an agent and give your company's name.

Professionalism with buyers

- At the initial meeting with a buyer, establish your relationship as their sole representation in real estate transactions.
- Stay within the guidelines of price, area, and style that the buyer establishes.
- Verify all information on the listing sheet when showing buyers a property.
- Give buyers all forms, disclosures, and printouts available on home.
- Be sure buyer is prequalified by lender before presenting a contract on a property.
- Comply with all agency disclosures and state law and stay within relationship boundaries throughout the transaction.
- When writing a purchase agreement, be sure it reflects *exactly* what the buyers and sellers are asking for.
- Double-check all figures to be sure the earnest money, mortgage amount, and down payment total the selling price.
- Explain the arbitration agreement, if it applies to buyers.
- Prior to the closing, arrange to have a final walk-through.
- Be sure you have the buyer's written permission before sending new neighbor cards to residents of the neighborhood.
- Give all earnest money checks to your company to be placed in an interest-bearing account, unless otherwise specified.
- If for some reason buyer's contract is canceled, be sure all copies are given to both parties, both buyer and seller.
- Prior to closing, check and double-check with title company to be sure loan is processing without problems.
- Prior to closing, be sure buyer has arranged for utilities; telephone, water, electric, and cable service.
- If possible, provide buyer with a list of moving companies.
- Attend the closing and bring your buyer a token of appreciation.

C H A P T E R   1 5

Professional Attitudes

- Dress professionally whenever showing a property, meeting with client, or calling on a seller. Wear business attire for all business appointments.

- Before showing a property that is not your listing, contact the other real estate company first.

- If the buyer decides not to see a property upon arrival at the property, leave your card and notify the listing office.

- Always leave your BUSINESS CARD with the date and time you showed a property. There could be others showing the same day, and if another agent left the home unlocked, this is your proof of when you were there.

- When showing a property, always knock on any doors that are closed within the house.

- If the seller is home, always ask before you use any of their facilities, such as the bathroom.

- Always be prompt for appointments.

- Avoid eating and drinking in front of sellers and buyers. It is best to decline offers of alcoholic beverages during BUSINESS situations.

- Get permission before videotaping the interior of a home.

- When showing a home with pets, always refrain from letting them out of the house and make sure they are not locked in another room before you leave.

- If it is impossible to lock home, or if there is a problem with lockbox, call the listing company immediately to report. Do not assume the next agent or the listing agent will take care of the problem.

- Do not provide information about topics relative to the home unless you are certain of the information.

- While showing a property, avoid talking to the seller about the price, terms, and closing date. Discuss these topics with listing agent.

- When you leave a property, leave the doors that were closed, closed. Leave blinds that were pulled, pulled. Leave lights that were off or on the way that you found them.

- Do not let unlicensed people show properties for you at any time!

Later...

Professionalism: Case Study #1

Michael had a listing at 1200 North Ninth Street.

Sheryl, an agent with a different company, called Michael within the last week, expressing interest in the listing on behalf of a buyer she was working with. She asked Michael to call her if any offers came in because her buyer expressed interest in writing an offer if there was any activity or offer on the home. Right or wrong, Michael agreed to comply with Sheryl's request and inform her of any offers.

The next day, Patty, a second multiple listing agent, called Michael and told him that she had an offer to present to Michael and the seller. Michael arranged an appointment and told Patty of the possibility of another offer coming in. Patty told Michael that if he notified the other agent that Patty's offer exists, Patty would withdraw the offer and advise her clients to purchase another home. Michael was concerned about proceeding, so he told the seller of Patty's statement. The seller didn't want to lose Patty's offer and told Michael not to call Sheryl about Patty's offer. Patty's offer was accepted by the seller.

Later the same day, Sheryl called Michael and told him that her clients had written an offer on the property. Michael then told Sheryl that the property was already under contract with another buyer.

Sheryl and her clients were very upset. Both Sheryl and her clients filed a complaint against Michael. They stated that he had violated the National Code of Ethics—a violation of Article 1—and that they were not treated honestly. Their complaint stated that Michael had promised to notify them in the event of another offer and he failed to do so.

* * *

Questions:

1. Do you think Michael can comply with Sheryl's request?
2. Do you think Michael is in violation of Article 1?
3. If Patty acted without her client's knowledge, do you think she is in violation of the code? What if Patty acted under instruction from her client?
4. Did Michael's sellers respond appropriately to the threat of the withdrawn offer? Did they have the right to do this?

Professionalism: Case Study #2

Rollie had a listing at 6925 Indian Way. It was very difficult to sell the house. There had been settlement problems in the basement in the past and the home was sinking. The property had been on the market for over 22 months.

One Saturday evening around 6:00 P.M., Rollie received a call from another agent. Barbara, let him know that she was bringing him an offer on Indian Way and would drop it off at his office within the next half-hour.

Rollie was a great movie buff and had tickets to the opening of a new show. He had been waiting a long time to get tickets to this particular event. The show started at 7:30 P.M. and he was already running late. He told Barbara to drop the offer in the mail slot at his office.

Rollie went to the premier of his show. As he was leaving he ran into some old friends, who invited him backstage to a prestigious party. It was a once-in-a-lifetime opportunity, and he did not get home until after midnight. He knew he couldn't call his seller at that hour, so he decided to call first thing in the morning.

The following morning at 7:00 A.M. Rollie got a call from Barbara at home. She informed him that the buyers had slept on the offer and changed their minds because of the settlement problems in the basement. She stated they were withdrawing their offer. Within the next half-hour Barbara delivered a written revocation of the offer, signed by the buyers.

The seller later learned about the revoked offer and filed a complaint in violation of the Code of Ethics, against Rollie.

*   *   *

Questions:

1. What articles or standards of practice apply to this case?
2. Do you think Rollie is in violation of any Code?
3. What should Rollie have done differently?

Professionalism: Case Study #3

David owned a discount broker real estate company. A seller had signed a contract with him to list their property in MLS for a certain amount of money. However, this was not an open listing. The seller was forced to handle all aspects of the listing, including: advertising, negotiation, contract writing, and closing. David's agreement gave specific permission to all participants of MLS to deal directly with the seller, and David's MLS insert stated exactly this under "remarks."

Suzanne was an agent representing a buyer who wrote an offer on another of David's listings, 9000 Frontback Trail. Although she would have preferred to work with David, he explained to her that she must call the seller directly with her offer. She set up the appointment and arrived at the seller's home to present her buyer's offer. The seller began to ask her questions about their position, the contract language, the closing process, and other important items. Essentially, the seller was seeking her advice about what they should do.

Whereas Suzanne tried to direct the seller to David, the seller dismissed this idea and continued to press her for answers. He indicated that he could not proceed with the offer until he got her feelings about his questions. She did not want to hurt her buyer's offer or their position, so she complied with the seller's requests, and she gave her opinion. She gave as much advice and counsel on all the questions as possible.

Suzanne and the seller finally came to terms and they made a deal. Throughout the ensuing weeks and up to the closing, problems arose. They buyer became extremely dissatisfied with several aspects of the transaction and asserted that Suzanne did not watch out for his interests. The buyer filed an ethics complaint against Suzanne and all of the above information was revealed at the hearing.

* * *

Questions:

1. What articles of the Code of Ethics might be applied here?
2. Is Suzanne in violation of the Code of Ethics?
3. Does Suzanne have any possible legal liability?

**These questions may be answered by looking in your own Code of Ethics and Standards of Practice from the National Association of Realtors.

Professional Ways to Stay Out of Trouble

Many steps are involved in a real estate transaction. Here are some pointers to follow for problem-free transactions.

1. Verify everything that you are told about a home.
2. Believe nothing you are told until you see proof.
3. Get everything regarding a listing/purchase in writing.
4. Take nothing for granted regarding real estate property.
5. Disclose all information about a property in writing.
6. Always keep an open line of communication with clients.
7. There is always a duty to the client to disclose.
8. There is an unwritten duty to the client to investigate.
9. Deposit earnest money with company as soon as possible.
10. Never, under any circumstances, fill out the disclosure on a property. This is up to the sellers.
11. Do not recommend what to include and what to leave out.
12. Do not dismiss defects that may have been corrected by current seller or by a prior seller. Disclose every detail to new buyers!

Simple keys to success

- Be aware that seller may be left with a huge liability and no equity.
- Be careful when accepting a small down payment. Can a buyer perform?
- A spouse can act as a power of attorney for a spouse.
- Let the buyer fill out all buyer information sheets.
- Never exaggerate or guess at square footage on a listing.
- Do not rely on information from other agent on a listing.
- Always give townhouse buyers a copy of Association Bylaws and Rules.
- An offer or a counter can be withdrawn at any time until acted on.
- Give the buyer names of several inspection companies to choose from.
- Financing is the key to whether or not closing is a success.
- It pays to have a foundation of goodwill with buyer and seller.

I should tell my seller to talk to an attorney if he wants legal advice!

I should have read *Real Estate Field Manual* first!!

Stay Out of Trouble and Out of Court!

1. Disclose if you were involved in a prior sale with seller.
2. Disclose if you sell your own home and act as an agent.
3. Send a written list of prospects to seller when listing expires.
4. Ask seller whether they are involved in foreclosure.
5. Check with date of sheriff's sale and redemption date on foreclosed property.
6. Check with sellers/buyers regarding whether they have declared bankruptcy.
7. Double check for assumption of mortgages on home.
8. Are contracts for deed available for creative financing?
9. Do not act as power of attorney for buyer/seller if you are the agent in the transaction.
10. A power of attorney ceases upon death.
11. Show seller in writing that buyer is preapproved or prequalified for a mortgage.
12. Know what is required in which municipality for each listing to diminish the liability.
13. Do not exaggerate or guess on fact sheets regarding a listed property.
14. *Do not rely on information from a previous listing sheet.*
15. Always document recommendations and defects.
16. Should you disclose if there is a murder/suicide in a home?
17. An offer or counter can be withdrawn anytime until such time as it has been acted on.
18. It is the duty of the agent to relay any/all pertinent facts regarding the property.

Disclosure and Professionalism

In Texas especially, no legislation has influenced the practice of real estate more than the Deceptive Trade Practices Act (DTPA). The initial 1973 statute, found in Chapter 7 of the Texas Business and Commerce Code, did not affect real estate transactions until 1975. Although minor revisions have been made to the act, extensive changes were implemented in 1979 and 1995.

The 1995 legislative changes made an attempt to level the playing field somewhat. They protect consumers in the marketplace while guarding defendants against groundless and false claims.

Basically, the act is designed to provide efficient, economical procedures to protect consumers against three offenses:

1. FALSE MISLEADING PRACTICES
2. UNCONSCIONABLE ACTIONS
3. BREACH OF WARRANTY

This law is a very powerful tool for consumers. Proving that a deceptive act has occurred is easier under this law than under previous real estate statutes or common law. The law provides that consumers may recover more than their actual losses. Although an injured party can recover punitive damages for fraud, the Deceptive Trade Practices Act does not require proof that the defendant intended to deceive or mislead. The result of a deceptive act can be a cause for damages beyond simple economic loss.

Breach of warranty of the sale of new homes was where the DTPA was initially used. The original draft of the law allowed a consumer to recover three times the amount of actual damages suffered as a result of defective or shoddy construction in a new home purchase. This generous remedy prompted consumers to bring all breach-of-warranty cases under the DTPA. Most recently, the law has been used by consumers against sellers of used homes, brokers, and lenders. The law allows for a recovery of damages in excess of actual economic loss, but no longer provides for the automatic trebling of damages.

Consumer Protection

The act protects consumers. Consumer means an "individual, a partnership, or a corporation in this state or a subdivision or agency of the state that seeks or acquires by purchase or lease any goods or services." Specifically excluded are business consumers with assets of $25 million or more. Goods include both real and personal property; services include any type of labor or work performed for another and for which compensation is received.

Deceptive acts

False, misleading, and deceptive business practices are not defined, but are described by a list of 25 practices.

Deception is wrong, no matter where you live. However, the Texas Deceptive Practices Act, Section 17.46(b), states that consumers must prove that the defendant engaged in one of the practices, that it was the producing cause of their damages, and that they relied on the practice to their detriment.

Following are deceptive practices relevant to real estate transactions:

- Misrepresenting or causing confusion and misunderstanding regarding the source approval, certification, or affiliation of goods or services.
- Misrepresenting that goods are new.
- Disparaging the goods, services, or business of another by misleading or making false representations.

No, the roof does not leak!

Except when it rains!

- Placing misleading advertising, such as advertising goods or services for sale with intent not to sell as advertised or advertising fraudulently that one is going out of business.
- Making false or misleading statements concerning the reasons for a price reduction.
- Misrepresenting the authority of an agent to negotiate the final terms of a consumer transaction.
- Representing that a contract, an agreement, a warranty, or a guaranty confers rights or benefits that it does not.
- Representing that work or services have been performed when they have not.
- Failing to disclose information concerning goods or services that was known at the time of the transaction if the purpose of the lack of disclosure was to induce the consumer in a transaction into which the consumer would not have entered had the information been disclosed.
- Taking advantage of a disaster declared by the governor by demanding or collecting an exorbitant or excessive price for the sale or lease of fuel, food, medicine, or another necessity. (1995 addition)

No law requires that the consumer prove that the offending party intended to deceive or misrepresent. The fact that misrepresentation occurred is sufficient cause. It is not a defense to a lawsuit brought under this act for the defendant to say he or she did not know his or her action was illegal. The act prohibits not only misrepresentations, but also misleading statements. (A misleading statement is one that leads the consumer to believe something other than true facts.)

Unconscionable action

An unconscionable action is one that takes advantage of the consumer's lack of knowledge, ability, experience, or capacity to a grossly unfair degree. With the passage of new amendments to the DPTA in 1995, the definition no longer includes transactions in which the value received and the consideration paid result in gross disparity.

The act does not create nor detail the warranties encompassed by the DTPA. Case law indicates that the DTPA is breached by a violation of an implied or express warranty described in the Uniform Commercial Code or an implied warranty declared by the courts.

Producing cause

Under the DTPA, the consumer must prove that a misleading, deceptive, or fraudulent act was a producing cause of loss. A producing cause is a contributing factor that, in a natural sequence, produces injury or damage. Under the DTPA, the consumer is not required to prove that the deceptive act related to material fact or that the consumer relied on that misrepresentation. A consumer needs to prove only the amount of actual damages caused by the deceptive act.

Defenses under the DTPA

There are several defenses to damages under the Deceptive Trade Practices Act. If the defendant can prove that, before consummation of the transaction, he gave reasonable and timely notice to the plaintiff on the defendant's reliance on a third party generating the false or misleading information, the defendant escapes liability by proving all of the following:

- The producing cause of the alleged offense stems from the information written by a third party and given to the defendant.
- The party supplying the information reasonably anticipated the information would be given to a consumer.

- The information related to the transaction in question was false or inaccurate.
- The defendant did not or could not have reasonably known of its falsity or inaccuracy.
- The defendant informed the consumer in writing prior to consummating the contract that he or she was merely the messenger, not the originator of the information.

Apparently the phrase "and could not reasonably have known of the falsity or inaccuracy" imposes upon the real estate broker this duty of care to at least investigate the information to determine whether or not it is true.

An agent should and must give the various parties notices for inspections and representation very early in the transaction since no definition to "consummation of the transaction" is apparent. Providing this notice prior to the earnest money contract would be the safest course rather than at the time of closing. While the defendant can escape liability, the third party supplying the information can be sued even though no contract existed with the plaintiff.

Seller disclosure form

Most states now have some form of a disclosure form. An excellent one to refer to is the following, outlined for the state of Texas.

The disclosure form is to be completed with the best of the seller's knowledge and belief as of the date the notice is completed and signed. If the information required is unknown to the seller, the seller should indicate that fact on the notice and stay in compliance with the Section. This probably does not mean, however, that the seller can ignore an obvious defect and say "I don't know." Disclosure of a defect is required for a broker under 15A (6) (a) of the License Act, which states: "The commission may suspend or revoke a license issued under the provisions of this act at any time at which it has been determined that a licensee made a material misrepresentation or failed to disclose to a potential purchaser, any latent structural defect known to the broker or salesman. Latent structural defects and other defects do not refer to trivial or insignificant defects, but refer to those defects that would be a significant factor to a reasonable and prudent purchaser in making a decision to purchase."

DISCLOSURE IS ESSENTIAL REGARDLESS WHERE YOU LIVE

The following Sellers Disclosure Form for Property Condition is for the state of Texas. However, most seller disclosure forms embrace the same principle: Let the buyer know the truth.

ALWAYS LET THE SELLER FILL IN THIS FORM COMPLETELY!
AGENT SHOULD NOT FILL OUT FORM

SELLER'S DISCLOSURE OF PROPERTY CONDITION

CONCERNING THE PROPERTY AT _____
(Street Address and City)

THIS NOTICE IS A DISCLOSURE OF SELLER'S KNOWLEDGE OF THE CONDITION OF THE PROPERTY AS OF THE DATE SIGNED BY SELLER AND IS NOT A SUBSTITUTE FOR ANY INSPECTIONS OR WARRANTIES THE PURCHASER MAY WISH TO OBTAIN. IT IS NOT A WARRANTY OF ANY KIND BY SELLER OR SELLER'S AGENTS.

Seller ☐ is ☐ is not occupying the Property. If unoccupied, how long since Seller has occupied the Property? _____

1. The Property has the items checked below [Write Yes (Y), No (N), or Unknown (U)]:

__ Range	__ Oven	__ Microwave
__ Dishwasher	__ Trash Compactor	__ Disposal
__ Washer/Dryer Hookups	__ Window Screens	__ Rain Gutters
__ Security System	__ Fire Detection Equipment	__ Intercom System
__ TV Antenna	__ Cable TV Wiring	__ Satellite Dish
__ Ceiling Fan(s)	__ Attic Fan(s)	__ Exhaust Fan(s)
__ Central A/C	__ Central Heating	__ Wall/Window Air Conditioning
__ Plumbing System	__ Septic System	__ Public Sewer System
__ Patio/Decking	__ Outdoor Grill	__ Fences

SELLER'S DISCLOSURE OF PROPERTY CONDITION P. 2

__ Pool	__ Sauna	__ Spa __ Hot Tub
__ Pool Equipment	__ Pool Heater	__ Automatic Lawn Sprinkler
__ Fireplace(s) & Chimney (Woodburning)	__ Fireplace(s) & Chimney (Mock)	System
		__ Gas Lines (Nat./LP)
__ Gas Fixtures:	Garage: __ Attached	__ Carport
	__ Not Attached	
Garage Door Opener(s):	__ Electronic	__ Control(s)
Water Heater:	__ Gas	__ Electric
Water Supply: __ City	__ Well	__ Co-op
	__ MUD	

Roof Type: _____   Age: _____ (approx)

Are you (Seller) aware of any of the above items that are not in working condition, that have known defects, or that are in need of repair? ☐ Yes ☐ No ☐ Unknown. If yes, then describe (Attach additional sheets if necessary): _____
_____
_____

2. Are you (Seller) aware of any known defects/malfunctions in any of the following? Write Yes (Y) if you are aware, write No (N) if you are not aware.

__ Interior Walls	__ Ceilings	__ Floors
__ Exterior Walls	__ Doors	__ Windows
__ Roof	__ Foundation/Slab(s)	__ Basement
__ Walls/Fences	__ Driveways	__ Sidewalks
__ Plumbing/Sewers/Septics	__ Electrical Systems	__ Lighting Fixtures
__ Other Structural Components (Describe) _____		

_____
_____

Seller's Disclosure Notice Concerning the Property at _____
(Street Address and City)

If the answer to any of the above is yes, explain. (Attach additional sheets if necessary): _____
_____
_____

3. Are you (Seller) aware of any of the following conditions? Write Yes (Y) if you are aware, write No (N) if you are not aware.

__ Active Termites (includes wood-destroying insects)	__ Termite or Wood Rot Damage Needing Repair	__ Previous Termite Damage
__ Previous Termite Treatment	__ Previous Flooding	__ Improper Drainage
__ Water Penetration	__ Located in 100-Year Floodplain	__ Present Flood Insurance Coverage
__ Previous Structural or Roof Repair	__ Hazardous or Toxic Waste	__ Asbestos Components
__ Urea-formaldehyde Insulation	__ Radon Gas	__ Lead Based Paint
__ Aluminum Wiring	__ Previous Fires	__ Unplatted Easements
__ Landfill, Settling, Soil Movement, Fault Lines	__ Subsurface Structure or Pits	

If the answer to any of the above is yes, explain. (Attach additional sheets if necessary): _____
_____
_____

4. Are you (Seller) aware of any item, equipment, or system in or on the Property that is need of repair? ☐ Yes (if you are aware)   ☐ No (if you are not aware).
    If yes, explain (attach additional sheets as necessary). _____
_____
_____

5. Are you (Seller) aware of any of the following? Write Yes (Y) if you are aware, write No (N) if you are not aware.

SELLER'S DISCLOSURE OF PROPERTY CONDITION P. 3

___ Room additions, structural modifications, or other alterations or repairs made without necessary permits or not in compliance with building codes in effect at that time.
___ Homeowners' Association or maintenance fees or assessments.
___ Any "common area" (facilities such as pools, tennis courts, walkways, or other areas) co-owned in undivided interest with others.
___ Any notices of violations of deed restrictions or governmental ordinances affecting the condition or use of the Property.
___ Any lawsuits directly or indirectly affecting the Property.
___ Any condition on the Property which materially affects the physical health or safety of an individual.

If the answer to any of the above is yes, explain. (Attach additional sheets if necessary): _____
_____
_____

_____   _____
Date   Signature of Seller   Date   Signature of Seller

The undersigned purchaser hereby acknowledges receipt of the foregoing notice.

_____   _____
Date   Signature of Purchaser   Date   Signature of Purchaser

In Texas, the Deceptive Trade Practices Act does not apply to the following:

- any new home sale
- any type of government entity
- a sale in which the value of property does not exceed 5 percent profit
- a sale from one co-owner to another co-owner
- a sale by a guardian, a conservator, or a trust
- a sale by a mortgagee or a beneficiary under a deed of trust who reclaimed the property by foreclosure
- a sale by a borrower back to a lender
- a sale by a trustee in bankruptcy
- a sale by court order
- a sale between spouses in a divorce or legal separation
- a sale made by a spouse or to a person(s) in initial line by relationship by blood of one or more of the transferees.

This notice must be delivered by the seller to the buyer on or before the effective date of a contract binding the buyer to purchase the property. (In Texas the broker must fill in the effective date on the Texas Real Estate Code forms.) If the contract is entered into without the seller providing this required notice, the buyer can terminate the contract for any reason within 7 days after receiving notice.

A specific part of the statute shows a similar change in the Texas Real Estate License Act: that a seller or a seller's agent has no duty to make a disclosure or even to release any information relating to whether a death was by natural causes, by suicide, or by accident, whether or not the death is related to the condition of the property, and whether the death occurred on the property.

This Texas Real Estate License Act says that a licensee (agent) has no duty to inquire about whether a death occurred on the property under these circumstances. Recent development of property inspections helps agents out tremendously. In Texas, the law says that when a buyer uses the services of an inspector, the buyer is relying on the inspection and removes or reduces the reliance on the listing (selling) broker.

Texas notice and inspection

A buyer (consumer) should give written notice to the person at least 60 days before filing a suit. This advises the person in detail of the buyer's complaints and the amount of economic damage, damage for mental anguish, and expenses involved.

In Texas, the property must be available for inspection and there must be a request made in writing. This should be done within the 60-day period.

Under the Deceptive Trade Practices Act, if a person receives this written notice from a consumer (buyer) prior to filing a suit, an offer of settlement may be brought about at any time during this 60-day period. Then, if the parties have decided not to mediate (come to terms with each other) by the end of this 60-day period, they must answer the notice and file it by the end of the 90th day after the original date. If they decide to mediate, the person whom the claim is against can offer a settlement beginning on the day after the date of mediation and ending 20 days after that date.

It seems a bit confusing, and you may think that this could never happen to you. But in today's real estate industry, there are more and more lawsuits over issues of negligence and— above all—misrepresentation by the licensee.

In the long run, it is far better to be factual, honest, and precise. The defendant may be found not guilty by being willing to pay for the damages, especially for economic damages and damages for mental anguish, including attorneys' fees claimed by the consumer within 30 days of receiving this notice. The good thing about this law is that, just because you are willing to settle, does not mean you are guilty. On the other hand, if the court finds that the case is groundless or brought about in bad faith or any way harassing in nature, the court will reward the defendant's reasonable and necessary attorney's fees and court costs.

Deceptive trades act mediation

The new Texas amendment provides for any party to mediate. It also offers the opportunity of settlement through mediation. Under this new procedure, a party may, not later than the 90th day after the date of service from pleading, file a motion to mediate in a dispute. After this motion is filed, the court must, not later than 30 days after the motion is filed, sign an order setting the time and place to mediate. This mediation must be held within 30 days after the date the order is signed, unless the parties agree otherwise.

A party cannot insist on mediation if the economic damages are less than $15,000.00 unless that party agrees to pay all the costs of the mediation.

Indemnity or contribution

Again in Texas, there is a provision that allows the defendant in a suit to extend indemnity (protection or security against damage) and contributions to other parties. A defendant may shift some or even all of the liability to the seller, property inspector, or anyone else it is determined to have contributed to a damaging act toward a consumer, whether by statute or common law.

Vicarious liability

Vicarious liability means that a party is not liable for misrepresentation concealing a material fact made by the licensee in a real estate transaction unless the party knew of the falsity of the misrepresentation or concealment and failed to disclose knowledge of the falsity of the misrepresentation or the concealment.

A *licensee* (agent) is not liable for a misrepresentation or a concealment of a material fact made by a party in a real estate transaction unless the licensee knew of the falsity of the misrepresentation or concealment and failed to disclose the licensee's knowledge of the falsity of the misrepresentation.

A *party* or a *licensee* is not liable for a misrepresentation or a concealment of a fact made by a subagent in a real estate transaction unless the party or the licensee knew of the falsity of the misrepresentation or the concealment and failed to disclose the party's or the licensee's knowledge of the falsity of the misrepresentation or concealment.

Whether the party or the licensee should have known of the falsity of the misrepresentations or concealment is not an issue under this new statute. But this does not mean the broker, as well as the licensee, does not have a responsibility to act in an honorable fashion.

Buyer's broker: no liability

Because the buyer's broker has an agency relationship with the buyer, the buyer's broker is not vicariously liable for the acts of the seller or the listing broker. The buyer's broker usually verifies the information about the property given by the listing broker, or requires that the seller give certain warranties or representations concerning conditions of the property (roof, plumbing, heating, cooling, etc.). The broker's exposure is reduced to claims for misrepresentation, for concealing material defects, or for failure to discover material facts. There is now less chance of the buyer's broker being sued for conditions that are not the broker's fault. But in Texas, especially, the buyer's broker has an increased responsibility to the client to use every means of finding problems.

Waivers

The legislature made major changes in the Deceptive Trade Practices Act as it pertained to waivers. A waiver is now valid and *enforceable* if the waiver is in writing and signed by the customer (and the consumer is not in a significant bargaining position). Additionally, the consumer must be seeking or requiring the goods and services and is represented by legal counsel not counsel directly or indirectly identified, or selected by the defendant (or agent).

To be effective, this waiver must be: (1) *conspicuous* and in boldface type (minimum ten points in size) and (2) identified by the heading "Waiver of Consumer Rights" or words of similar meaning in the following form:

> **I waive my rights under the Deceptive Trade Practices-Consumer Protection Act, *Section 17.41 et. seq.,* Business & Commerce Code, a law that gives consumers special rights and protections. After consultation with an attorney of my selection, I voluntarily consent to this waiver.**

The statute does *not* require the signature of the consumer's attorney.

Professional services

An amendment now prohibits a claim for damages based on the rendering of professional services, that being the rendering of advice, judgment, opinion, or similar professional skill. This exemption could and was intended to apply to real estate brokers. Only time and litigation will tell if the courts consider real estate brokerage a "professional service." The exemption does not apply, however, to the omission or an express misrepresentation of a material fact, unconscionable action, or course of action, the failure to disclose information and violation or a breach of an express warranty that cannot be characterized as advice, judgment, or opinion.

> NOTE:
> *Make sure that there will be no surprises at the final walk-through,* such as a stove that does not work, lights that won't go on, or faucets that will not turn, *that could circumvent the closing and cause delays.*

The amendment also prohibits a claim for damages, for a claim arising out of written contract, if the contract relates to a transaction involving total consideration by the consumer of more than $100,000 if the consumer is represented by legal counsel and the contract does not involve the consumer's residence. The Act also exempts claims arising from a transaction, a project, or a set of transactions relating to the same project, involving total consideration by the consumer of more than $500,000 other than a cause of action involving a consumer's residence, even if the consumer is not represented by a legal counsel.

Relief for consumers

The statutory damages recoverable under the **Deceptive Trade Practices Act** were changed and now include:

Lorayne thinks she can show me up...I'll show her. I've got my new book, now I can be professional!

1. The DTPA provides that a prevailing consumer can recover his or her *economic damages,* attorney fees, and court costs. The new changes redefined actual damages to mean economic damages that do not include mental anguish, pain and suffering, and loss of consortium. But, if the defendant is found to have **knowingly** committed the act, then mental anguish may be awarded. Those damages for mental anguish may then be given if the defendant is found to have committed the act **intentionally**. "Intentionally" is actual awareness or obvious disregard of fair business practices, *intending* that the consumer rely on false information or deceptive acts.

2. Orders necessary to restore to any part of the suit any money or property, real or personal, which may have been acquired in violation of the sub chapter.

Neil is always trying to be one-up on me...wait till he sees my new book! I give professional service!

3. Any other relief which the court deems proper, including the appointment of a receiver or the revocation of a licensee or certificate authorizing the person who engages in business in this state if the judgment has not been satisfied within three months of the date of final judgment. **The court may not revoke or suspend a license to do business in the state or appoint a receiver to take over the affairs of the person who has failed to satisfy judgment if the person is a licensee of or regulated by a state agency which has the statutory authority to revoke or suspend a license or to appoint a receiver or trustee.** Changes to the DTPA make the award of trebled damages discretionary with the court and not an automatic award.

Chapter Summary

Never overprice a listing. Give the seller the whole truth. If You are asked about another agent, ALWALYS be kind and fair. Companies are Starting to add "exceptional service" Communication is the greatest concern. If Buyers and sellers are having a problem, they want to know that they can talk it Over with their real estate agent. They want to see how their agent deals with the Problem. Keep everything documented and keep records of all conversations with Clients. Be consise and fair in providing the seller disclosure forms at the onset. At the initial meeting with the buyer, establish your relationship as their sole Representation in real estate transactions. Dress professionally whenever showing Property, meeting a client or calling on a seller. Where business attire for all Business appointments. Do not let unlicensed people show properties for you at Any time! Verify everything that you are told about a home. There is always a duty To a client to disclose. Take othig for granted regarding real estate property. Get Everything regarding a listing/purchase in writing. Do not exaggerate or guess on Fact sheets regarding a listed property. Do not rely on information from a previous Listing sheet. Always document recommendations and defects. It is the duty of the Agent to relay any/all pertinent facts regarding the property. Under the DTPA Act, the consumer must prove that a misleading, deceptive or fraudulent act was a Producing cause of loss. Most states now have some form of a disclosure form. Always let the sellers fill out this form, agents should not fill out this form! In the Long run, it is far better to be factual, honest and precise. Vicarious Liability means. That a party is not liable for misrepresentation concealing a materal fact made by. The licensee in a real estate transaction unless the party knew of the falsity of the Misrepresentation or concealment and failed to disclose the licensee's knowledge of

The falsity of the misrepresentation.

Because a buyers broker has an agency relationship with the buyer, the buyers Broker is not vicariously liable for the acts of the seller or the listing agent. Make Sure there are no surprises on the final walk through that could circumvent the Closing and cause delays!

CHAPTER 16

REAL ESTATE STRESS: "TAKING CARE OF ME"

big deal by Lorayne n' Neil

There comes a time in every real estate agent's work life when stress and fatigue become overpowering, and the agent comes to the conclusion, "I am drained, I am spent, I can't do this anymore." An agent's emotional tank is "empty."

But it is particularly frustrating that there is no other plan in sight, and you still have things to do, such as:

- appointments to set up
- clients to call and reschedule
- open house ads to write
- marketing plans to develop
- new listings to check on
- "solds" to check on

And that is not all! Besides work-related obligations, the agent needs to attend to family obligations as well, like:

- Grocery shopping
- Washing the car
- Picking up dry cleaning
- Banking
- Doing laundry
- Cleaning

What a list! And personal needs still have not been addressed. When you are so busy taking care of everyone else, you forget to take care of yourself. YOU get left behind!

It is important to remember that the best person to take care of you is YOU! No one else knows how each real estate deal affects you.

"It's your job to take care of you." No other person can feel the pressure or the pleasure you get from each real estate transaction. Only you know how it feels to face rejection head on!

When you lose your buyer, when a deal falls through, when one listing after another just sits on the market because the market has slowed, stress creeps in.

The stress warning signs are evident, and it's important to recognize them:

- Becoming overtired
- Extreme fatigue
- Doing too many things at once
- Making too many mistakes
- Doing all you can do, but getting nowhere
- Losing your temper easily
- Misplacing things over and over again
- Showing up late, missing appointments
- Developing shortness of breath (sighing a lot)
- Not getting enough sleep
- More rapid heartbeat

Yesterday was packed with appointments. I'm glad I get my massage and facial today!

This is when it is time to regroup. Maybe deciding to find a new real estate partner or even assigning jobs to a new office assistant is the best bet. Maybe you are working with the wrong kind of buyers. Maybe you are in an area that is already overworked by other real estate agents. Whatever is happening, recognize that when the stress keeps growing, you have to sit down, take a deep breath, and think through the problem.

Experienced real estate agents will verify that in order to be successful, there are three essential ingredients:

- DAILY DISCIPLINE
- STRUCTURED PLAN
- EXECUTION OF THE PLAN

> The ingredients of daily discipline, a structured plan and execution of the plan are, in essence, the same ingredients critical to your plan for eliminating stressors.

A real estate agent's plan for a structured day:

7:00 A.M.	Wake up and get ready for the day
8:00 A.M.	Early morning walk/meditation/eat nutritious food
9:00 A.M.	Go to work—confident your day will run smoothly
10:00 A.M.	Follow a structured plan for the day
12:00 P.M.	Take at least 30 minutes to relax/lunch and regroup
12:30 P.M.	Make/take telephone calls and new appointments
1:30 P.M.	Go on appointments and secure listings
5:30 P.M.	Take time out again (personal/relaxation/exercise, family time/dinner and so on)
6:30 P.M.	Arrange for new appointments with clients and write up new listings, develop copy for ads and so on
8:00 P.M.	Retire from a day of work

You are the only person who can guarantee this organized schedule. Now let's look at some stressors that can interrupt the structured, organized plan for the day.

Do you recognize any of these stressors?

- Waking up just in time to make it to work and to an important appointment (rushing frantically to catch up)
- Leaving the bedroom cluttered (and the closet to match)
- Leaving dirty clothes all over the floor
- Leaving old newspapers and junk mail stacked around
- Leaving the kitchen dirty with dishes and cluttered counters
- Leaving the apartment or home in shambles (then thinking about the mess all day long)
- Leaving pets without daily feedings and/or daily clean up
- Getting into an unclean car, filled with clutter

- Facing traffic or a long commute
- Poor diet, eating too many meals on the go
- Not having enough time to eat, working while hungry

Understanding Real Estate Stress

Ken Pelletier, a professor of psychiatry at the University of California in San Francisco, found that most people in the workplace generally want to help and train in handling stress. And a real estate agent is one of the greatest candidates for stress. Why? Selling real estate is unpredictable, and because unexpected events are highly stressful, the real estate agent is most likely to encounter stressors on the job.

> Work-related stress can contribute to heart disease, hypertension (high blood pressure), alcoholism, drug abuse, ulcers, and extreme anxiety.

If stress continues for long periods of time, burnout follows. Long periods of burnout lead directly to poor job performance.

So, it is a fact that the real estate agent can never live a completely stress-free life. Continued exposure to stress can exceed the ability to cope with daily activities.

In order to avoid future job stress, the agent needs to analyze the job in relation to an honest assessment of his or her personal needs. This is the only way agents can realize their own expectations and avoid the harmful side effects of stress. It is the only real way the agent can take good care of him or herself in the real estate industry today. As the market shifts, real estate home sales may slow down and commissions may stop coming in. A plan to stabilize and gain balance must be in place.

Balance can best be achieved by the agent asking some probing self-assessment questions:

- How does my job as a real estate agent fit in with my company?
- How does selling real estate meet my own personal needs?
- How can I survive financially if there is a real estate slump?
- How will my need for recognition and self esteem be satisfied if a contract I have written falls through?
- How will I address the issue of a client who doesn't list with me as previously planned?
- When people ask me: "What do you do?" can I proudly state, "I sell homes for XYZ Real Estate Company"?
- Do I feel that the perceived value that society places on selling property is consistent with my needs for self esteem and status?
- Is it important for me to sell only exclusive properties (distinctive homes that range over a million dollars) because these sales are more prestigious, or can I sell any property and be proud of my accomplishments?
- Is the marketing involved in closing listings and sales consistent with the kinds of things I love to do (developing virtual tours, planning and writing ads, preparing promotional brochures, holding open houses, setting up signs for open houses and so on)?

> SO WHAT DOES ONE DO WITH BALANCE?
> OR TO BE BALANCED?
>
> YOU GO TO BURNOUT NEXT.

> Burnout is an emotional state that a real estate sales person might experience as a result of continued periods of stress (personal and job-related).

Burnout is emotional exhaustion. Real estate agents who experienced burnout feel that there is nothing else inside of them to give to the job. They think their work is useless, and they feel there is nothing they can do that is right.

Real estate agents burdened by long periods of stress and burnout can become uncaring, depersonalized, and unproductive. They say to themselves over and over again, "What difference does it make?" until they eventually start to believe there is no difference.

> People who succeed in real estate careers find a way to apply discipline in their lives on a daily basis in order to cope with stress. They move on!

Successful real estate agents remove themselves from their work occasionally for short periods of time. They cut down their workload and take much needed breaks during the day. What these agents do is to follow a disciplined routine to wipe away the problems of each day's work. They offset the build-up of daily stress and therefore reduce chances for burnout.

The following diversions from work will allow agents an opportunity to reduce the effects of work stress.

Suggested stress reducers

- Sit quietly, close your eyes, take 10 long, deep breaths. Feel yourself relax.
- Take a scenic drive to a place where there is water, country, quiet, and peace.
- Play relaxing music (such as George Winston's "Autumn") for 20 minutes.
- Read an uplifting book such as *Great Thoughts* by Geo. Seldes.
- Play golf.
- Make a reservation at a nice hotel, even if it is close by.
- Walk very hard and fast outside in the fresh air.
- Do exercise of some kind for no less than 20 minutes.

(continued)

- Go for a swim at a local health club for at least 15 minutes.
- Go for a bicycle ride for a half hour.
- Take time to meditate and be all alone.
- Go window shopping and people watching at a mall.
- Get a massage, pedicure, facial and/or haircut.
- Play cards. Learn a new card game.
- Stop working earlier and do something with family.
- Go for a short vacation.
- Go out dancing.
- Go to a comedy movie—even alone. Laugh a little.
- Go somewhere quiet and private to pray/meditate.
- Curl up with a cozy blanket/crackling fire.
- Learn to play the piano or an instrument.
- Take up drawing lessons or painting.
- Go to a craft store and learn to do a new project.
- Go to a health food store and explore options of healthy eating.
- Reorganize your closets, your bedroom, your kitchen.
- Reorganize the furniture in a room in your house or apartment.
- Learn to play tennis or a new sport.
- Use self-learning tapes and inspirational videos.
- Volunteer to work at an organization that needs help. The quickest way to forget your problems is to help someone!
- Reflect on things you used to like to do for fun! IT IS POSSIBE TO DO THIS NOW!

I balance my day and my business is booming!

Do some of these suggested diversions right now (don't procrastinate!). As you plan these diversions, also plan to structure your work goals in such a way that will allow you an opportunity to eliminate job stress.

- Stay focused on the fact that stress (or challenge) cannot be completely eliminated, so don't try to remove all stress.
- Remember that the right amount of stress often brings out the best in a person.
- No mater what happens, don't give up! If you cannot reach a particular real estate goal (for whatever reason), look for an alternative way to get to your goal. Other ways almost always exist.
- Consider bringing in other real estate minds for consultation and ask them to join you in touring an existing property that may not be selling.
- Hopefully, as you become successful in one transaction and move on to the next, you will assess your own needs and how they can be satisfied. Become aware of what makes you anxious when you are with clients. (These are all ways to look inwardly and achieve introspection.)
- If you can avoid stressors with care and forethought, do so. This isn't necessarily running away from a real estate problem; this is saving your strength for coping with unavoidable stressors. In other words, pick your battles carefully.
- Find positive ways each day to deal with real estate rejection. If a sale falls through, if a buyer says "no," if a listing goes to a different broker, try to let go, and learn valuable lessons from why this may have happened.
- Focus on positive things in your life, such as family, friends, previous professional successes that got you where you are.

Try to remember that sometimes it is important to confront the stressful situation. It may be that your fear is unfounded or surmountable; for example, you may be afraid to just plain close a sale. If so, gain additional training in closing a buyer/seller sale. (One way to do this is to shadow local peers who are successful in closing sales.) Each time you try again, it becomes a little bit easier. This is not to say that the stress goes away, but it lessens the anxieties until you are able to successfully close on a real estate transaction with minimum stress.

- Increase your physical activities and find relaxing alternatives so that you can try to change your view of a particular real estate situation.
- Look in the mirror. Do you feel that you need a new look? When you take care of how you look, you gain confidence.
- Relax. Hot showers and soothing baths help to reduce stressful feelings.
- Associate with other positive, high-spirited agents. Spend time with people who motivate you to become better than you already are.
- Keep your car organized, filled with gas, ready to do business at a moment's notice. This helps to eliminate stress when a buyer wants to sign a contract right away. Have the contracts in your car.
- Get as much sleep as you can every night! Getting at least 7 to 8 hours of sleep every night will help eliminate the stress that builds up inside of you from being overly tired.
- Practice deep breathing and happy thoughts throughout the day. Learn to replace a negative thought with a positive one!
- Tell yourself, "Listening to my clients is more important than talking." (I will slow down, take deep breaths, and listen.")
- Pace yourself with the right number of appointments that you know you can handle. Don't try to overdo it. Stress comes when you plan to do too much and can't handle it!
- Keep note pads around the house and in your car and wherever you have a telephone. Practice writing notes to yourself. This helps eliminate the stress of trying to remember everything!
- Balance your day and plan it wisely. Make a schedule that works for you! Sticking to it is a good accomplishment that will help relieve stress.

> Besides reducing stress in life with diversions, and setting structured work-related goals, the successful real estate agent also works on developing a positive work attitude.

Researchers at Mayo Clinic conducted a 30-year study, which found that optimistic, positive people live about 19 percent longer than pessimists do. This finding comes from studying 839 people living in Minnesota. Optimistic people had better survival rates, less depression, and took better care of themselves.

TAKE DEEP BREATHS ALL DAY LONG

- Practice good posture, stand tall, walk briskly, and take big steps.
- Apply discipline and balance all day.
- Begin each day with a structured plan for selling.
- Create an environment that motivates and inspires with a cheerful voice.
- Deliver answers to buyers/sellers without dodging the tough ones.
- Be truthful.
- Weigh your thoughts and make the right statement at the right time.
- Focus on solutions.
- Follow through after a sale to keep up contacts.
- Guarantee top performance in everything you do.
- Have heart in the business at hand at all times.
- Be sincerely interested in the client and ask a lot of questions.
- Be a good role model.
- Integrate buyer/seller values to instigate a good match.
- Know what to do for your clients each day and keep in touch with them every day if possible.
- Look at all possible alternatives in a transaction.
- Manage your business in a professional manner.
- Prioritize To-Do items every single day.
- Organize your time wisely in order to make valuable appointments that lead to sales.
- Praise yourself for your excellent effort.
- Don't give up until the entire job is completed.
- Realize success in real estate is hard work.
- Service your clients with 100 percent dedication.
- Manage your time in all of your endeavors.

An old client just gave me a brand new lead!

Other key tips:

- Understand the situation of buyers and sellers.
- Understand that market downswings are inevitable and usually temporary.
- Jot down all necessary information as clients reveal their needs and wants.
- Revise yearly goals and ambitions, reorganize files.
- Develop zest, whole-hearted interest, gusto, and love for life!

> Psychologists believe that stress that is challenging is actually beneficial—even necessary—but remember constant stress can be both mentally and physically harmful.

So, it is understood that some stress is important to help people stay motivated—to do a good job. There are even some psychologists who believe that some stress can energize a person to even do a better job. This is called an "optimal level of arousal." In real estate, this is a good thing. Without any challenge, there would be no arousal. More than anything else, a real estate agent is stimulated by a good challenge. "Can I make that sale today?" "Will the buyer say yes?" "Can I get at least four listings for the month ahead?" "Can I close this buyer?" Challenge helps to keep you focused.

If real estate agents are able to face stress head-on and channel the stress to a more creative action rather than to give in to self-destructive tendencies, they will be on the right track. Take time out of your busy day to think about eliminating stressors from your work and personal life. You are the only one who can accomplish this.

- ORGANIZE your day
- DECIDE the next days calender each night
- BALANCE personal and professional life with structured time tables
- Stay focused
- Let yesterdays PROBLEMS GO-work on positive solutions today!

Chapter Summary

Like most professions, real estate agents face stress. Stress is not always negative, but too much stress is harmful. Sometimes stress is physical and sometimes it is a perception of a situation. Sometimes you can decide to fight or flee from stress.

We have seen that a real estate agent's personal life can become unhappy if the excessive stress continues. When stress is taken home, anger and anxiety are sure to affect family life as well.

Real estate agents who work non-stop getting as many listings as possible and closing sale after sale without regard for family or personal needs will eventually bankrupt their emotions. If agents invest all of their emotions in their jobs with no regard for their other needs, the isolated loss of a listing or sale could devastate them.

Oh yes, expectations that are not met and rewards that are not realized will cause the real estate agent to be stressed out and burned out. Whatever agents decide to do, they must find relaxing alternatives. They must learn not to invest all of their emotions in only one phase of their lives. Be it work, family, leisure activities, or friendships, balance is the key factor!

Abstract of Title—A history of the title of one piece of real estate going back to the original owner.

Acceleration Clause—In a mortgage, a clause that allows the lender to state that the "entire mortgage is due and payable immediately because of default."

Acceptance—A person accepting the terms of an offer.

Access Easement—Allowing some other person use of property for access only.

Accrued Depreciation—The loss of value that has accrued since the beginning of construction. The difference between the appraised value and the replacement value.

Acre—Land that equals 43,560 sq. ft. or 4,840 sq. yds.

Addendum—Altering a contract with added provision; addition to a contract that is referred to in the contract.

Adjacent—Laying beside, but not necessarily touching.

Adjustable Rate Mortgage (ARM)—A mortgage where the interest rate can change according to the index it is tied to. A 5-year ARM is FIXED for 5 years and then can escalate accordingly.

Adverse Possession—Acquiring property through unauthorized use of someone else's property.

Agency Relationship—Where the client is represented by the agent and the agent acts on his/her own behalf.

Agent—A person that is given authority to represent another.

Alienation—The transfer of property from one person to another voluntarily or involuntarily.

Alienation Clause—A mortgage clause that allows the lender to declare all principle unpaid balance and interest due and payable if the borrower transfers the title of the property to another person.

Amenities—The special features or aspects of a property that make it stand out, especially in value.

Amortization—The paying off of a debt by making periodic payments to the lender.

Amortization Schedule—A graph that shows a person how much of the loan payment is applied toward the principle with each payment made for the life of the loan.

Appraiser—A person who decides the value of a property at a specific time period.

Appraised Value—An appraiser's opinion of the value of a property. An appraiser usually uses 3 comparable properties.

Arbitration binding—A legal process that replaces going to court, wherein the parties involved agree in writing.

Assignment—Transferring the interest/rights from one to another.

Assumption Mortgage—Acquired title to a property where the owner's original mortgage is assumed by the new buyer.

Attachment—Process where the court takes the property until a debt against it has been satisfied.

Balloon Mortgage—Loan where the final payment is due at the end of the mortgage after periodic payments are made.

Bankruptcy—A process where a person relieves themselves of debts and loans by filing in federal court. A common type is Chapter 7 or Chapter 11.

Bequest—Personal property that is given by a will.

Bill of Sale—Written agreement that transfers personal property (does not transfer real estate).

Binder—Accompanies earnest money in the purchase price as a written agreement showing "good faith."

Blanket Mortgage—Where more than one piece of real estate is covered with a single debt.

Bono Fide—In honest and good faith.

Bond—Showing personal debt secured by a lien on real estate.

Breach of Contract—Violating any conditions of a contract without a good legal reason.

Bridge Loan—A short-term loan in expectation of permanent long-term financing.

Broker—The real estate owner of a business that brings together the parties involved, for a fee.

Broker's Open—Open house for all the agents as opposed to the open house for the public at large.

Building Code—The regulations and rules that control building and construction of property based on safety and health regulations.

Buyer's Broker—A real estate broker that is employed by the buyer. The broker owes the buyer fiduciary duties.

By Laws—Usually referred to in condo/townhome associations as to the rules and regulations.

CC&Rs—Conditions, covenants, and restrictions.

Cancellation Clause—A part of a lease that allows one of the parties to cancel and/or terminate the lease.

Canvessing—Looking for clients, making cold calls.

Cap—The ceiling on an interest rate with regards to ARMs (Adjustable Rate Mortgages).

Capitol Gains Tax—Tax that is charged on the profit you make from selling a piece of real estate—long-term.

Cash Flow—Monies left over after deducting operating expenses from the gross income.

Caveat Emptor—Buyer beware.

Certificate of Eligibility—Usually refers to a document issued by the Veteran's Administration (VA). This allows the veteran to get a VA loan.

Certificate of Reasonable Value (CRV)—The VA issues this after the appraisal has been done on a property.

Chain of Title—Recorded history of one piece of property.

Clear Title—A title that is free from liens and encumbrances.

Closing—The part of a real estate transaction where the seller gives the deed to the new buyer and the property is transferred from seller to buyer.

Closing Costs—These costs are, for the most part, itemized on a good-faith estimate usually after 3 days of securing a new mortgage application.

Closing Professional—The professional (attorney sometimes) who handles the transaction of the closing.

Closing Statement—This is also known as a settlement statement. This gives an accurate detailed account of the buyer's and seller's obligations of debt and credit for the real estate sale. The buyer and seller each receive a separate closing statement.

Competitive Market Analysis (CMA)—A report done (usually with 3 similar properties) to give the seller the range of list price and sold price.

Condominium—Each owner has a separate, specific interest in a multi-unit building, yet shares ownership of the common areas.

Contingency—Condition of a contract that is "conditional upon an agreement that must be met" before the contract can be completely binding.

Cooperative—Ownership of a property where each person owns a percentage of the corporation but not the title.

Counter-offer—An offer that is given in response to one already made. Usually it is accepted, rejected, or countered with a different price, terms, and so on.

Credit History—A thorough record of one person's debt history.

Cul de sac—No outlet; a curved circular area, turnaround.

Damages—Monies that are owed/given to a person that has been hurt by the actions of another person.

Decedent—Someone who has died.

Deed—A written document that conveys title to a property.

Deed of Trust—A document that is used to secure interest in a property.

Default—When a person misses or does not meet their obligations; failure to perfom.

Deficiency Judgment—When the funds are not produced from the sale of a foreclosed property to pay off mortgage, a claim is made.

Delinquency—When payments are due; failure to pay on time.

Depreciation—A tax deduction, attributing the cost of an improvement over a lifetime. Can also refer to a property that has become run-down and is physically deteriorating.

Devise—Using a will to transfer real estate.

Discount rate—A rate that the lender pays for a mortgage fund.

Down payment—Usually the earnest money or the part that the buyer pays in cash and not financed.

Dual Agent—A real estate agent that represents both the buyer and the seller in a real estate transaction.

Due on Sale Clause—A condition in a mortgage where the lender demands payment in full if the borrower tries to sell the property.

Duress—Unlawfully forcing a person against their will.

Earnest Money—Monies given as a down payment for the purchase of a new property they are buying.

Easement—The right to use property of another person for a specific purpose.

Eminent Domain—Governmental rights to take a person's private property for public usage after they have compensated the owner with a fair market price.

Encroachment—Trespassing onto another property or space by use of a wall, fence, or any structure.

Equity—The difference between what a property is valued at and how much is owed against it.

Equity of Redemption—Borrower's right to stop foreclosure.

Errors and omissions insurance (E & O insurance)—Insurance that a broker real estate agent carries to protect against claims.

Escalation Clause—Part of a lease allowing the landlord to increase the rent owed based on cost of living increases.

Escheat—State claims against property when owner dies and there are no heirs.

Escrow—A third party (independent) that holds all funds for the buyer and seller and prepares documents.

Estate—All the total property owned by a person.

Estate Tax—Federal tax against a property after death.

Estoppel Certificate—A statement that shows the total amount owing on a mortgage (includes interest).

Et al—And another.

Et ux—And wife.

Et vir—And husband.

Eviction—removing a tenant/person from a property.

Examination of Title—Reviewing an abstract to see the current condition of the title.

Exchange (1031)—Also known as tax-free exchange where the profit is deferred for real estate owners who are selling investment property and buying investment real estate.

Exclusive Agency Listing—Contractual agreement between a property owner and broker where the broker is given a specific fee to sell the property in a certain amount of time with certain conditions applying. Yet the owner can still produce his or her own buyer and not pay a broker's fee.

Exclusive right to sell listing—Contractual agreement between a property owner and agent where the agent gets a commission even if property is sold by someone else during the terms/conditions of listing.

Execution—Signing a contract.

Executor—Person who administers an estate.

Extension agreement—Agreement between the mortgagee and mortgagor which extends the life of the mortgage beyond when it is due.

Fair Market Value—What the buyer will pay for and the seller will sell for.

Fannie Mae—Largest congressional privately owned corporation that supplies funds for home mortgages.

Federal Housing Administration (FHA)—An agency inside the Department of Housing and Urban Development (HUD) that insures home mortgages by FHA-approved lenders who make loans available to buyers that have limited means.

Fee simple—The highest, most complete form of ownership in a property.

Feng shui—An ancient Chinese way of balancing the elements and furniture placement in a room.

Fiduciary Duty—A requirement to act in a "trusting way." In real estate terms; a broker/agent acts with integrity, honesty, confidentiality, and loyalty. This is a legel relationship between the agent and client.

Finders fee—A commission paid to a broker for finding a home for a buyer.

Fixed rate mortgage—Obtaining a mortgage wherein the interest rate stays the same for the duration of the mortgage.

Floor time—Rotating agents at the real estate office to answer floor calls or service walk-ins regarding real estate. The individual agent on "floor duty" responds to traffic.

Foreclosure—Legal process where the borrower of a mortgage is in default, there is usually a forced sale of the property, and the proceeds go to paying off the mortgage.

For Sale by Owner (FSBO)—Owner selling property without an agent.

Franchising—Licensing other people to use your business/name for a specific fee.

Fraud—Intending to not tell the truth; misrepresenting fact.

General agent—Agent authorized to act for the principle.

Goodwill—Value that a business has developed as a result of intangibles (business name, reputation, length of time in business).

Government National Mortgage Association (Ginnie Mae)—A mortgage company owned within the U.S. Department of Housing and Urban Development (HUD), Ginnie Mae manages and liquidates loans and Assist HUD in lending procedures.

Grant Deed—Deed that transfers title to the property and ensures that the title is guaranteed.

Grantee—A person who received title to real property.

Grantor—The person who gives title to real property; owner.

Handheld organizer—Minicomputer; holds MLS data, emails, etc.

Heir—A person legally entitled to property when owner dies.

Home Equity Conversion Mortgage (HECM)—This is also called a reverse annuity Mortgage. The lender makes payments to the owner. Allows owners to take equity now in home and convert to cash; usually monthly installments.

Home Inspection—A professional person that evaluates the entire structure of a property and its condition.

Homestead—A particular piece of property that is the owners' prime residence.

Improvement—Structural, cosmetic additions to a piece of property; man-made.

Independent Contractor—A person who has the right to control the way that he or she works. Retained by an owner to sell property in a real estate sense—receives a fee.

Independent contractors pay their own taxes and obtain no employee benefits.

Inflation—Increase in the amount of money/ credit available related to the goods and services available. This causes overall goods and services to go up.

Inspection Contingency—Right of the buyer to perform an inspection (usually within 10 days) to completely check over the entire condition of property.

Insured Mortgage—This mortgage is protected by the Federal Housing Administration (FHA) or a private mortgage insurance (PMI). If the borrower defaults on the loan, the insurer must pay the lender the insured amount.

Interest—Fee that is charged by the lender for use of money.

Interest rate—Percentage on which the interest accumulates on the mortgage.

Intestate—When a person dies with no will.

Invalid—Contractual agreement not enforceable.

Investment property—Not occupied by the owner.

Joint Tenancy—A method of holding title. The co-owner gets the deceased co-owner's interest without going to probate court. Co-owners do not need to be married.

Judgment—Court action in a lawsuit.

Judgment lien—A lien against the property, from a judgment.

Lease—Contract between landlord and tenant where the landlord receives monies for a certain time.

Lease Option—Allows the buyer the right to occupy the property for a fixed fee and the right to buy it later.

Lessee—A person who receives the right to occupy a property usually for a fixed amount of monies and terms.

Lessor—The owner of a property who gives possession to the lessee.

Levy—To collect a tax.

Lien—A legal claim against a property.

Listing agent—Broker who acts for the seller.

Listing agreement—Contract between the seller and broker that outlines what the broker will do for seller and length of listing period.

Lock box—An attachment to the property (door) that contains a key, which allows agents to access a home.

Lock in period—Time during which the lender guarantees interest rate.

Margin—Difference between interest rate and index on ARM (adjustable rate mortgage) Margin stays stable. Index fluctuates.

Market Value—Amount that seller expects to obtain for selling.

Mechanic liens—Lien against property by workmen/labor for supplying labor and materials to improve property.

Mediation—Settlement process that is outside of court, precedes legal action and usually is agreed upon in the purchase agreement by both parties.

Metes and bounds—A method of identifying a property by reference to boundaries, direction, distance, and shape.

Multiple Listing Service—Database where properties are listed for sale and rent at a specific location and is available to all those who participate in the MLS.

Negative Amortization—Monthly payment is not sufficient to cover principal/interest that is due. This difference creates a negative amortization.

Net proceeds sheet—A summary itemizing the closing costs of a sale and how much the seller will "net" at the closing. This sheet is usually given to the seller by the agent.

Net worth—The total value of a person's assets.

Notarize—To be certified by a notary public.

Note—Promissory I.O.U of a debt to be paid.

Offer—Making a bid on a piece of real estate property.

Open house—A set date and time when an agent holds a home open for the public at large.

Option—The right of a buyer to purchase a property within a certain time period.

Ordinance—Regulation within a municipality.

Origination Fee—The amount the lender charges for originating the loan and putting the loan package together.

Owner Financed—The seller supplies the financing for the buyer.

Parcel—A specified piece of real estate within a large one.

Partnership—Two parties that agree to come together for a business relationship for profit.

Passive Loss—On a rental property, the loss that exceeds income.

Personal Property—All the parts of real estate with in a property that are not "affixed" or attached to the property.

PITI—The monthly payment of principle, interest, tax, and insurance in a mortgage payment.

Plat—A subdivided land map that shows the boundaries.

PMI—Private Mortgage Insurance.

Power of Attorney—The authorization of a specified person to act on one's behalf with complete or limited legal authority.

Prepayment Penalty—Lender charging a penalty for paying off a mortgage before it expires.

Prequalification—A lender meets with a buyer and prequalifies them prior to buying a piece of property. However, this does not necessarily confirm it.

Principle—Amount that is borrowed separate from interest; one of the parties to a transaction; one who authorizes someone else to act on their behalf.

Prorate—The division of property taxes/ maintenance between buyer and seller at closing.

Prorations—The division of property expenses between the buyer and the seller at closing.

Purchase Agreement—A signed written contract between buyer and seller stating the term and conditions of a property.

Quitclaim Deed—A deed that transfers interest in a property from the grantor to the grantee but with no warranty of good title.

Real Estate Agent—A real estate broker that is assigned to represent a buyer/seller in a real estate transaction.

Real Property—Land, the earth, all its rights and anything attached permanently to the land.

Recording—Entering information regarding the title into public records.

Referral Fee—A specified fee that is paid for referring a client to another real estate broker.

Rent—Payments made by the lessee to the landlord for the use of property.

Replacement Cost—Current cost of replacing a building.

RESPA (Real Estate Settlement Procedures Act)—Protects the consumer/ buyer by requiring the lender to give them advanced notice of all closing costs and prohibits lender against abusive practices.

Reverse Annuity Mortgage—Seller of a home receives monthly checks or a large sum with no obligation to repay until property is sold.

Reversion—Return of interest or the title to the grantor on a life estate.

Right of Redemption—The statutory right of a seller to reclaim the ownership after there has been a foreclosure sale.

Right of Survivorship—This occurs in joint tenancy where the right of the survivor owns the property over the one joint tenant that is deceased.

Safety Clause—Part of the listing contract that states that after the expiration of the listing "if there is a buyer that was introduced to the listing by the agent, that agent should be compensated."

Salesperson—An individual who works for a broker and is licensed to sell real estate in a specific area.

Satisfaction—An instrument stating that a debt/mortgage has been paid in full.

Second Mortgage—A mortgage that takes second place to the first mortgage.

Selling Broker—Sometimes known as the "listing broker/agent." Also known as the "buyer's agent."

Set back—Agreement between neighbors stating how far an improvement can be affixed from a certain point (established by zoning law).

Settlement Statement (HUD)—This statement is covered by RESPA and itemizes all costs relating to the closing of a residential transaction.

Special Assessments—A special tax that has to do with public street improvements or sewer. May be assessed by an association for homeowner improvements for a new roof, etc. or for common areas of the association.

Subdivision—A specific area of land that is divided into lots that are publicly recorded within the guideline's state/local regulations.

Survey—A map that shows exact boundaries of a property. This map reflects improvements/easements and all other features of the property.

Survivorship—When a co-owner dies, the other co-owner automatically receives title without probate.

Tax Lien—A claim against a property by law that takes seniority over any other lien.

Tenants by Entirety—The ownership of a husband and wife during marriage where the surviving spouse gets the interest of the deceased.

Tenants in Common—Two or more co-owners of a property hold undivided interest in a property. This does not have the right of survivorship.

Title Company—The company that does the title search and makes up a report for the buyer to see.

Title Insurance—A policy that guarantees the title is clear of liens except what is noted in the policy, and is legally owned by the seller.

Timesharing—Ownership of real estate for a certain part of a year.

Torrens System—Establishes clear title to property with a certificate through governmental authority.

Trust Account—A bank account that hold the funds that clients have pledged to a real estate broker on their behalf.

Trustee—The person who holds the title to a property for someone else who is the beneficiary.

Truth-in-Lending Law—This is also known as "Regulation Z." It requires all lenders to make a full disclosure regarding all terms and conditions of a loan made.

Undivided Interest—The interest of co-owners to use an entire property regardless of any small amount of interest owned.

Unsecured Loan—A loan that does not have any security or collateral to back it.

Usuary—Charging interest on a loan that is above that which is allowed by law.

VA Guaranteed Loan—A mortgage made to a veteran guaranteed by the Department of Veterans Affairs.

Valid Contract—A real estate contract that is legally binding and enforceable on all parties involved.

Variance—Zoning authority's permission to build a structure outside of the current zoning laws.

Vendee—The buyer.

Vendor—The seller.

Virtual Tour—A 360-degree depiction of a property as though it were photographed with a video camera.

Voidable Contract—A contract that is subject to cancellation by either the buyer or the seller.

Warranty Deed—A deed where the seller guarantees that the title is free and clear and good.

Wraparound Mortgage—A mortgage that not only includes the existing balance, but also additional amounts. Payments on the total are made in a wraparound mortgage to the mortgagee (then forwarded on to the first mortgagee).

Yield—Interest earned on a real estate investment.

Zoning—Government regulation regarding the use of a property.

Zoning Ordinance—Regulating and controlling the use of a property with zoning laws in a city.